Making Music With Your PC

A Beginner's Guide

Available Now!

WINDOWS Magazine Presents: Access from the Ground Up
CorelDRAW! 5 Revealed!
Create Wealth with Quicken
Cruising America Online
DOS 6.2: Everything You Need to Know
WINDOWS Magazine Presents: Encyclopedia for Windows
Excel 5 for Windows By Example (with 3 ½" disk)
Free Electronic Networks
WINDOWS Magazine Presents: Freelance Graphics for Windows: The Art of Presentation
Harvard Graphics for Windows: The Art of Presentation
Improv 2.1 Revealed! (with 3 ½" disk)
Internet After Hours
Lotus Notes 3 Revealed!
Making Movies with Your PC
Microsoft Office in Concert
Microsoft Works for Windows By Example
Novell NetWare Lite: Simplified Network Solutions
PageMaker 5 for the Mac: Everything You Need to Know
PageMaker 5 for Windows: Everything You Need to Know
Paradox for DOS Revealed!
WINDOWS Magazine Presents: The Power of Windows and DOS Together, 2nd Edition
Quattro Pro 4: Everything You Need to Know
Quicken 3 for Windows: The Visual Learning Guide
QuickTime: Making Movies with Your Macintosh
The Slightly Skewed Computer Dictionary
Smalltalk Programming for Windows (with 3 ½" disk)
The Software Developers Complete Legal Companion
Software: What's Hot! What's Not!
Superbase Revealed!
Thom Duncan's Guide to Netware Shareware (with 3 ½" disk)
WinFax PRO 4: The Visual Learning Guide
Word for Windows 6: The Visual Learning Guide
WordPerfect 5.1 for Windows Desktop Publishing By Example
WordPerfect 6 for DOS By Example
WordPerfect 6 for Windows By Example
WordPerfect 6 for Windows: How Do I...?
Your FoxPro for Windows Consultant (with 3 ½" disk)

Upcoming Books

Act! 2.0 for Windows: The Visual Learning Guide
The CD-ROM Revolution
Create Wealth with Quicken, Second Edition
IBM Smalltalk Programming for Windows & OS/2 (with 3 ½" disk)
Internet for Windows: America Online Edition
Paradox for Windows Essential Power Pro (with 3 ½" disk)
Procomm Plus for Windows: The Visual Learning Guide

How to Order:

Individual orders and quantity discounts are available from the publisher, Prima Publishing, P.O. Box 1260BK, Rocklin, CA 95677-1260; (916) 632-4400. For quantity orders, include information on your letterhead concerning the intended use of the books and the number of books you wish to purchase. For individual orders, turn to the back of the book for more information.

Making Music With Your PC

A Beginner's Guide

Warren Sirota

Prima Publishing
P.O. Box 1260BK
Rocklin, CA 95677-1260

Prima Computer Books is an imprint of Prima Publishing, Rocklin, California 95677.

Managing Editor: Paula Munier-Lee
Acquisitions Editor: Sherri Morningstar
Cover Production Coordinator: Anne Johnson
Copyeditor: Joyce Armor
Technical Reviewer: John Melcher
Production: A-R Editions
Indexer: Katherine Stimson
Book Designer: A-R Editions
Cover Designer: Page Design, Inc.

ISBN: 1-55958-595-1
Library of Congress Catalog Card Number: 94-66735
Printed in the United States of America
95 96 97 RRD 10 9 8 7 6 5 4 3 2 1

Table of Contents

For Denise, with all my love

Introduction

Making Music With Your PC

Until recently, most PCs were silent. We used them mainly for administrative tasks—writing letters and reports, keeping records, and summing columns of numbers. The only people with sound cards were computer gaming enthusiasts and serious musicians. But in November, 1990, the Microsoft Multimedia Conference fired a shot heard 'round the world, publishing the specifications for the Multimedia PC (MPC). This standard, which requires a sound card, CD-ROM drive, Microsoft Windows, and a reasonably fast computer, has been responsible for transforming the PC from a simple "work processor" into a fun machine that offers all of us personal rewards via new forms of entertainment and education.

One of the most rewarding and entertaining aspects of this multimedia revolution has been the liberation of sound on the PC. Sound cards are continually costing less and sounding better, and programs that use sound are popping up everywhere. The variety is extraordinary, with programs aimed at children, adults, game players of all ages, musical novices, and musical professionals. Follow along for a taste of what's available.

Music For Everyone

Music is one of our greatest gifts. It can make us feel awe at the majesty of the universe or just make us want to get up and dance. With a PC and sound card, you can be a participant in the creative process, or you can simply become a more involved listener. Experience the thrill of creating new sounds and new pieces, or take a walking tour through the history of music. Learn to play the piano or to sing in tune. Compose music interactively with a program that creates drum, bass, and piano parts in styles that you choose. If you have a fast computer and Windows, you can even add music, dialogue, and background sounds to video clips. And if you have a child (an ever-more-popular computer peripheral), you can create and enjoy music together, which can be a deeply rewarding experience for both of you.

The possibilities multiply if you have both a sound card and a CD-ROM drive. Play games that incorporate realistic video sequences and well-crafted, mood-enhancing music. Learn about music from Beethoven to Afro-Pop in a fun, interactive way that leaves most music textbooks and lectures in the dust. Catalog your audio CDs and create custom playlists so that you can hear your favorite songs in any order you choose, with the titles of the pieces appearing on your screen as they play. Experience new forms of interactive multimedia art from creative giants such as Todd Rundgren, Peter Gabriel, and the Residents.

If you delve more deeply into making music and sound on your computer, you'll learn what professional musicians have known for years—that computers can be put to simply marvelous uses. That's why they have become omnipresent in the music industry; no recording studio is without them, and they are used in the production of most of today's hit songs.

Take existing music files (which you can obtain from bulletin-board services such as CompuServe or from vendors) and bend and shape them to your will—make them slower or faster, higher or lower, change the piano sound to an electric guitar, or eliminate the accordion altogether (yes, it's a common fantasy). Create a saxophone solo so impossibly fast that no mere mortal could ever play it. If you have a synthesizer keyboard, record your own performance of a song, remove any mistakes with surgical precision, and layer different parts together to create complete, polished, professional results. Record your own pots, pans and pets, and then add echo, change the pitch, and play them backwards. Record talk-show hosts, politicians and advertisements from TV and radio, and dice and slice them to create devastating satires. Assemble outlandish sound collages. Playing with music and sound on your PC is a great way to let your imagination run wild and have Big Fun—don't miss out on it!

What's in This Book?

This book will guide you through the possibilities and help you avoid the pitfalls of using music on your PC. You'll learn how to choose a sound card and speakers, and you'll learn scores of ways to use them. You'll find out about the different types of programs (both for Windows and for DOS) that are available for music and sound, and which ones are right for you. You'll see how to test your sound setup, how to connect your PC to your home stereo system, and how to get the best sound quality out of your setup. You'll learn about digital audio recording and the mysterious MIDI, and you'll discover important undocumented facts about Windows' MIDI Mapper. Above all, you'll learn how to create and edit music and sound with some extremely powerful tools.

The chapters in this book are designed to be as independent as possible so that you can go directly to the chapters that are most interesting to you and read the others later. Most people will benefit by reading Chapter 1 first, in order to get the big picture. After that, please go where your fancy leads you. Turn to the Glossary or Index if you encounter terms that you don't understand.

Here's what you'll find in the various chapters:

Chapter 1 talks about the evolution of music on the PC, the MPC specification, and the differences in the ways DOS and Windows handle sound.

Chapter 2 is an overview of the different types of cool audio gear that are out there. It'll help you to decide which components you want and which you don't need.

Chapter 3 deals with the all-important task of choosing a sound card. It tells you what to look for in a sound card, and when to consider replacing or adding to your current sound card. It also discusses parallel-port sound devices for laptop users and external sound modules for serious musicians.

Chapter 4 deals with choosing sound peripherals to let you listen to and record sounds—speakers, headphones, and microphones.

Chapter 5 gives you some easy ways to test your setup to make sure that it's working properly, and some immediate fixes for the most common problems that you're likely to encounter. For less common problems, or ones that are specific to particular sound boards, this chapter will help you to identify the problem clearly and make it easier for you to get help from your sound card manufacturer's technical support department.

If your PC is near your stereo receiver, check out *Chapter 6* for some tips on hooking the two together. You can either save yourself the cost of a pair of specialized PC speakers or greatly enhance the sound by using both systems in tandem. Don't read this chapter if you share an office with people who need to concentrate on their work.

Chapter 7 offers some little-known tips for getting the best sound quality out of the equipment that you already have. Enjoy better sound without spending a dime on upgrading!

Chapter 8 is where you'll dig into the guts of digital audio. It shows how to record and edit dialogue, music, and sound effects and save them into .WAV or .VOC files, and points out the many uses of these files. You'll find out how to create all kinds of special effects, and also how to listen to recordings backwards in order to decipher secret messages.

Chapters 9 and *10* focus on an incredibly powerful tool for making music—the Musical Instrument Digital Interface (MIDI) and the programs that create and manipulate MIDI music. *Chapter 9* gives you a solid background in MIDI concepts and terminology, and *Chapter 10* introduces you to the programs that use it. If you're interested in composing music or playing along with a computerized backup band, these are the most important chapters for you.

Some of the most innovative multimedia software is in the area of education, the subject of *Chapter 11.* Music education, in particular, can be quite enjoyable and effective when text, audio, and interactivity are combined.

Finally, in *Chapter 12,* we cover an assortment of audio applications that don't fit neatly into the other categories: speech recognition and talking computers, drum patterns and rhythm editors, and other software descriptions are spread before you in this buffet table of audio software.

You'll find additional technical details in the *Appendices,* along with the names and addresses of various manufacturers and software companies, and pointers to good sources of audio shareware.

I've attempted to make this book appealing to a wide range of readers, explaining all concepts from the ground up but not shying away from applications and evaluations that may be news to veterans of computer-based music making. My goal in writing this book was to have it be like the rapids in a good river—clear, deep, and exciting. I hope that I've succeeded.

Warren Sirota
Jacksonville, Oregon

Chapter 1

Music on the PC— An Overview

Over the past thirteen years, PCs have evolved from sightless, speechless business machines into multimedia megalomaniacs, complete with video cameras for eyes, microphones for ears, and speakers for mouths. In many ways, the additional "sensory organs" and "limbs"—input and output devices—that we've added to our computers have transformed them from computing machines into personal communications enhancers. We've added modems and fax-modems for instant long-distance communications, mice that enable us to communicate gestures in addition to the plain text of typing, laser printers to extend our "broadcast range" to the paper-oriented world, and sound cards and synthesizer keyboards to enable a full range of musical communications.

The need to communicate in ever-richer, ever-denser media has driven the development of new forms of hardware. The popularity of the CD-ROM stems from its ability to communicate images, sounds, and video clips that are simply too large to fit onto a floppy disk or to transmit easily over telephone lines. And, as you'll soon see, sound cards and synthesizers evolved to meet the needs of game programmers and musicians (both amateur and professional) to extend the reach and improve the quality of their communications by providing richer and more involving experiences to their audiences.

You, too, can extend the reach and improve the quality of your communications with music. But before we dive into detailed descriptions of the various tricks and tools, let's look at the big picture. In this chapter, you'll learn about the basic hardware and software involved in making music on the PC. You'll read about the history of synthesizers and sound cards, audio CDs and CD-ROMs, and the significance of the Multimedia PC (MPC) standard.

The Evolution of Music on the PC

The history of music on the PC is a story that shows how technologies developed for radically different purposes can come together, when the time is right, to give rise to explosively exciting products never dreamed of by the original creators. Sound on the PC is the result of the convergence of computer gaming, music synthesis, audio CD and CD-ROM technology, and Windows.

Computer gamers were (and are) the advance scouts of the multimedia revolution. Early on, they developed a hunger for better PC sounds, an appetite that spurred the development of the first sound cards by AdLib and Creative Labs. Those sound cards used synthesizer technology that had been developed for the professional music market. The Sound Blaster combined this with the ability to digitally record and play back car crashes, sword clashes, demonic laughs, and other sounds important to gamers.

In the meantime, Bill Gates and Microsoft had been promoting the CD-ROM concept for years, although it didn't seem that many people were listening. There was a kind of chicken-and-egg problem— developers weren't getting excited until they saw a market, and the market wasn't getting excited until it saw some fantastic titles. When the MPC specification came out in 1990, however, the groundwork was laid for mass acceptance of the new media. When Creative and other manufacturers added CD-ROM control to their sound cards and started releasing "multimedia upgrade kits" that included both a sound card and a CD-ROM drive at an economical price, consumers noticed. When developers saw that more and more consumers were buying CD-ROM drives and that there was a standard programming interface to write to (instead of having to write separate subroutines for every drive on the market), multimedia titles started to appear in stores. When consumers started seeing titles in stores, they bought more CD-ROM drives, which encouraged the title explosion that we're now experiencing. This forward motion was further encouraged by the recent addition of video clips to many CD-ROM titles. Although the quality of the video is less than ideal, its uses in interactive multimedia have already been compelling enough to spark a tremendous surge of CD-ROM growth, with no signs of diminishing in the next several years.

Sound card users have been beneficiaries of increased interest in multimedia. Since sound cards are essential components of MPCs, they have been selling in ever-increasing numbers. Competition among sound card manufacturers is fierce. This is excellent for you and me, who can purchase better-sounding cards for less money than ever before.

To understand the background of these forces, let's take a short step back in time.

In the Beginning Was the Beep

The first personal computer was the Altair, released in 1975 by MITS, a small company in Albuquerque, New Mexico. This computer had no sound card or speaker (indeed, not even a keyboard or display), but it was soon the starring performer in a music recital, thanks to the ingenuity of an early computer enthusiast named Steve Dompier. In April,

1975, Steve brought one of the first Altairs to Menlo Park to show to his friends in the Homebrew Computer Club, the informal group that acted as a catalyst for much of the early activity in Silicon Valley.

The Altair was a primitive affair by our standards, although a wonder for its time. It was a bare-bones computer, without even a display or keyboard. The only way to communicate with it was to enter each instruction into memory by flipping switches on the front panel. The only feedback the computer could give one was by turning a row of lights on and off. It's quite incredible to believe that this was considered usable in any way at any time, but it was a necessary first step along a road that has taken us to multimedia-equipped personal computers in less than twenty years.

What could one do with such limited material that would make a good group demonstration? Dompier came up with an ingenious idea. He noticed that the computer produced a lot of static on his radio and figured out how to control it. He programmed the computer (entering it in front of a roomful of people, since there was no disk or tape storage) to play melodies using radio static as a sound source!

Steve wouldn't have had long to wait for speakers. As the programmers of mainframe computers already knew, it's important to be able to beep at the user once in a while. If you initiate a long task, it's nice to be able to turn to some other activity while the computer does its thing and to get an audible alert when it's finished. Also, beeps are useful for telling you when a program disagrees with you over the appropriateness of a mouse click or keystroke. And finally, beeps provide an important safety valve for the computer's own frustrations, allowing it to take out its ill-feelings on you instead of your data. The terminals attached to mainframes already had speakers, and the first personal computer to gain significant popularity, the Apple II, released in 1977, was similarly equipped. This set the standards for all future personal computers, which had at least rudimentary sound capabilities.

By the time the first IBM PC was manufactured in 1981, a host of other personal computers were already on the market and were being used extensively for (among other things) games. Programmers were creating simple melodies on the PC and, perhaps more importantly, were creating the sounds of different weapons for the primitive Star Trek games that circulated on college campuses and bulletin board systems. For adventurous musicians, there were even synthesizer sound cards that plugged into the Apple II, made by alphaSyntauri and several other companies. These cards, which offered the general public the ability to compose music on a computer for the first time, fired the imaginations of many musicians. Even though they were expensive, they enjoyed a fair degree of success until MIDI and economically-priced digital synthesizers entered the market in 1983.

Meanwhile, sound on the PC remained relegated to system beeps and photon torpedo blasts for several years. During this time, synthesizers were evolving rapidly. MIDI brought these two forces together with a resounding crash heard in recording studios everywhere. And those studios were not always happy about it. But we need to backtrack a few years—to the 1890s, in fact—in order to understand why synthesizers suddenly became important in 1983.

Synthesis

All sound is the result of vibrations in the air. Acoustic instruments use vibrating strings, drumheads, rattles, or other physical means to create these vibrations. Electric instruments rely on an amplifier and speakers to move large volumes of air for them, but the original source of the vibration is a physical object whose motion is sensed by a pickup or a microphone. In an electronic instrument, however, the original source of the vibration is either a special oscillator circuit or, in digital synthesizers, a program loop residing in a sound chip's memory. Electronic sounds breathe their first life emanating from speaker systems.

These sounds are said to be synthesized, which literally means "produced by combining separate elements." By that definition, of course, a vegetable omelette is synthesized; perhaps we'd better rely on the meaning of the word that came into being along with chemistry: "produced by combining elements that are unrecognizable in the final product; man-made; artificial." And, of course, a synthesizer is anything that produces synthesized sounds.

Synthesizers take many forms, including sound cards, electronic keyboards, sound modules (small boxes containing synths that are "slaved" to a keyboard or computer), and drum machines. Synthesizers need controllers to trigger them. A controller is anything that sends MIDI messages to a synthesizer telling it to make sound (or to shut up, for that matter). Yamaha's DX-7 and most other electronic keyboard instruments include both a controller (the keyboard itself) and a synthesizer (the actual sound-producing hardware), although the entire instrument is often simply called a synthesizer. However, there are also stand-alone keyboard controllers that don't include synthesizers. These are often expensive "master" keyboards with weighted wooden keys (for the feel of an acoustic piano). It makes sense for an excellent keyboard player to buy just one of these and use it to control multiple sound modules.

Other MIDI controllers abound. Electronic drum pads are quite common—stick hits trigger sounds (usually drum sounds) in an external synthesizer module. Guitar controllers are less common—a special pickup attaches to a guitar and converts the notes that you play into MIDI messages and sends them to a synth. This technology is less than perfect, which has led to its less-than-widespread acceptance.

And last, but far from least, your computer is a MIDI controller if you have a MIDI interface attached to it.

The Roots of Synthesis

Synthesized music has actually been around since the turn of the century, although it took the advent of the digital computer in the last two decades to tame the unruly beast. Thaddeus Cahill's Telharmonium, patented in 1897, weighed about 200 tons and filled six railway cars. It created sounds by mechanical and electrical means but was never produced commercially, for obvious reasons.

Cahill's device drew upon an astounding conclusion from the realms of mathematics and physics. A French mathematician named Joseph Fourier had shown, early in the 19th century, that all periodic waves could be approximated to any degree of accuracy desired by a sum of simple sine waves (see Figure 1-1). A periodic wave is one which repeats; all pitched musical tones (as opposed to unpitched percussive tones) are, physically, periodic pressure waves in the air. This theorem states that all notes can be constructed from sine waves. This was a dramatic advance for the theory of sound, on a par with stating that all matter is composed of atoms.

This guiding concept has fueled many attempts at additive synthesis over the years, including Cahill's, as inventors attempted to develop instruments capable of creating any sound. Unfortunately, such instruments have proven impractical thus far, because the actual computations necessary to analyze sounds into their component sine waves, manipulate the components, and recreate the sounds are both too daunting for even today's computers and too musically unintuitive to be very useful for composers or performers.

In 1924, a Russian physicist named Leo Theremin took an alternate path to Cahill's and invented the electronic instrument that bears his name. The theremin, producer of the weird swoops used in the Beach Boys' hit "Good Vibrations" and in countless science fiction and

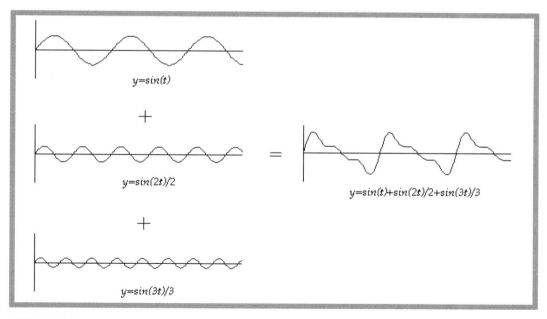

▶ **FIGURE 1-1**

Three simple sine waves are added together to create a richer, more complex sound.

suspense films, was played by waving your arms at a pair of anten-nae—one that controlled the pitch and one that controlled the volume. This instrument gained a certain amount of exposure and notoriety, and even produced one bona fide virtuoso, Clara Rockmore (her record, The Art Of The Theremin, is available on the Delos label). Theremin himself was abducted from the United States by Soviet agents in 1938 and remained cloistered in the Soviet Union for most of his life, emerging for one final visit to the United States in 1989. He died in Moscow in November, 1993.

A more significant milepost in synthesizer development, from the point of view of its impact on popular culture, was the introduction of the Hammond organ in 1939. It produces its sound by means of spin-ning metal discs, a technique pioneered in the Telharmonium but made much more compact for this use. Hammond organs evolved into tremendously expressive and rich-sounding instruments and became mainstays of jazz, rhythm 'n' blues, soul, and 60s rock groups. Ham-monds derive much of their soulful sound from their pairing with Leslie speaker cabinets, which include motorized speakers that spin rapidly around, adding depth and liveliness to the sound. Electronic effects that musicians today know as phase shifters and chorus stem from attempts to create similar sounds in boxes that are a manageable size, for although Hammond organs and Leslies are considerably more portable than their pipe organ ancestors, it's still no picnic moving them from club to club. Nonetheless, many keyboardists swear by their B-3s (the most popular model) to this day, claiming that no modern synthesizer can capture their sound and feel.

The Analog Age

The Hammond organ isn't what we generally think of when we talk about synthesizers. Although it is capable of producing a wide variety of sounds, all of them are recognizable as organ sounds. Today's syn-thesizers can produce many original timbres, and also many that mimic various acoustic and electric instruments. They have evolved along different lines than the Hammond, starting with the analog synthesizers developed by Dr. Robert Moog and others in the mid-'60s.

Moog was the first person to develop and market voltage-controlled oscillators (VCOs). These are electronic circuits that produce a steady pitch when their output is amplified and sent to a speaker. By sending different voltages to the inputs of these oscillators, you change their pitch. By combining VCOs with an organ-like keyboard which sent out different control voltages, depending on which key you pressed, Moog created a new musical instrument.

This description is somewhat oversimplified. Voltage-controlled oscillators can only produce a few simple timbres (timbre describes the tone quality of an instrument, as opposed to the pitch. A clarinet and a piano can play notes at the same pitch, but they will have different timbres). In Moog's earliest synthesizers, and in many more produced by Moog and his competitors in the following years, other voltage-controlled modules were used to shape the VCO's output into something more interesting. Also, devices other than keyboards, such as Sample-and-Hold modules, were used to create and process the voltages that controlled the pitch. In fact, analog synthesizer systems in the late 1960s became virtual hand-wired computer systems in their own right, with a dozen or more independent modules to process control voltages and audio signals, all interconnected with messy tangles of "patch cords." Despite all that complexity, these instruments were monophonic—capable of producing only one note at a time. The earliest synthesizers were better-suited to engineers than to musicians, but they laid the groundwork for everything to come.

Moog's instruments gained worldwide recognition when Walter Carlos (now Wendy Carlos) used them to record *Switched-On Bach*, a purely-electronic realization of many of Johann Sebastian Bach's greatest pieces. The record quickly became the best-selling classical music record of all time, and impressed the public tremendously with the ability of the new timbres to accentuate the many independent musical lines in Bach's music.

Switched-On Bach paved the way for Moog's next creation, the Minimoog. This synthesizer was designed specifically for live performance, and included the most important analog modules, pre-wired in a way that eliminated the need for patch cords. You didn't get the full flexibility of the earlier systems, but the Minimoog was usable onstage and produced a bass sound that synthesizer manufacturers try to emulate to this day, usually with mediocre results. The Minimoog was used extensively by some of the more prominent rock keyboard players who were tired of playing second fiddle to the guitar gods of the '60s. The most notable of these new keyboard virtuosi was Keith Emerson, originally of The Nice and later the key member of Emerson, Lake and Palmer. Other prominent synthesizer players were Rick Wakeman of Yes, Stevie Wonder, Herbie Hancock, and Joe Zawinul of Weather Report. Groups such as Pink Floyd and Tangerine Dream used synthesizers to create other-worldly textures, while Kraftwerk used them to create mechanistic aural backdrops symbolic of the Industrial Age.

Synthesizers waned in popularity somewhat through the mid and late 1970s due to their considerable expense, difficulty of use, and unreliability. Changing sounds was quite time-consuming and involved setting many dials to exact positions and sometimes changing the configuration of patch cords—not very practical for live performances. In addition, the tuning of these instruments tended to drift along with temperature changes (exacerbated by hot stage lights), and the complex electronic components were often not "roadworthy" (able to survive a six-foot toss into the back of a tour van).

Digital Synthesizers and MIDI

All of this changed in the early 1980s, due to several factors. The first of these was the advent of digital synthesizers. These synthesizers used computer chips and digital-to-analog converters (DACs) to create their sounds. When the synthesizer's processor detects that a key has been played, it generates a stream of numbers representing a sound wave based on which key was pressed, how hard it was pressed (called velocity in synthesizer terms) and the particular program or sound algorithm that you've chosen. It sends these numbers to a DAC, and the DAC produces voltages that form an audio signal (see Figure 1-2). The voltage produced by each number is held until the next number arrives, resulting in a staircase-like output. This is smoothed out by an analog filter, as shown in the diagram.

FIGURE 1-2

*The inner workings of a
digital synthesizer.*

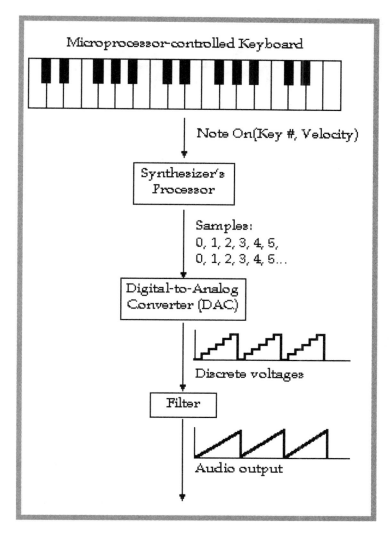

Digital synthesizers are far more stable in their tuning than their analog counterparts, far more roadworthy, and far more programmable. They're also usually less expensive. In short, they address all of the imperfections of analog synthesizers—except, for some purist tastes, the quality of the sound. For most of us, though, the advantages of digital synthesizers far outweigh the disadvantages, which is why almost every synthesizer that you can buy new today is digital.

The second major factor in the synth boom of the '80s was MIDI—the Musical Instrument Digital Interface. This was a communications standard developed by a group of synthesizer manufacturers in 1983 to help their customers solve a common problem—an excessive proliferation of keyboards onstage. Prior to MIDI, you couldn't connect equipment from different manufacturers together in any useful way. Consequently, once you purchased a keyboard from one manufacturer, you were more or less locked into purchasing expansion modules (for additional sounds) from that same manufacturer, unless you wanted to purchase an extra keyboard. You might end up with a stack of five keyboards that you'd have to carry to each gig and set up. Plus, you'd need five pairs of hands to play them all together. MIDI lets you mix and match keyboards and sound modules to your heart's content. With MIDI, you can press a key on a single keyboard and get a really massive sound from five sound modules responding at once ("fat" sounds seem to be the ultimate goal of many keyboard players). The first MIDI keyboards were the Prophet 600 from Sequential Circuits and the JP-6 from Roland.

For all the benefits that MIDI offered to performing keyboardists, it also had an unexpected use that has proven to be far more significant: MIDI is a digital data stream that essentially tells synthesizers when to turn notes on and off. If you put a computer in the middle of that stream and capture a record of the messages as they pass by, you can play back that stream at a later time (see Figure 1-3). It's important to understand that you're recording the actual keypresses of the performer on her controller and not the sounds that they trigger in the synthesizer.

Once the computer has a record of the MIDI messages in a performance, you can recreate that performance exactly at a later time by sending the messages to a sound module or back to the original keyboard synthesizer. When MIDI interfaces for computers first came out, along with the sequencing software to record and play back MIDI messages, a new world was born for musicians.

With a computer, a sequencing program, and a few sound modules, your average Jill could have a mini-recording studio in any unused corner of the house. Sequencers are extremely powerful—a

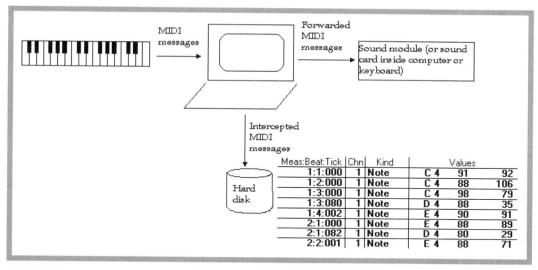

▶ **FIGURE 1-3**

Recording a performance with a MIDI sequencer. The list of notes shows the starting time of each note in the leftmost column.

single musician can record track after track and end up sounding like a large band. Sequencers give you a level of control over your music that tape recorders never will. If you record a wrong note with a sequencer, you can actually drag it with a mouse or type a few keystrokes to turn it into the right one. If you wish, you can play back your solos at double speed without any change in nuance or pitch, turning yourself into an instant virtual virtuoso.

The instant popularity of MIDI caused big changes in the recording industry. It was responsible for the rise of many project studios, small operations capable of producing commercial projects, to the dismay of many established recording studios. However, the majors have little to fear, because their superb microphones, isolation booths, and expensive, top-of-the-line signal processing gear are still necessary for recording live music of all kinds. A common hit-making procedure nowadays is for an artist or producer to create the synthesized tracks at his own home studio, and then bring the MIDI files into a professional studio where he can lay down the vocal tracks. It saves a lot of money for artists, who can experiment with different versions of their songs at home instead of using expensive studio time for songwriting and arranging purposes. And, as you'll no doubt discover for yourself, your home MIDI studio is available day and night, whenever inspiration strikes.

For a long time, before Windows achieved its current popularity, the Apple Macintosh was the computer of choice for musicians. A graphical interface is extremely useful for sequencing, although there are also many musicians who swear by their favorite DOS-based, non-graphical sequencers. Currently, Windows and the Macintosh are the most popular platforms for sequencing.

Most of us can make great music (within the limits of our talents and imaginations) with MIDI. The bag of tricks that MIDI programs offer is virtually unlimited, and gobs of fun. We'll cover many of them in detail in Chapter 10.

The Rise of Sound Cards

When digital synthesizers first became popular, their sonic palette was still pretty limited. They were great for sweeps and whooshes, did credible organ imitations, and produced a variety of other useful sounds, but musicians had a great hunger for a broader selection. A group of researchers at Stanford University, led by Dr. John Chowning, developed a technique called Frequency Modulation (FM) that produced rich, complex sounds inexpensively. This technique was soon licensed to Yamaha, who produced the enormously popular DX-7 synthesizer. This was the instrument that truly brought synthesis to the masses. Within a year of its creation, you could hardly find a rock band that didn't have one of these keyboards. Later, a simplified version of this synthesizer made it into the chips that form the heart of the Sound Blaster and many other sound cards, so it's well worth taking a few minutes to explore the details of FM.

Frequency modulation is an extreme case of vibrato, which is a warble in pitch that singers and instrumentalists use to add interest to sustained notes. Early on, analog synthesizer manufacturers used Low-Frequency Oscillators (LFOs) to simulate these effects. An LFO is just like a VCO, only slower. It typically produces a sine wave (or wave with another shape) that varies too slowly to be heard by itself (only waves that go through their complete cycle 20 to 20,000 times each second are audible to humans. You can't, for instance, wave your hand quickly enough in the air to create an audible tone).

Even though an LFO by itself can't create a tone, if you connect it to the pitch control input of an oscillator, it can cause the VCO's output to warble (see Figure 1-4). But strange things start to happen if you push this effect to the limit by increasing the speed of the LFO. First, when your ears can no longer track the precise ups and downs of the pitch changes, the warble becomes a rough buzz. Then, as the LFO speed increases further still (into the audible range, where it would more correctly be viewed as a second VCO), the buzz seems to smooth out, and you're left with the sensation of a continuous tone that has a more complex and interesting timbre than the original oscillator's output.

In this example, all the sound that you hear comes from the original VCO. In FM terms this VCO is called the carrier, while the LFO is called the modulator. Modulation means change, and this LFO is the

FIGURE 1-4

When an LFO is used to alter the frequency of a VCO, the VCO's pitch will increase when the LFO's value is positive (peaks of the wave are close to each other) and decrease when the LFO's value is negative (peaks of the wave are farther apart).

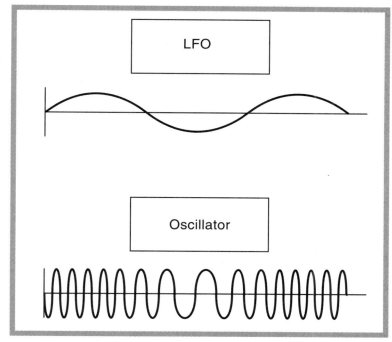

thing that causes change. The overall technique, in a nutshell, is that one oscillator modulates the other oscillator's frequency (hence the term "frequency modulation") in order to create a change in the tone that you hear. By changing either the amount of modulation (cutting it in half, for instance) or the frequency of the modulator, you can get a wide variety of timbres from two simple sine-wave oscillators—a much wider variety than you could if you mixed their outputs in an attempt at additive synthesis, for example.

Each of these oscillators is called an operator, and the pair of them together constitute a two-operator system, such as that used in the original AdLib and Sound Blaster cards on the PC. The professional musicians' DX-7, by contrast, had six operators that could be interconnected in many ways, creating a vast number of new sonic possibilities.

Still, two-operator FM sound was revolutionary on the PC, especially when AdLib released it in on an inexpensive card in August, 1987. It quickly became a standard when Taito of America, a major game publisher at the time, started writing games explicitly for the card. AdLib developed a virtual monopoly in the sound card market, one that clearly demonstrated the power of being first in line and establishing a standard. Other sound card manufacturers entered the market with incompatible cards and failed to convince programmers to support them, causing them to fail in the marketplace as well. It wasn't until a new competitor, Creative Labs, put forth the first Sound Blaster in early 1990 that AdLib had any competition. The Sound Blaster featured AdLib compatibility, along with improved features and value, and was an instant success.

The most important new feature introduced with the Sound Blaster was the ability to record and play back digital audio. For gamers, this introduced a whole new dimension of fun—car crashes, screams, laughs, cannon blasts, and a myriad of other noises were now in the realm of possibility. This, in combination with the MIDI interface built into the Sound Blaster, made it a very attractive proposition for buyers, who abandoned the AdLib fold in droves. AdLib was eventually driven out of business when they were unable to deliver an answer to the Sound Blaster challenge due to problems with their chip suppliers.

These days, sound cards no longer have to be AdLib-compatible. The standard has shifted, and they now must be Sound Blaster compatible. But, of course, as you now know, any card that is Sound Blaster compatible is automatically AdLib compatible (but not vice-versa). And, as we'll discuss in more detail below, this type of compatibility is gradually becoming less important as Windows applications become more dominant and DOS applications recede.

At this point, you might be wondering why a sound card is necessary at all. Couldn't the CPU do all the calculations involved in synthesis and drive the speaker by itself? The answer is yes, theoretically it could. But the sound generation calculations would have to take precedence over everything else going on in the computer, because precise timing is essential in order to produce accurate pitches. This wouldn't leave much power left over for putting graphics on the screen or performing calculations, so it's better to have a custom-designed chip on a card do all the work and leave the CPU free for other tasks.

The CD Revolution

Meanwhile, the digital sound concept was invading the world of consumer electronics as well. Audio compact discs (CDs), first announced in 1982, use the same principles as digital synthesizers to produce (or, in this case, reproduce) sound. As we've seen, digital synthesizers work by sending numbers to DACs, which are then converted into voltages that eventually drive speakers and create music. CD players do the exact same thing, except that they read those numbers with a laser beam from a spinning disc instead of calculating them with oscillator-simulating subroutines.

The quality of digital sound is directly dependent on the sample rate, which is the rate at which numbers are fed to the DAC. As it turns out (according to a piece of mathematical analysis called Nyquist's theorem), in order to accurately represent a frequency digitally, you need to have a sample rate that is at least twice the frequency. Since we can hear frequencies up to 20,000 Hz (Hertz, abbreviated Hz, is the same as cycles per second), a sampling frequency of at least 40,000 samples per second is necessary to reproduce the full range of audible sound. The designers at Sony and Phillips who developed the compact disc added some breathing room to allow for filters to screen out some potentially audible extraneous noises produced by the process and decided on a sampling rate of 44,100 samples per second (44.1 kHz).

The precision of lasers, which are used both to create and play CDs, are necessary in order to handle the massive storage requirements of high-quality digital audio. At a sample rate of 44.1 kHz, each minute of stereo sound requires 10 megabytes of data. An entire 200-megabyte hard disk can only hold about 1/3 the data contained on a typical audio CD.

The CD was quickly adopted by great numbers of music fans due to its high-quality sound and, perhaps more importantly, its freedom from the annoying pops and clicks that had plagued vinyl records for decades. It is indeed possible to scratch and damage a CD, but most minor scratches will have no audible effect.

Once CDs containing digital audio data entered the marketplace in significant quantities in the early eighties, it was but a short step to conceive of CDs containing other forms of data. If the computer industry had been able to create a removable disc that could hold 640 megabytes of data that you could read from and write to just like the most massive diskette you've ever imagined (but working much more quickly), it would have built the ultimate storage device. However, reality reared its ugly head and a technology was born that offered some, but not all of these features: CD-ROM.

As you probably know, the "ROM" in CD-ROM stands for Read-Only Memory. Of course, a disc isn't really memory, but at least the "Read-Only" part is accurate. You can read information, music, pictures or whatever from a CD-ROM, but you can't ever change its contents. These contents are burned into the discs at the pressing plant. The CD-ROM technology is a publishing medium, not a personal storage medium.

You can put CD-ROMs into audio CD players, but the first track will be an ugly static noise that might just blow your speakers. That's the sound of data—the track actually contains a directory and files, just like your hard disk. If there are tracks beyond the first, they contain standard CD audio data—music or sound that can be played on any CD player, but that are generally meant to be accessed under control of the programs contained in the first track.

The uses of CD-ROM are only beginning to be explored. We'll look at them in depth in Chapter 11.

Enter Windows and the MPC

Windows took a number of years to become the standard that it is today. Before it could become truly popular, it had to evolve and improve through many versions with glaring imperfections, and it needed the glut of inexpensive 80386-based computers that became available around 1991. Or, just maybe, it needed a compelling and valuable reason to exist, and the Multimedia PC (MPC) specification that Microsoft released in November, 1990, provided that reason.

Not surprisingly, the MPC specification was built around Microsoft Windows. At first, the recommended system software for multimedia was Windows 3.0 with the additional Multimedia Extensions (MME). These pieces were soon consolidated and improved, and released as Windows 3.1.

For a computer system to qualify as an MPC Level 1 system, it needs at least a 386SX processor, a CD-ROM drive, a sound card with both digital audio and MIDI playback capabilities and a pair of speakers. In the time since the Level 1 specification was announced, video clips on CD-ROM have clearly demonstrated the need for faster processors and CD-ROMs. Now there is an MPC Level 2 specification, which requires a double-speed CD-ROM and at least a 486SX processor. To be quite frank, though, if you're thinking about purchasing a new computer and you want good video quality, you should exceed even these specifications. Get a computer with a 486DX2 chip running at 50MHz, or a faster model. They're not much more expensive than the 486SX computers, and they're significantly more powerful.

The MPC specification officially recognizes three kinds of audio: CD audio (also called "Red Book" audio), digital audio in the form of wave (.WAV) files, and synthesized audio in the form of MIDI (.MID) files. It also specifies that MPC computers must have a mixer to control the relative volumes of these music sources.

You're already familiar with CD audio. As we discussed, it is stored in tracks other than the first track on a CD-ROM. However, CD audio alone is not sufficient for developing multimedia applications. For instance, a typical use of audio in a multimedia title might be to provide transition music while the computer finds an animation file on the CD-ROM and prepares to play it. Unfortunately, if the CD-ROM is currently playing an audio track, the search for the animation file will have to interrupt the music—the CD-ROM drive can't read from two parts of the disc simultaneously. Instead, many titles copy MIDI files and/or wave files to the hard disk and play them from that location to entertain you while the CD-ROM spins.

Because of the size of CD audio files, it would be impractical to copy them to the hard disk. But wave files are more flexible and can sacrifice some sound quality in order to shrink themselves. A wave file can be stereo or mono, can be sampled at a wide range of sample rates that are slower than CD rates, and can use eight-bit samples instead of 16-bit ones. All of these measures result in lower quality audio, but you can fit a 30-second wave file into half a megabyte or less, instead of the five megabytes that a CD audio cut of the same length would occupy.

MIDI files are smaller still; in fact, they are practically negligible, mere specks by multimedia standards. That's because they don't contain any direct representations of sound; instead, they contain instructions, much like the paper rolls that control player pianos. A minute of MIDI music could easily fit into 25KB or less.

The most significant aspect of the MPC specification may have been one that is invisible to most end-users. Windows 3.1 provides an Application Program Interface (API) that gives programmers the ability to write hardware-independent multimedia code. It's an abstract concept, but it has a profound effect on encouraging competition, which determines which products are available to you and me and how much they cost.

Under Windows, a programmer doesn't have to know which sound card is installed in order to use it. Instead, she simply sends a command such as "PLAY MYFILE.MID" to the Media Control Interface (MCI) component of Windows, and Windows handles the details of the playback. In order to accomplish this, Windows issues to a driver that is installed by the Setup or Install program for your sound card. Figure 1-5 shows the difference between the two coding approaches.

With the old approach, thousands of application programs would have to include support for a variety of sound cards and would have to be periodically updated as new sound cards entered the market. The consequences are clear—no one would support anything other than the Sound Blaster standard. It would be impossible for any non-Sound

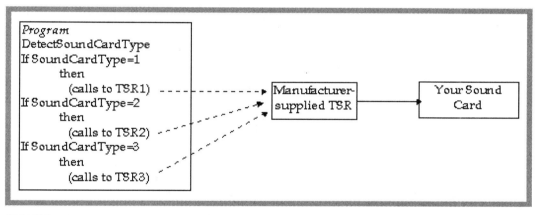

▶ **FIGURE 1-5A**

DOS programs must support different sound cards explicitly by calling subroutines installed into memory by Terminate and Stay Resident (TSR) programs.

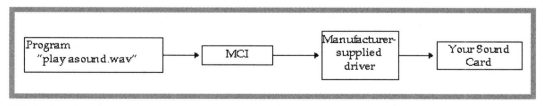

▶ **FIGURE 1-5B**

Windows programs issue a single call to the Media Control Interface (MCI), which calls the manufacturer's driver to execute the command.

Blaster compatible sound card, no matter what its virtues, to succeed in the market. Instead, we have a situation in which each manufacturer only has to supply a driver that is compatible with Windows 3.1 guidelines, and every Windows program will automatically work with it correctly. Sound Blaster compatibility is still important for non-Windows applications, but that is becoming less compelling every day. The net result is that you and I have more and better sound cards to choose from (a bewildering array, in fact, as you'll discover in Chapter 3).

DOS or Windows?

The increasing popularity of Windows 3.1 may make you think that you must move to that platform immediately. This is not true. You can have a great time with music on your PC whether you're a DOS fan or a Windows fanatic. Many software developers create separate versions of their products that will work in either environment. Windows is definitely the wave of the future, especially for multimedia and sound-oriented products, and many of the newest, hottest products will only come out in Windows versions. Still, there are millions of computers out there that aren't fast enough to run Windows, and an ample supply of DOS software available for them to satisfy most musical needs.

In today's computing world, Windows and DOS share the spotlight. The old war-horse is DOS, and it will still run efficiently on computers that are five years old or older. Windows is the glamorous newcomer with the pretty face. It comes pre-installed on just about all new PCs. At the time of this writing, Windows is installed "on top of" DOS and still relies on the older system to handle many low-level functions. That is changing, though, and newer releases of Windows will dispense with DOS altogether. Whether many users will want to move to an all-Windows world, however, is debatable. There are still good reasons to keep ol' DOS around.

The overwhelming reason for DOS' continued existence is performance. Windows is a vast operating environment that offers many services to developers and users, and coordinates multiple programs running simultaneously. There is a lot of overhead involved in these services, and programs running under Windows don't have access to all the raw power of your computer. That's why most game programs are written to run under DOS—these programs need to squeeze every last bit of performance out of your computer in order to produce lightning-fast responses to your finely-honed reflexes and to create computation-intensive effects such as three-dimensional environments that scroll on the screen as you move your mouse or joystick. Even state-of-the-art, CD-ROM-based games such as The Seventh Guest rely on DOS rather than Windows.

On the other hand, there are many reasons for developers—especially non-game developers—to concentrate on Windows. Performance is often not as important as convenience and ease-of-use, and that is what Windows delivers in spades. From a developer's point of view, writing a graphically-oriented applications program is infinitely easier when a robust framework such as Windows already exists. Programmers don't have to reinvent the wheel for each program, and program development time is greatly shortened. From a user's point of view, not only do you get easier-to-use, more affordable programs more quickly, but you also benefit from the synergy of having them work together smoothly. You can cut and paste calculations from your spreadsheet and drawings from your painting program into a word processing document, for instance. In addition, Windows programs share a common set of interface standards that make basic keystrokes and menu choices consistent from application to application, making it much easier to learn new programs.

The ideal strategy is to get a computer that can run both DOS and Windows and to use each one when it's most appropriate.

Chapter 2

Swinging Through The Equipment Jungle

There are a surprising number of components that make up a fully-equipped musical PC, and a number of bundles that mix them harmoniously and economically for you. In this chapter, we'll take a look at the different hardware components that you might want, at the most common package deals, at which setups are right for which purchases, and at the various types of equipment dealers. When you've finished the chapter, you'll know the full range of your options and have a good idea of which ones might be right for you.

As a long-time consumer of music technology, I know that it's important to consider long-term equipment needs rather than buying the hottest new gear on impulse. A planned approach can prevent you from purchasing the wrong piece of equipment and can also allow you to save money by buying several related pieces at once from a single source, instead of buying them piecemeal as you uncover new needs. Even if you can't afford everything you want at once, a vision of your dream system will make your current purchases serve your long-term goals.

Sound Hardware

In this section we'll talk about all the different types of music gear that can add to your PC and the major varieties that exist within each type. Our approach will be that of a broad overview. You'll learn the function of each component and the type of person who will get the best use from it. Later chapters will delve into finer detail and present specific evaluation criteria.

Sound Cards and Daughterboards

Everyone who wants to make music on a PC needs a sound card, with the single exception of laptop owners who are only interested in MIDI and have no use for CD-ROM or digital audio. Sound cards are the heart of a multimedia system—they typically contain a synthesizer, CD-ROM controller, digital audio playback and recording hardware, and an audio mixer for combining all these sound sources. Furthermore, MIDI interfaces are often included or available as inexpensive options.

Fully-loaded multimedia sound cards as described above are the most popular, but there is another variety—the synthesizer-only sound card. The Roland SCC-1 Sound Canvas was the first of these, and the Turtle Beach Maui is another. These cards are meant to function in conjunction with a Sound Blaster or other general-purpose sound card; they specialize in providing high-quality synthesizer sounds and leave all the remaining functions to your original card. They make sense as an upgrade path from an older FM card.

Similar to the synthesizer-only sound card is the daughterboard, a synthesizer-only sound card that plugs into a socket on an existing sound card instead of into a computer slot. The most popular daughterboard is Creative Labs' Wave Blaster. This chip plugs into the Sound Blaster 16 and provides it with wavetable synthesis.

Many sound cards include a CD-ROM controller; if you already have a CD-ROM drive and plan to change sound cards, it is important to make sure that the new controller will be compatible with your drive. Check with the sound card manufacturer for more information.

Parallel Port and PCMCIA Sound "Cards"

These are devices intended to give sound card functionality to laptop and notebook owners. They are intended for Windows users and are generally not Sound Blaster-compatible. They all feature the ability to play back wave files, but the rest of their features vary quite a bit. Some offer FM synthesis, some offer wavetable synthesis, some have no synthesizer, some offer a MIDI interface, and some offer a built-in speaker and/or microphone. Some of the parallel port devices offer "passthrough" connections that enable you to connect a printer without unplugging the sound device.

MIDI Interfaces

These are devices that allow your computer to communicate with MIDI keyboards and other sound peripherals. They are often built into sound cards but may require the purchase of an optional connector cable that attaches to the card's joystick port.

Long before sound cards, MIDI interfaces existed for the PC. In fact, the musical equipment manufacturer Roland set the standard in 1984 when it released the MPU-401. This consisted of a card designed to plug into a PC slot, and an external connector box with MIDI In and Out ports and tape synchronization jacks. These synchronization facilities were designed to let musicians lock sequences to analog instrumental tracks recorded on tape. They have largely been supplanted in the world of serious musicians by newer technology (MIDI/SMPTE converters, used by recording studio professionals everywhere, and compatible with any MIDI interface), which is one of the reasons that they are not included on the newer sound card MIDI interfaces.

The MPU-401 dominated the world of MIDI interfaces for many years, even though it was severely overdesigned for its market (it featured a "smart mode" which no commercial programs of note ever took advantage of, because it just wasn't smart enough and developers found it more prudent to let their software be smart and use the interface in "dumb" mode). In the DOS-dominated world that existed until recently, it was hard for any non-MPU-401-compatible interface to get support from software developers. Even the Sound Blaster's MIDI interface is MPU-401-compatible.

For most people today, there is no point in purchasing a separate MIDI interface—for the same price, you can buy a sound card and get the interface in addition to all the card's other features. The one exception to this is anyone who needs to connect external MIDI modules to a laptop computer (although even these folks have the option of purchasing one several good sound modules that include a built-in serial port MIDI interface). Since most portable sound devices don't provide MIDI ports, this function requires a serial- or parallel-port MIDI interface in order to talk to the outside world. Generally, the parallel port interfaces are more reliable and accurate in their timing than the serial ones, but also more expensive.

Powered Speakers

The musical computing experience is greatly enhanced by a pair of powered speakers connected to your sound card's output, although you can use your existing stereo system for this purpose if it is conveniently positioned. You could, of course, avoid this purchase and use only headphones (which may be your only option if your music computer is in an office environment), but headphones are fatiguing after an hour or two of listening.

Use only shielded, powered speakers designed for computer systems near your computer. Unshielded speakers produce magnetic fields which can damage your monitor or any diskettes that you unthinkingly lay on top of them.

It's a general truism in speaker design that the larger the speaker, the better the bass response—that's why bass guitarists use huge cabinets with one or more 15-inch speakers in them. You don't have to go this far for your system, but ordinary weak-powered speaker sets usually have pretty anemic bass response. For this reason, I highly recommend purchasing a speaker system with a subwoofer, if you can afford one. This is a separate speaker enclosure (with its own amplifier) designed to reproduce bass frequencies well. You can place one of these under your desk and enjoy stomach-pounding bass while the two high-frequency speakers (called, in a subwoofer-based system, satellite speakers) give you crystal-clear highs and stereo separation.

You will find many more details about speaker systems in Chapter 4.

Microphones

Microphones are useful for recording voice annotations to spreadsheets, e-mail and other multimedia documents (if you already work in an "office of the future"), and they're also useful for recording acoustic instruments and vocalists. There is an extremely wide range of microphone quality, from the 50-cent microphone in your answering machine to the $2,000 microphone that Barbra Streisand might use in a recording studio. You don't have to spend much on a microphone for ordinary business use, but a decent microphone for recording music will cost between $40 and $100. Even so, you'll have to invest in a small mixer or microphone preamplifier in order to make high-quality musical recordings with a microphone, as explained in detail in Chapter 8.

Headphones

Headphones are uncomfortable and inconvenient for daily, routine use (you don't want to don them just to hear your system beeps), but they are great for listening to fine details of the music. A good pair of "cans," as recording engineers call them, is essential for checking the fine points of instrument volume, stereo placement, and ambient effects in a musical composition or soundscape. With the improvements that have been made in headphone technology in the past few years, even an extremely inexpensive set can provide pretty good sound and get your irate co-workers off your case for a while.

The lightweight, Walkman-style headphones that have become popular during the last few years offer surprisingly good quality at low prices, and they allow you to hear outside sounds such as your co-workers talking to you. The heavier padded and enclosed-style headphones, on the other hand, insulate you from outside sounds to a greater extent and provide still greater fidelity and bass response.

CD-ROM Drives

These are essential multimedia components. They come in both internal and external varieties, and also in single, double, triple and quadruple-speed varieties. A CD-ROM needs a controller, which is typically built into your sound card for internal CD-ROMs. (If you purchase a multimedia upgrade kit, you're assured of compatibility. Otherwise, check with your sound card manufacturer before you purchase a CD-ROM drive). External CD-ROMs attach either to a parallel port, to a parallel-port-to-SCSI adapter, or to a controller card provided by the manufacturer (often at extra cost).

Currently, double-speed CD-ROM drives offer the best balance of value and performance. Single-speed drives are rapidly becoming obsolescent—don't buy one unless it's practically free! And, since most software these days is targeted for double-speed drives, you may not reap major benefits by paying for quadruple-speed performance.

Professional (and Semi-Professional) Musical Equipment

There's a wealth of great-sounding musical gear that you can attach to your PC—musicians and composers have been doing so for years. If you're already an instrumentalist, you'll want to seriously consider purchasing a MIDI controller in order to have a means to play your performances into the computer. If you're not a player but the quality of your MIDI music is very important to you, consider purchasing an external MIDI sound module—there are some pretty fantastic-sounding units out there.

MIDI Equipment

MIDI controllers and sound modules have been circulating in the musical community since 1984, and they've evolved to meet the needs of some pretty picky people—professional musicians. A MIDI controller is a necessity for anyone who is serious about sequencing—

entering notes into the computer with a mouse is many times harder and less natural than playing them in, even if you're only a mediocre performer. Although MIDI sound modules are often more expensive than their sound card counterparts, they also deliver better-quality sound than all but the most expensive sound cards.

Keyboards

MIDI was developed for the convenience of keyboard players, and keyboards remain the most versatile and capable of MIDI controllers. Most have a built-in sound module, and many have built-in sequencing programs (which are redundant for you, who will most likely use a more powerful and convenient PC-based sequencer). Most MIDI keyboards have 61 weighted plastic keys, although more expensive controllers with 88 wooden keys are available for those who desire a feel more similar to that of an acoustic piano.

The MIDI keyboards range in price from small, no-frills units costing less than $200 to multi-thousand dollar top-of-the-line sonic extravaganzas.

Percussion Controllers

For those who would rather pound rubber than tickle the ivories (or the "plastics," as the case may be), percussion controllers are available that will send out MIDI messages when you strike them with sticks. These are less flexible than keyboards in a number of ways but suit some people very well.

Percussion controllers usually have about eight pads that you can strike. Their main musical limitations are that chords are difficult, if not impossible, to play and that there is no natural means of creating notes of differing durations. (On a keyboard, you hold a key down and then release it when you want it to stop. In contrast, on a percussion controller, you strike a pad and the physical release follows immediately as the stick leaves the pad.) In short, percussion controllers are great for pounding out rhythm tracks but far from ideal for other purposes.

Percussion controllers come in several shapes. As with keyboards, you can obtain percussion controllers with or without built-in sound generators. Most percussion controllers have their pads laid out on some kind of box, but some come in the form of traditional drum sets, with skins and cymbals replaced by sensor pads.

At long last, it's possible to practice drumming without disturbing the entire neighborhood—just pull out the electronic drums, plug in the headphones, and pound away.

Guitar Controllers

Guitar players, unfortunately, don't have it as easy as keyboard players or drummers when it comes to engaging in musical dialogues with their computers. It is relatively simple technology for a keyboard's computer chip to tell exactly which keys are pressed at any given instant, and it is equally easy for a percussion controller to respond with accuracy. However, in order for a guitar controller to translate a picker's playing into MIDI messages, it must actually "listen" to the sound of the strings and attempt to deduce from that exactly which notes were played. This turns out to be a pretty knotty problem, both because virtually instantaneous analysis is required and because guitarists tend to play a lot of "pseudo-notes"—damped notes, ghost notes, and "chicken-picked" notes have more percussive content than melodic content and are quite difficult for a controller to analyze.

The upshot of all this is that MIDI guitars are less reliable than MIDI keyboards or drums and invariably include a slight time delay that many players have difficulty accepting.

Although there are several competing technologies that have been used for guitar controllers, the most popular one consists of a special hexaphonic pickup that mounts on any steel-string acoustic or electric guitar, and a converter box which analyzes the signals from the pickup and turns them into MIDI messages. Roland is the most successful manufacturer of guitar controllers, and its current offerings all include built-in synthesizer sound modules.

Other Controllers

MIDI controllers have also been designed for wind players, violinists, and other instrumentalists, although they have not attained the massive popularity that keyboards and percussion controllers have. Keep your eye on Keyboard and Electronic Musician magazines for news and advertisements related to these, if they interest you, and keep an eye out for the phrase "alternate controllers."

Sound Modules

A tremendous variety of sounds is available in the form of MIDI sound modules. These boxes range from units about the size of a laptop computer to devices that are closer in size to stereo receivers or amplifiers. Some of them even include interfaces that allow you to connect them directly to your computer, without the need for a separate MIDI interface. The criteria that we'll give in Chapter 3 for evaluating the synthesizer sections of sound cards apply to these units.

Packages

Now that you know all the different pieces that you might want, let's take a look at some of the common bundling options and see which ones are cool and which are not.

Multimedia Upgrade Kits

If you're ready for both a sound card and a CD-ROM player at the same time, this is definitely the way to go. You can be certain that the drive and the sound card are compatible, that the right software drivers are provided, and that the installation process will be relatively easy. Plus, if you need technical support, you'll be able to get it from a single source. Many of these packages include a selection of CD-ROM titles, making the entire package a good bargain (if the titles are ones that appeal to you). Some of these upgrade kits also include powered speakers. These speakers are often the weakest part of the kit, and the cheap microphones and headphones that may also be thrown in are usually no great bargains. Stick to the basics—a sound card, CD-ROM drive, and some titles—and buy the other pieces separately.

Multimedia Computer Systems

Buying a brand-new computer system complete with sound card, CD-ROM drive, and speakers is the most hassle-free way of getting a multimedia-enabled system. The drawback is that these packages tend to include mid-level or inexpensive sound cards and speakers. If you go for one of these, make sure you know which kind of sound card you're getting, as well as which speakers. If your interest is quality sound, you'd be better off adding these components yourself or having a dealer put together a custom package for you.

Teaching Bundles (Don't Expect A Miracle)

Some teaching systems (most notably the Miracle Piano System from The Software Toolworks) come complete with a keyboard, MIDI interface, and computer software. While this can be an excellent deal for a beginner, you may soon become dissatisfied with the entry-level keyboard and wish that you had purchased the software and a better keyboard as separate components.

Who Are You?

"Different strokes for different folks," is the way Sly Stone put it in his song "Dance To The Music." Before you run off on a computer sound peripheral spending spree, decide whether your main interest is computer gaming, "edutainment" and education, sequencing, performing, or multimedia production. This section will help you to focus on the most important equipment for your needs in each of those categories.

Computer Gaming

If you want a sound card primarily to enhance your enjoyment of computer games, you need a desktop computer and a Sound Blaster-compatible sound card, and you'll probably want a CD-ROM drive, either now or in the future. If it's within your budget, a wavetable synthesizer can really increase your enjoyment of games.

If you already have an FM-based Sound Blaster-compatible card and are ready to upgrade, then consider a synthesizer-only sound card or daughterboard.

Edutainment and Education

In this category CD-ROMs are the wave of the future, so you'll probably want a multimedia upgrade kit. The actual sound quality of the synthesizer may not be of primary importance to you, since most of the sound in CD-ROM titles currently comes from wave files and CD audio tracks.

If one of the things you want to learn is how to play the piano, then you'll want a MIDI keyboard, and you'll want to make sure that the multimedia upgrade kit that you purchase includes a MIDI interface.

Musical practicing is another form of education, one that is applicable to all instrumentalists and vocalists, MIDI'd or not. With MIDI software such as Band-In-A-Box or SuperJam (described in Chapter 10), you can have the computer play backing parts at any speed while you practice your best licks or exercises. It's a great way to polish your instrumental skills and doesn't require any equipment except a sound card and the right software.

For more information about music education of your PC, turn to Chapter 11.

Sequencing

If you can play an instrument and sequencing or producing music notation is your main interest, then you'll want to use a MIDI controller to play your music into the computer. In order to do this, you'll need a MIDI interface on your computer, so get a sound card with a MIDI interface. An inexpensive sound card will probably suit your needs just fine, since the synthesizer in your keyboard is likely to be your sound source of choice.

Performing

If your goal is the specialized one of performing live while the computer handles the drum, bass and other backing tracks, then you'll undoubtedly want a notebook computer. The multimedia capabilities of a sound card won't be that important to you; instead, you'll want either a parallel- or serial-port MIDI interface, or a sound module that comes with a computer connection.

Multimedia Production

Although MIDI capabilities can be important, it is often digital audio that takes the spotlight in this theater, because it accompanies the all-important digital video. Digital video requires a fast machine and CD-ROM drive, so put your extra money into these items, and don't worry about wavetable synthesis. In fact, if you use synthesis at all, you'll probably want to develop it on the most popular sound card in order to optimize it for the greatest number of users. At the time of this writing, that means you should get a Sound Blaster 16.

Where to Buy

You can buy sound cards, upgrade kits and multimedia computers by mail order or from your local computer dealer. Mail order will often be less expensive than local purchases, but you may not get much installation support, which can be an issue with these items. You'll have to deal with interrupts, DMA channels, and I/O port addresses during the installation process. It's not that horrible, and the defaults that the sound card setup programs offer will work in most systems. Furthermore, Chapter 5 will help you with the process. Still, if you're uncomfortable with the idea of changing a jumper on a board or editing your CONFIG.SYS file, your local dealer may well be your best bet. It's quite possible that he will match any printed price in a mail-order catalog.

If you have a large warehouse store near you, shopping at it will be much like purchasing from a mail-order operation, except that you'll have fewer choices and no access to anyone even remotely knowledgeable. I don't recommend these as sources of computer hardware unless you really know what you're doing. On the other hand, they can be good places to purchase top-selling software at substantial discounts.

You can find 800 numbers and advertisements for mail-order operations in any PC-oriented magazine. Your local computer dealer, of course, can be found in your Yellow Pages.

Keyboard synthesizers are another matter. For these, visit a music store or order from a musical mail-order catalog (advertised in music magazines such as Keyboard and Electronic Musician). The keyboards that are found in computer and consumer electronics catalogs are often low-end, discontinued models that may well disappoint you. Your local music dealer will be able to let you compare the sounds on various keyboards and advise you on the capabilities of each instrument.

Chapter **3**

Sound Cards

In this chapter we'll take a close look at sound cards and give you enough information to judge any card's appropriateness for your purposes. Most of the significant differences will be found in the synthesizer sections of these cards, but there are also important differences in the digital audio areas and in CD-ROM compatibility and bundled software.

Digital Audio Section

Digital audio capability, as we've discussed, refers to the ability of a sound card to record and play back digital representations of sound waves. In a Windows environment, these are *wave* files and have a .WAV filename extension, while the slightly-different digital audio files that have become popular for DOS applications are called *voice* files and have a .VOC extension. In addition, the audio tracks for animation and video files are all played back using your sound card's digital audio facilities, which makes this aspect of the card quite significant.

In this section, you'll learn the details of how sound cards differ in their digital audio implementations, and how these differences may affect you.

Number of Bits

Sound cards come in both 8- and 16-bit flavors. I strongly recommend purchasing a 16-bit sound card, because the difference in the quality of the sound is dramatic. A 16-bit card can play 8-bit files, but an 8-bit card can't play 16-bit files. In fact, the existence of a large, installed base of 8-bit cards is a drag on the market, sometimes forcing title developers to conform to the lowest common denominator and release their sounds in the 8-bit format.

To understand the difference between 8- and 16-bit sound, let's consider some fundamentals.

Bits, Bytes, and Words

All the information that a computer can handle—which means everything on your hard disk, diskettes, or CD-ROMs—is stored in the form of numbers. You don't normally think of them that way because application programs interpret them and display them for you in formats that are more meaningful to humans. Word processors, for instance, translate the characters that you type into numbers (the letter "A" is represented by its *ASCII* code—the number 65) and store them on disks. Later, they retrieve the streams of numbers and reinterpret them into characters, page breaks, font choices, and all the other elements that make up a document.

However, this is not the whole story. When we dig a little deeper, down to the physical level of what is actually happening on your hard drive, we learn that each data location is a tiny area of the drive that can either be magnetized in one direction or the other. In other words, the smallest "atom" of information on a hard disk can only have two states. Therefore, it can represent at most two numbers. If we decide to interpret these numbers as 0 and 1, we can build up larger numbers by stringing these data atoms, called *bits*, together.

Our familiar number system is known technically as a *positional number system with base 10*. This mysterious mouthful actually means something that is quite obvious when you apply it to a common example. Consider the number 3219. It's what you get when you add up 9 ones, 1 ten, 2 hundreds, and 3 thousands. Each digit represents a different value depending upon its position; 13 is not the same as 31. The value of the position starts at 1 for the rightmost position and is multi-plied by 10 each time you move to the left by one digit.

Computers are based on bits, which can only take on two values, 0 and 1. When these bits are combined into larger numbers, the numbers must consist of strings of 0s and 1s, such as 100010, 111, or 100001. How can the number 3 be stored in a computer? It's easy if you use a positional number system with base 2 (called the *binary* system). In this system, the various positions have the values shown in Figure 3-1. Since 3 is 1x1+1x2, its binary representation is 11.

```
  1   0   0   1   0   1   1   1    = 1x128 + 0x64 + 0x32 + 1x16 + 0x8 + 1x4 + 1x2 + 1x1 = 151
128  64  32  16   8   4   2   1
```

▶ **FIGURE 3-1**

Each position in the binary number system has a value double that of the position to its right.

In computers, each set of 8 bits is called a *byte*. The smallest byte is the number 00000000, which simply represents 0, while the largest is 11111111, which represents 1+2+4+8+16+32+64+128, or 255. (If you know about exponents, you can take a shortcut: the largest number that can be represented by n bits is $2n$ -1). As one more example (one with mixed 0s and 1s), the number 1001 in the binary system represents 1x1+0x2+0x4+1x8, which adds up to 9 in our usual decimal system.

Similarly, a collection of 16 bits is called a *word* (an unfortunate choice of terminology due to the standard English meaning of "word," but we're stuck with it). The smallest value a word can have is 0, while the largest is 65,535. And, just for the sake of completeness, we'll mention that a collection of 4 bits is called a *nybble* (half a byte is a nybble—get it?) and can represent numbers from 0 to 15.

So far, we've been talking about positive numbers. When we want to represent waveforms and other types of data that can have both positive and negative values, we use the first bit in a number to represent its sign, leaving the rest for the actual data. In this way, bytes can represent numbers from −128 to 127, and words can represent numbers from −32,768 to 32,767.

Number of Bits and Sound Quality

In Chapter 1, we talked about the playback of digital audio files. Now we'll reverse the process and talk about the recording of digital audio files in order to demonstrate the differences between 8- and 16-bit recording.

A digital audio file is created by *sampling* an audio signal at a fixed rate (see Figure 3-2). An audio signal enters a chip called an *Analog-to-Digital Converter* (ADC), which is the opposite of the DAC that we discussed earlier. The sound card's controller chip requests a value from that ADC thousands of times each second, and the ADC returns a number representing the voltage of the audio signal (positive or negative) at the time of the request. An 8-bit ADC returns a byte, while a 16-bit ADC returns a word.

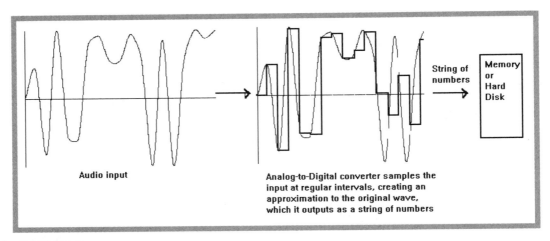

▶ **FIGURE 3-2**
Capturing a sound wave as a digital audio file.

An 8-bit ADC can only return one out of 256 different numbers; it effectively divides up the sound wave into 256 horizontal slices, while a 16-bit ADC divides it up into over 65,000 slices. The latter is far more accurate (like measuring with a ruler marked in inches versus one marked in yards) and results in far less audible noise and an improved dynamic range—the difference between the softest and loudest sounds—during playback.

Sixteen-bit cards are the way to go, and they're not very expensive. Furthermore, you needn't worry about obsolescence. If you're thinking, "They used to tell me I needed an 8-bit card, and now they tell me 16 bits are required. Right after I buy one, they'll up the ante to 32 bits," don't worry. Sixteen bits are used in audio CDs, and there's no need for sound cards to exceed that quality. The difference couldn't be heard by any but the most "golden" ears, and then only under pristine listening conditions that are not likely to apply on your desktop.

Compression and Decompression

Sound cards can squeeze extra sound quality out of a fixed number of bits, or lower the number of bits (and hence disk space) required for a fixed sound quality, by using *compression*. There are several techniques used for accomplishing this, but the most common is called *Adaptive Delta Pulse Code Modulation* (ADPCM), which works by storing the differences between the values of successive samples instead of the actual samples themselves.

Sound card compression is especially useful if you're going to be recording a lot of digital audio music or voice for your own use. It is less useful for distributed applications such as networked, voice-annotated documents or commercial software distribution unless you can be sure that all your intended recipients have sound cards with compatible decompression hardware. In short, it's not a critical feature.

3-D Sound

Several sound cards offer 3-D sound processing built into their chips. This is a bit of psychoacoustic wizardry (involving the science that relates sound to the ways in which the brain processes it) designed to fool you into thinking that sound from a single pair of speakers is really coming from above, below, and behind you.

There are at least three different flavors of 3-D processing available. One, SRS, used in products from Media Vision and NuReality, among others, is a surround-sound technology similar to that available in many home theater-oriented receivers. It processes the entire signal and increases the feeling of immersion. On the plus side, cards with this technology can apply it to CD audio, wave audio, and synthesizer sounds. On the minus side, this technology cannot precisely locate individual sounds in 3-D space, so game manufacturers won't use it to make spaceships seem to sneak up on you from behind, and neither will you be able to insert commands into your sequences that place an oboist in the right balcony.

Q-Sound is available on all Creative Labs 16-bit boards that have the ASP signal processor, and on their AWE32 board. This expands the sound field to a full 180° semicircle rather than the smaller triangle formed by your head and the speakers. This processing is available to you when you create MIDI sequences. Q-sound makes notes that are panned full left (using a 0 value for the Pan Continuous Controller, as described in Chapter 10) sound as if they're coming from an instrument off to your left rather than from the left speaker.

Focal Point 3-D sound claims to be a true 3-D surround technology that works best with headphones. Available primarily for the Advanced Gravis Ultrasound line of cards, Focal Point is mainly a tool for developers. Game designers preprocess sounds (using a utility that Advanced Gravis supplies to them in their Developer's Kit) to seem as if they're coming from any location in a sphere surrounding your head—above, below, behind, on the sides, or in front. The first game to make use of this technique is *Hired Guns* by Psygnosis. It can be a very exciting effect for games and virtual reality, but it is likely to remain inaccessible to the average computer musician.

Sampling Rates

While the number of bits determines how the incoming signal is sliced horizontally, the sampling rate determines how it is sliced vertically. Most 16-bit cards support the CD-quality sampling rate of 44.1 kHz (samples taken 44,100 times per second), but certain older cards do not, so it is worth examining this feature.

Sampling Rates and Frequencies

There is a strong relationship between the sampling rate and the frequencies that can be represented. Figure 3-3 shows the effects of different sampling rates on two different sound waves. Wave B completes three cycles in the time it takes Wave A to complete one. This means that its frequency is three times as high; musically, it would sound an octave and a half (an octave plus a perfect fifth, to be exact) higher than Wave A. The figure shows that, at sample rate one, neither wave is recorded well. At sample rate two, Wave A is recorded reasonably well, but the digital representation of Wave B would be misleading.

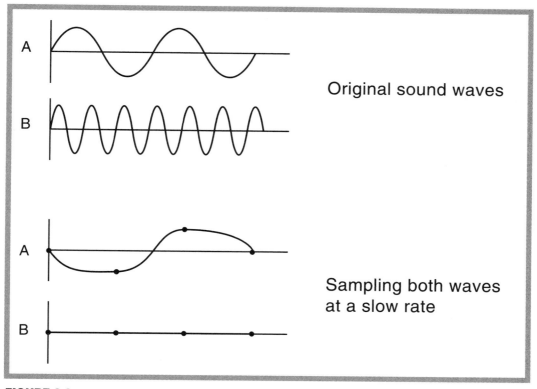

▶ **FIGURE 3-3**

The effects of different sampling rates on two different sound waves.

The conclusion to draw from this example is that we need a sampling rate high enough to adequately represent the highest frequencies that we can hear, which is about 20,000 Hz. As we mentioned in Chapter 1, Nyquist's Theorem tells us that we have to sample at least twice as fast as this (40,000 times per second) for good results. In fact, from examining this figure, it may seem surprising that sampling twice per cycle is adequate; however, it has been proven to be so mathematically and in the real world, on compact discs.

Different Rates for Different Reasons

Although a sampling rate of 44.1 kHz is ideal for audiophile purposes, there are several reasons to use lower rates—notably for space and compatibility considerations. A 16-bit stereo digital audio file recorded at 44.1 kHz consumes 10MB of disk space for every minute of sound. A 60-minute recording would take up 600MB (which, not coincidentally, is approximately the amount of storage a CD-ROM offers. Longer recordings can be stored on audio CDs, which lack the formatting overhead of CD-ROMs). If you want to record background music for a multimedia production, you can get good results at 22 kHz, with half the storage requirements. You can cut these requirements in half again by recording in mono instead of stereo, getting down to an almost-reasonable 2.5MB per minute. Human speech can be adequately reproduced at an 11kHz sampling rate, and mono is generally quite suitable, so you're down to a little over 1.25MB per minute.

If you're recording digital audio for widespread distribution, you'll have to take into account the large number of 8-bit cards out there that can't play 16-bit audio. In that case, you'll wind up with noisier recordings, but you can cut all of the above storage numbers in half.

Analog Section

Your sound card is not just a digital sound producer—it outputs sound in an analog electrical form that your speakers can amplify. It also records sounds from analog sources such as microphones and *line-level* (a standard-strength electrical signal that is used to pass sound among stereo components such as receivers and cassette decks) inputs. In addition, the mixer section of your sound card, which is responsible for combining CD, wave, and digital audio, is analog. The mixer section may also include *filters* or *equalization* (EQ), used to vary the amounts of treble and bass to your taste.

Analog components, unfortunately, are not perfect. They are all subject to interference from electrical signals. Furthermore, they all have certain limitations when it comes to reproducing portions of the sonic spectrum; they tend to exaggerate certain frequencies and weaken others. *These characteristics affect every sound passing through your card, including synthesized sounds, wave audio, and CD audio.*

Unfortunately, the analog characteristics of different sound cards (and, as we'll see later, speakers) are difficult to compare, except with either expensive test equipment or your own ears. The manufacturers' specifications, if they are published at all, are often unreliable and based upon differing standards, test equipment, and test conditions.

The good news is that most sound card analog sections are fine for most purposes. However, the differences are significant enough that it doesn't take a record producer to tell the difference between the best and the worst, or even between the worst and the majority of cards that lie in the middle ground. If you're a multimedia producer or someone who cares deeply about music and sound quality, then it will be worth the effort for you to pay attention to these characteristics.

But how can you judge noise and frequency response if you can't trust the specifications? If top-notch sound is your goal, then go for one of the top-dollar sound cards from a respected pro-audio manufacturer. (Both Turtle Beach and Roland are known to consistently produce products with excellent audio characteristics.) In the mid-range, the best advice we can give you, in a field where new products are introduced more rapidly than they can be tested, is to follow the magazine reviews closely. Both *Multimedia World* and *New Media* magazines frequently survey the field of sound cards. Take these reviews with a grain of salt, however. The noise and frequency response rating are only reliable if they have been carefully tested with professional equipment or rated in controlled, comparative listening tests. Tables that merely reprint manufacturers' specifications for these factors have little, if any, meaning.

We'll explore these characteristics in detail in the pages that follow.

Signal-to-Noise (S/N) Ratio

Intuitively, the S/N ratio of a card is simply the ratio of the signal (i.e., the desired sound) to the noise (i.e., extraneous, undesired sounds such as hums, hisses, and distortions not in the original signal). This simple, intuitive definition, however, is far from simple in the real world. The S/N ratio of a card varies according to the frequency content of the musical material that it's reproducing, and also according to the environment that it's placed in.

The big problem for sound card manufacturers is that the inside of your computer is a raging volcano of molten electromagnetic lava. The computer's chassis prevents the interference that all those chips generate from leaking into the outside world, but the universe inside the case is a different story entirely. Any sound card that aspires to produce professional music must be carefully shielded. The vast majority of low- to mid-priced sound cards opt for economy over ultra-quiet sound.

Frequency Response

Not only do the analog stages inevitably add a certain amount of noise, but they also amplify different frequencies by different amounts. Figure 3-4 shows a frequency response graph for a hypothetical sound card. It shows the relative strength of the output signal as an input signal sweeps the audible frequency range. It is measured in *decibels* (dB), a standard measure of audio signal strength. Perfect frequency response would be indicated by a flat line at 0 dB, indicating that the device adds or subtracts nothing from the input signal.

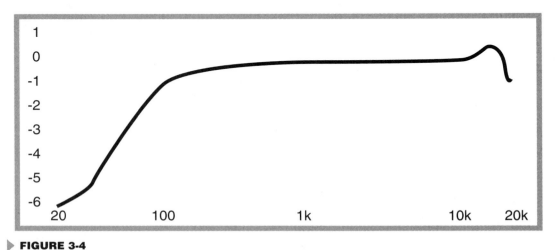

▶ **FIGURE 3-4**

A frequency response graph.

The graph shown in Figure 3-4 is certainly not perfect, although it is nearly flat for the most common listening frequencies, from 200 Hz to 8 kHz. As you can see, this card has a pronounced "bump" between 10 kHz and 20 kHz, indicating that it exaggerates those high frequencies, and it falls off rapidly below 100 Hz, indicating that it doesn't have much bass response. The bump is mild and would probably only be noticeable because this card would sound fairly bright when compared to other cards. The bass falloff (also known as *attenuation*, or weakening) would be quite noticeable to people with subwoofer-equipped speaker systems, but ordinary small-powered speakers wouldn't reproduce those frequencies well even if the sound card output them strongly.

Frequency response ranges are often summarized instead of graphed. The card graphed in Figure 3-4 could be described as having any one of the following ranges, depending upon the amount of error included in the quote:

- 95 Hz-20 kHz ± 1 dB
- 60 Hz-20 kHz ± 2 dB
- 45 Hz-20 kHz ± 3 dB

Can you see how these numbers are derived from the figure?

None of these quotes reveals the high-frequency bump, which is less than 1 dB in magnitude. As you can see, cards look better (i.e., have a wider range) when they're quoted with higher margins. A card quoted at ± 3 dB could have substantial bumps and dips that you wouldn't know about until you listened to it in comparison with other cards. Let the buyer beware.

Filters and Equalization (EQ)

Both filters and equalization (EQ) are just fancy terms for *tone controls*. The term "filter" is derived from its non-electronic meaning, which is "to strain or remove impurities." Originally, sound filters worked by removing part of the signal, but now they can generally either remove or boost frequencies.

Every sound card uses low-pass filters (filters that remove high-frequency signals) to smooth the output of the DACs before sending it to the mixer. The quality of these filters varies and is reflected in the frequency response and S/N ratio of the card. However, you and I have little direct concern with these filters; what are more important to us are tone controls that we can tweak.

You can tell whether a sound card has tone controls by looking at its mixer applet. If it has tone controls, sliders for bass, treble, and possibly mid-range sound control will appear there. The middle position on these sliders represents a neutral position, while higher positions will boost these frequencies and lower positions will cut them.

The tone controls in a sound card can add a tiny amount of noise (the fewer circuits a signal passes through, the less noise it picks up), and they also may be redundant—most powered speakers have tone controls. However, depending upon exactly where your speakers are situated, it can be more convenient to have these controls right on-screen, only a mouse-click away.

Synthesizer Section

In Chapter 1, we discussed the basics of FM synthesis, the most common type of synthesis method found in sound cards today. In this section, we'll talk about today's other prevalent synthesis method, *wavetable synthesis*, and also about features and characteristics that are common to both forms. We'll give you a perspective on the important topics of polyphony, digital effects processing, and General MIDI so you can judge for yourself which sound card will work best for you.

General MIDI

Purchasing a sound card that supports General MIDI assures you of getting a complete palette of instrumental sounds that is compatible with virtually all MIDI music produced today. General MIDI was created to assure that sequences that sound good on one General MIDI synthesizer will sound at least similar on any other, and it has been wildly successful at this task. We'll delve deeply into the General MIDI specification in Chapter 10; for now, we'll just present an overview.

Any General MIDI synthesizer is fundamentally a MIDI synthesizer which contains a full set of instrument emulations kept in standard locations. For instance, under General MIDI, Program Change 1 will always call up an acoustic piano sound, Program Change 36 will invoke a fretless bass, and Program Change 31 will call up a distorted guitar sound—all regardless of the sound card involved. One synthesizer's distorted guitar will not quite sound like another's, but they will be similar enough to let sequences created for one General MIDI synthesizer sound reasonably good on any other. A complete list of General MIDI instruments and their Program Change numbers (called The *General MIDI Patch Map*) can be found in Appendix A.

Finally, even if you have an older, 8-bit sound card, there is a way to get it to conform to General MIDI sound conventions under Windows. Simply download the shareware file FMSYN.ZIP from CompuServe or another BBS and install it as a new driver for your sound card. In addition, Voyetra has created several drivers which can add General MIDI capabilities to FM sound cards. Contact your card's manufacturer for information.

Polyphony

One important criterion for distinguishing synthesizers from one another is *polyphony*, or the number of simultaneous distinct notes that the instrument is capable of playing. This is measured in *voices*; a synthesizer will be said to have 11-, 20-, or 32-voice polyphony. A voice is like a note, except that sometimes several voices are combined to form a single note. This cuts down on your effective polyphony; Twenty-voice polyphony may only mean 16 simultaneous notes if some of them use particularly rich sounds.

Polyphony won't make any difference to you when you sequence a flute solo, but play back a dense, multi-part arrangement (or, on older cards, even a not-so-dense multi-part arrangement) and you'll quickly become acquainted with the phenomenon known as *voice stealing*. When your computer asks a sound card to play a note but the card is completely maxed out from notes that are already sustaining, the card generally shuts off the note that has been sustaining for the longest time in order to give the new guy a chance. Sometimes it doesn't make much difference to the music, and sometimes the bottom seems to fall out.

The above scenario may sound a little farfetched, but in reality it doesn't take much to get into voice-stealing situations on some cards. Older cards had only 11-voice polyphony. Play a six-note piano chord and hold it (in a sequence), then play a four-note guitar chord on the next beat while the piano is still sounding, hit a bass note, and that's it. There's no place for any drums or any other notes until one of the chords or the bass note ends.

You're especially likely to run into voice-stealing problems when using FM sound cards. Although the newer FM sound cards nominally boast 20-voice polyphony, the real polyphony that you'll experience depends on the driver that you use and your panning requirements. The Yamaha OPL3 sound chips that are found on these cards can handle five percussion sounds plus 15 two-operator melodic voices at once; however, many of the drivers available for these cards utilize the richer four-operator voices for melodic parts, cutting your effective polyphony to somewhere between six and nine melodic voices (plus the percussion voices), depending on the cleverness of the driver. Furthermore, any sound that isn't panned to the center, hard (all the way) left, or hard right requires an extra voice. So you may well run out of voices with FM cards sooner than you expect.

Further cutting down on effective polyphony is the fact that many synthesizers reserve a certain number of voices for drum parts and the rest for pitched instruments, so that you may have less room to maneuver than you'd hoped in a piece that is either heavily percussive or completely nonpercussive. It's like a restaurant with separate smoking and non-smoking sections—if the section you want is full, it doesn't help you that there are empty tables in the other one.

There are a number of tricks that you can use during sequencing to maximize your polyphony. (We'll give you details in Chapter 10.) Nonetheless, the bottom line is that added polyphony represents significant added value if MIDI is important to you, and that a 32-voice sound card really does offer 33% more power than a 24-voice synthesizer (all other things being equal) if creating fully-arranged musical compositions is your goal.

If playback (or creation) of multimedia titles is the only MIDI feature that's important to you, than the polyphony issue will be less significant to you. Since multimedia producers must target the large, installed base of sound cards already out there, MIDI sequences in multimedia titles will almost always play back well on 20-voice synthesizers. Actually, in order to conform to the MPC specification, they should be playable on 11-voice synthesizers without voice stealing, but many producers have ignored and will continue to ignore this draconian restriction.

Wavetable Synthesis

In Chapter 1, we discussed FM synthesis, in which a pair of oscillators are logically hooked together in order to produce complex timbres. While this was viewed by many musicians as a very exciting technology in the mid-1980s, many more were disappointed by its inability to convincingly emulate most acoustic instruments. Back then FM produced some pretty wild original sounds and was able to produce a good imitation of the weighty Fender Rhodes electric pianos that had become a staple of many groups, but it was pretty far off base when it came to imitating most other instruments.

When manufacturers came to believe that there was a larger market for instrument emulation than for way-out FM sounds, they started making *wavetable synthesizers*. The oscillators in these synths were precisely-timed program loops that would play back short digital recordings of real instruments stored in ROM. (The name "wavetable" comes from the fact that the loop reads values from a table that stores a digital recording of a note.)

Wavetable synthesizers were not a new idea. Their roots go back to drum machines made during the 1970s that used recordings of acoustic drums as their sound sources (or even further back, to the *Mellotron* of the 1960s, a keyboard that triggered the playback of different tape loops. It was used on recordings by the Beatles, the Beach Boys, and others). But the plummeting price of memory in the 1980s was a new factor, suddenly enabling more and longer recordings to be stored at a reasonable price. As you'll see, in a wavetable synthesizer, quality is almost synonymous with memory size. The declining price of memory led to an explosion of wavetable synthesizers, to the point where they now dominate the synthesizer keyboard and sound module markets.

An obvious enhancement to wavetable synthesis is to let the users record their own wavetables. Instruments that allow you to do this are called *samplers* and have had a tremendous impact on the world of pop music. Rock and rap from the late '80s to the present have been dominated by ultra-funky rhythm grooves created on samplers. Samplers have always been considerably more expensive than wavetable synthesizers, despite their similarities, due to the recording and editing hardware and software that they include. This situation has changed, however, in the sound card arena as several low- to mid-priced sound cards now include sampling capabilities.

The digital recordings stored in the memory of wavetable synthesizers are called *samples,* and the synthesizers themselves are sometimes called *sample-playback synthesizers.* We'll examine their most important features.

Wavetable ROM

The amount of memory on a wavetable card is perhaps the single most important indicator of both its quality and its price. The best-sounding cards are generally those with the longest samples and many *multi-sampled* instruments, as you'll see below. These cards have between 4MB and 8MB of ROM, and the numbers will no doubt continue to go up over time.

DEMANDS ON MEMORY. A General MIDI synthesizer must contain at least 150 samples to cover all the instrument and drum sounds mandated by the specification. With 1MB of memory on board, this would provide about 6.67KB per sample—less than 1/5 of a second at CD sampling rates. In reality, memory isn't divided up evenly among the instruments, and compression is used during sampling, so the actual samples can be several seconds long for critical instruments such as the piano. However, it's still a tight fit.

To further tighten the memory belt, many instruments require more than one sample in order to sound good. If you record a sample of a saxophone playing middle C and then try to play a melody line that's about two octaves higher, the results will be laughable. Your wavetable synthesizer will transpose that sample up to the desired range before playing it back, and it won't sound anything like a real sax. The music industry has a name for this undesirable effect: *munchkinization*. If you sample a normal speaking voice and play it back an octave or two higher, it will sound like the high-pitched munchkins in the movie *The Wizard of Oz*, hence the term.

The cure for munchkinization is *multi-sampling*, that is, making multiple recordings of each instrument across its normal playing range, and triggering the appropriate sample for each note played. Ideally, no sample would be transposed more than an octave or so. All professional MIDI wavetable sound modules use multi-samples, and so do the better-sounding wavetable sound cards.

Multi-sampling places, of course, another demand on sound card memory.

MEMORY CONSERVATION—JUMPING THROUGH LOOPS. Wavetable synthesizers use a technique called *looping* in order to create sustained notes. You can hold an organ note for 15 seconds, but you can be sure there's no 15-second organ sample on your sound card. Instead, for example, the card will play the first half second (for example) of its organ sample and then loop back to a point near, but not at, the beginning of the sample. It will continue to play back this loop for as long as you hold the note, a period of time called the *sustain phase* of the sample. On some synthesizers, when you release the note, playback continues past the endpoint of the loop all the way to the end of the sample. Other synthesizers simply continue playing the loop and fade the sound out quickly (but not instantly) when you let go of the key. Regardless of the technique used, this portion of each note is called the *release phase*. It is necessary in order to prevent notes from being cut off in an abrupt, unnatural fashion. This emulates the physical world of acoustic instruments, where all notes take a certain amount of time to die out, even if they're damped.

Sound Card RAM and Sampling

In order to get around the limitations of finite ROM and the samples that love to gobble it up, several cards provide either RAM (*random-access memory*), slots for user-supplied RAM, or both. Unlike ROM, whose contents can only be altered at the factory, RAM can be written to by programs under your control. By adding RAM to sound cards, some manufacturers have provided you with a means of loading new samples at will, in order to make the most of whatever memory is on the card. This, in effect, turns your entire hard disk into an extension of wavetable ROM and gives you the ability to create your own samples. With on-board memory slots that take standard SIMMs (or the newer SIPPs), you can increase the usefulness of your sound card at low, competitive memory prices (usually found in mail-order advertisements in magazines such as *Computer Shopper*).

Sound card RAM uses aren't limited to instrumental sounds. You can also record dialogue or advertisements from the radio or other sources and play them from your MIDI controller. I've recorded an aluminum pot, for instance, that sounds absolutely incredible when I trigger it from my MIDI guitar and bend the string. If you're a mad musical scientist type, you should definitely consider sound card RAM seriously. It's a gas!

PATCH CACHING. The first sound card to provide RAM was the Advanced Gravis UltraSound. The basic card comes with 256KB of memory, upgradeable to 1MB.

The UltraSound is an extreme example of the use of RAM. All instruments are loaded from "patch" (.PAT) files on your hard disk as they are needed. None are stored in ROM. This scheme has profound implications.

The first consequence of these RAM-based instruments is that different instrument files may easily be substituted for the standard set of .PAT files. These files can be created with patch editing software supplied by Advanced Gravis, or downloaded from CompuServe, the Internet, or other networks. Unlike ROM-only wavetable synthesizers, if you don't like a factory-supplied instrument sample, you can supply your own. Furthermore, if you compose a song for, say, solo piano, you can use all the card's memory to hold the longest, best piano sample available. Then, when you want to play back a multi-instrument arrangement, you can switch to a smaller piano sample.

There is a down side to this scheme, however. Unless you say the magic word (which we'll reveal in a moment), every sound is loaded from disk as you need it. If you're playing back a sequence with several instrument changes, this can result in playback interruptions while the disk is accessed. This is not a good situation.

To remedy this problem, you can use a feature called *patch caching* to preload all the samples that you'll need to use in a given song. You usually do this simply by selecting an "Update Cache" (the magic word referred to above) command in your sequencer program before playing back your sequence. This takes care of most problems; however, if the card doesn't have much memory and you have a lot of instrument changes, it is still possible to exceed memory capacity and cause delays.

ROM and RAM Together

An even better approach to on-board RAM is used in the Maui and Monterey cards from Turtle Beach. These cards have both ROM and RAM (or slots for RAM), providing you with a full set of high-quality General MIDI instruments as well as the ability to create your own. If you restrict yourself to the standard ROM sounds, you don't have to worry about patch caching or sequence interruptions. When you want to use your own samples, you load them directly into sound card RAM using convenient applets supplied by Turtle Beach.

The Creative Labs AWE32 card also provides sound card RAM and lets you load new samples in the form of Soft Fonts. Currently you cannot create your own Soft Fonts, although Creative plans to release a utility to give you this capability.

Digital Effects Processing

Digital effects processors are used primarily to add presence, ambiance (the sense of an instrument emanating from a real, physical room or hall), and thickness to sounds. Almost any synthesizer sounds better when given a little more character by a digital effects processor.

A few of today's sound cards include effects sections. These sections produce what are called *time-based* effects; in essence, they are all complex variants of the digital delays described below. You don't, however, get the ability to produce distortion such as that used with electric guitars. That's an analog effect, which you can experience, if you wish, by routing your sound card's output through a distortion box meant for guitarists. (It's definitely worth trying if your taste leans to rock.)

The range of digital effects has become fairly standardized over the past few years, although the actual sound of them varies from device to device. Here are the most common ones:

- **Reverberation (Reverb):** This is the most useful effect of all. It aims to "place" the instrument in a virtual room or hall by simulating the subtle and complex echoes that would be created as notes bounce off the walls and ceilings. You can usually choose from several room sizes and *decay times*, which describes how long the reflections of each sound take to die out. In addition, you can independently choose the amount of reverb to add to each instrument. Good reverb algorithms are highly proprietary, closely-guarded secrets of the companies that do them best at the professional level. You may not hear too much difference among sound card reverbs, but listen for warmth and spaciousness as opposed to a slightly metallic, ringing sound.

- **Delay:** This is the familiar echo effect that you've heard on many rock records. The most significant parameters are the maximum delay time (one second is typical; it depends on memory) and the number of *delay taps*. A single delay tap allows you to create standard echo effects, while multiple taps allow you to create complex rhythms by having several delays running at once with different delay times.

- **Chorus and Flange:** These effects are quite similar to each other. They are both created digitally by combining a large number of closely-spaced, extremely short delays. Adding chorus will thicken most sounds (a little like cornstarch) and make the sustained portion seem more lively by creating subtle variations.

Flanging does the same thing but also tends to add a little bit of a "whooshing" sound.

CD-ROM Interface

There are many varieties of CD-ROM interfaces available on sound cards. If you're planning to buy a multimedia upgrade kit with both a CD-ROM drive and a sound card, then this isn't an issue, but if you're buying either separately, it may well be. If you're purchasing a sound card and planning for a CD-ROM in the future, then buy a card with a SCSI-2 interface built in. This is the highest-performance interface currently available, able to easily handle triple- or quadruple-speed drives. If you purchase a sound card with a proprietary interface, make sure that you learn from the product literature or the manufacturer which drives are compatible with it. If you later decide to purchase a SCSI drive and don't have an interface for it, you'll have to buy an interface card separately, most likely for more than $100.

In the near future there may be yet another alternative—IDE CD-ROM interfaces. There is a large existing base of IDE hard disks, which have evolved due to the interface's low manufacturing cost and respectable efficiency. If IDE CD-ROM drives become available, they may well be an excellent, economical choice.

Bundled Software

Most sound cards are bundled with a basic set of software, including, at a minimum, an entry-level sequencer and digital audio editor. These programs are often surprisingly capable for freebies and can suit your needs for years. On the other hand, if you're a sound professional, you may outgrow them quickly. Older 8-bit cards may only come with DOS programs, so be careful if you're a Windows user purchasing one of these.

Additional software that is bundled with sound cards can include some of the composition-oriented software such as *Band In A Box* or

Power Chords, described in Chapter 10. Also common are text-to-speech and speech recognition programs such as those described in Chapter 12.

Listening Tests

In the final analysis, your ears are the best determinants of sound card quality. If you're a casual purchaser who doesn't have time to invest in an involved decision process, then you can simply abide by the criteria outlined in the Summary section at the end of this chapter. However, if you have some time to invest, you can minimize your purchasing risk and maximize your enjoyment by performing some tests yourself.

You can either test sound cards at your local computer dealer or at your home. You can test at home by mail-ordering various sound cards from companies that will guarantee you a 30-day unconditional refund. You will have to go through the noxious installation processes for a number of sound cards, but you will end up knowing which is the best for you. In this case, be sure to take good care of all packaging materials and documentation, and to return unwanted sound cards in as close to unopened condition as you can.

You may well be better off testing sound cards at your local computer dealer, especially if she has a variety of cards already installed in computers. Be aware, though, that if you take up a dealer's time with extensive testing, you have a moral obligation to purchase a product from that dealer, if she has one that suits your needs—even if it isn't priced at rock-bottom prices.

A great way to test is to take a couple of short MIDI and wave files down to the store with you and play them back on different sound cards. For instance, CANYON.MID, included with Windows, is a good test for a MIDI file, and there are many more available on networks. Networks are also an excellent source of wave files.

If you're modem-less and sound card-less, then you won't have any way to create test files. Your best bet would be to get a friend or colleague to lend some files to you. Failing that, you could always ask the salesperson at the computer store for sample files.

Summary

There is something for everyone in the vast selection of available sound cards, but you have to make an effort to ensure that you get the best value for your money. Not all sound cards are alike, not by a long shot.

If you're willing to spend top dollar, then it's hard to beat the products from Roland or Turtle Beach (and other excellent competitors may enter the fray by the time you read this, of course). In the mid- and low-price ranges, things are murkier. Generally speaking, wavetable synthesizers will provide better synthesized sounds than their FM counterparts. Check the comparative reviews in magazines, paying particular attention to their assessments of noise levels, and avoid purchasing sound cards that haven't been reviewed as parts of multimedia package deals.

Finally, if you have the time and energy, narrow your list of choices and audition the top candidates. This will tell you more than any specification sheet ever could.

Chapter **4**

Speakers and Headphones

The speakers and headphones that you use with your computer are truly "where the rubber meets the road" in terms of audio quality. No matter how good your sound card or how high the quality of your CDs and CD-ROM player, if you listen through inferior speakers or headphones, you won't hear good sound. This chapter will help you pick powered speakers and headphones that suit your needs and budget.

Headphones and Speakers—Who Needs 'Em?

Not everybody needs special headphones and/or speakers for his or her computer. If you're into sound, then you may already have a stereo system set up to entertain you while you're at your computer. If this is the case, then all you need are the right cables to connect your sound card's output to your receiver, amplifier, or mixer and you're ready to roll. In this case, you might want to skip right ahead to Chapter 6, which discusses integrating your computer with your stereo system. On the other hand, you may still want a set of powered speakers because they're small enough to be positioned for ideal stereo separation while you're seated at your computer or because you want portable sound. Or you may want a new pair of headphones to enjoy sounds in private or for recording purposes. In these cases, read on.

Do you need both headphones and powered speakers? The decision to get both is almost a no-brainer. Headphones in themselves, while wonderful for certain uses, are not sufficient for a number of reasons, such as:

- Most headphones—even the lightest ones—become uncomfortable after an hour or two of use.
- The cord limits your mobility.
- Headphones can isolate you from your co-workers (although some people will see this as an advantage rather than a disadvantage).
- It's hard to talk on the telephone when wearing headphones.
- It's hard to chew snacks while wearing headphones.

Despite the flippancy of these last two points, it's clear that headphones alone are not enough. Therefore, you need speakers. For most people, a set of powered speakers alone will do the job. Do you need a pair of headphones in addition? They can come in handy if you have an occasional need to not disturb co-workers, if you plan to record digital audio using a microphone, or if you just like to listen to music through headphones once in a while (I know I do). Otherwise, you don't need them. (However, if you're reading this book, the odds are that you already have a pair or two lying around the house). The privacy need can be fulfilled by very inexpensive headphones, while better ones are advisable for the other purposes mentioned. In either case, we'll give you some guidelines for choosing headphones in the next section.

Headphones

Listening to music through good headphones is a wonderful experience in small doses. Even a relatively inexpensive pair of headphones can reveal more details of the music than a much costlier set of speakers. And, if you're recording vocals or other acoustic instruments with a microphone, you must monitor (listen to the sound as you're recording, to check the sound quality) with headphones rather than speakers in order to avoid feedback and phase cancellation, a subject we'll cover in detail in Chapter 8.

Headphones have come a long way in the past thirty years. The average $20 set today provides sound quality that would have cost over $80 just a couple of decades ago. Still, not every pair of headphones provides both good sound and comfort, and there are substantial differences between professional models and consumer models.

Budget Headphones

It seems that new models of budget headphones are introduced every week. They're included free with many personal cassette players or radios and are available in just about every record store or department store music section. They're also included in many multimedia computer packages.

Budget headphones can deliver fairly impressive sound. They deliver excellent highs but are often somewhat lacking in low frequencies. I'd suggest bypassing the type of headphone with little "bud" speakers that fit in your ear in favor of units with larger, foam-enclosed speakers. Even in the world of budget headphones it's true that larger speakers deliver better bass.

Be cautious of the cord length when purchasing a new pair of budget 'phones. Many headphone cords are designed for exercisers and are cut just long enough to go from your belt to your ear without encumbering you with a lot of slack. These are great for jogging on the beach, but they can be a drag if your cord is plugged into the back of your computer and you have to reach down to the floor to pick up a piece of paper that you dropped. Make sure the headphones that you purchase have a cord that is at least three or four feet longer than the distance from your head to the headphone jack on your sound card.

Cords, by the way, are the major cause of budget headphone failure. They have a tendency to develop internal breaks which result in intermittent sound; usually, the sound on one side of the headphones cuts in and out depending on how the cord is bent. Look for cords that appear relatively thick and sturdy.

If the cord starts giving you trouble and you're handy with a soldering iron, then you can usually locate the section with the break and splice it out. Sometimes, however, you're better off just tossing the bad set out and buying a new one. As wasteful as that seems, it's certainly less expensive than finding someone to repair such a low-cost device.

Mid-Range Headphones

If you're willing to spend around $100, you can purchase a pair of headphones suitable for professional studio use (and for extremely pleasurable personal listening). These phones offer extended frequency response in the bass ranges, better fidelity across the line, and (if you want it) sealed enclosures. In addition, they're designed to be comfortable for longer listening sessions.

Sealed headphone enclosures serve several purposes. They accentuate the bass range and isolate the sound of the headphones from ambient sounds. The latter function is especially important if you intend to dub (record new tracks while listening to existing ones) acoustic or vocal tracks over prerecorded instrumental tracks. (Without sealed headphones, the sounds from the headphones will leak into the microphone.) In a pro setting, this impairs the "isolation" of the vocal track and makes the mix much more difficult. In your home studio, it might simply result in a weakening and distortion of the original musical tracks through the combination of those tracks with an out-of-phase version of themselves.

Among sealed headphones, many people swear by several sets in the Sony MDR series: the original MDR-6 (now discontinued) and its descendants, the MDR-V600 and the MDR-7506, are favorites in the $100 price range.

Unsealed headphones may be a better choice if you want top-quality sound but work in an office environment. Sealed headphones can be very isolating, and it may feel as if people are sneaking up on you when they tap you on the shoulder to talk to you. Unsealed headphones (the most famous ones are by Sennheiser and AKG) can provide you with true audiophile sound quality while still letting you remain aware of the sonic environment around you.

Powered Speakers

Powered speakers are the vital link between your sound card and your ears. They differ from standard stereo speakers in that they're generally smaller, contain their own small amplifiers (hence the term "powered"), and are shielded to prevent them from magnetically interfering with your computer's monitor.

There are a bewildering array of powered speaker choices available to you, with sounds that run the gamut from awful to awesome and prices that go from dirt-cheap to sky-high. In this section, we'll let you know "watts" important in choosing a pair of powered speakers.

Bass Response

It's an immutable law of speaker design that the bigger the speaker, the better the bass. Bass guitar players in bands routinely use massive speakers that have a 15-inch or larger diameter. When evaluating small speakers, you'll find that most of them reproduce high frequencies fairly well. Their bass response, however, varies radically.

As with sound cards, unfortunately, manufacturers' specifications are a poor guide to what you'll actually experience when you turn on your speakers. In fact, worse specifications may simply indicate that the speakers are from a more honest company, and thus may be preferable! A far better indication of bass response is the size (the diameter) of the speaker and whether a separate *subwoofer* is included. The term "subwoofer" comes from traditional speaker design. Before the advent of subwoofers (and probably even since that time), most speaker cabinets contained one large speaker for reproducing low- and mid-range sounds (the *woofer*) along with one or more small *tweeters* for reproducing treble sounds. Systems with subwoofers deliver the best bass response you can get.

Systems with subwoofers consist of three speaker enclosures—two conventional powered speakers, called *satellites* in this context, and a separate box called a subwoofer that is usually placed on the floor. The job of the subwoofer is to deliver the bass. It takes advantage of the fact that bass sounds are generally perceived as nondirectional (they don't seem to come from any given location) to deliver tremendous bass response at a very economical price.

Because the subwoofer enclosure isn't responsible for any treble sounds, it can be optimized to deliver bass. This is generally accomplished by sealed enclosures containing elongated, folded tubes that give the sound a longer distance to travel, producing the effect of larger speakers in a smaller box. Subwoofers are a great value for producing bass sounds because of their specialized design, because you only need one subwoofer instead of a pair of large speakers, and because they don't have to be shielded (they're designed to sit on the floor where they can't interfere with your computer's operations).

There are a number of systems available that include subwoofers, and also subwoofers that can be added to existing systems, available from Altec Lansing, Acoustic Research and other companies. The full systems that include subwoofers tend to also include high-quality satellite speakers and are generally more expensive than simple pairs of powered speakers. The listening satisfaction is well worth the investment, however, if you use your computer in an environment where you can listen to music at moderate volumes without disturbing others.

When it comes to the bass response of non–subwoofer systems, let speaker size be your guide (fortunately, unlike other specifications, speaker size can't be fudged), but also consult magazine reviews, friends, and computer dealers.

Power

You don't need a lot of watts to drive the small speakers that are found in most personal computer speakers, but a small reserve will go a long way toward avoiding distortion when the music peaks. Some powered speakers are rated as low as three watts per speaker; this is pretty paltry. Seven watts per channel or more gives you a comfortable amount of headroom. Subwoofers need more power, but they're generally well-designed for their intended usage so you don't have to worry about this.

Once again, beware of quoted specifications. The figures I've given above are measured with the conservative RMS (root-mean-squared) method. Wattages quoted in terms of "Peak Power" or "Music Power" are somewhat inflated compared to this standard.

Power Source

Some powered speakers can use batteries as their power source, which adds to their portability, and some require optional AC adapters in order to plug into a wall outlet, which adds to their expense. If portability is a need for you, choose a pair that can use batteries and, if possible, that comes with a carrying case.

Mounting Options

If space on your desktop is at a premium, consider mounting your speakers on the wall behind your computer. Wall mounts are available for a number of speakers, either in the package or as an inexpensive option.

Inputs

Extra inputs on your speakers give you extra flexibility. You can, for instance, plug your portable radio or cassette player into one of the inputs to enjoy your favorite programs or songs without headphones. Or, as you'll see in Chapter 6, you can hook up your stereo system to an input to enjoy your ideal positioning for stereo separation and, if you have one, your subwoofer, while you're at your computer. Several models of Roland speakers even have microphone inputs to let you sing along.

For convenience, each input should have its own volume control, or there should be a mix control on the speaker.

Controls

I view a volume control as essential, but some speaker manufacturers apparently do not. Many sound cards have an output volume control knob (although some do not), but locating it entails reaching around to the back of the computer and groping blindly. And every sound card comes with a mixer applet that lets you control the volume with software. Still, when the telephone rings, I need to be able to reach over and instantly turn down the sound from my normal (rather loud, according to my wife) listening levels, and a volume control is the only practical way to accomplish this.

An on/off switch is desirable but not necessary if you plug the speakers into a power strip or other type of controlled outlet. A balance control is important if you can't position your speakers symmetrically; otherwise, it would see occasional use at most.

Tone controls are very desirable in powered speakers. It's quite possible that a high-frequency hum or noise that would otherwise drive you crazy can be eliminated by cranking back the treble control. And bass boost can be a boon, especially without a subwoofer.

Traveling Case

If you're getting your act together and taking it on the road, then a convenient traveling case for your speakers, cables, and other accessories can be a handy accessory. Of course, you can always improvise this from a gym bag, oversized attaché case, used video camera case, or overnight bag, but a professional appearance and snug fit can be well worth the modest prices that manufacturers charge for this option, when it's available.

Bells and Whistles

Bells and whistles are big fun if you're in a samba band, but in powered speakers they're more or less excess baggage. As mentioned above, bass boosts are great if you have small speakers, and the dynamic EQ found in some systems is a variation on that theme. Beyond that, consider any extra features (such as the digital signal processing that some manufacturers include) to be a bonus; what counts the most are the factors discussed above.

Chapter **5**

Installing and Troubleshooting Sound Cards

I've already told you how great sound cards and synthesizers are today in comparison to a few years ago. Perhaps in a few years, after "Plug and Play" (a new Microsoft proposal) computers and cards have completely taken over the market, I'll be able to say the same thing about PC hardware installation. However, for now, this remains a difficult area for some users. In this chapter, you'll learn some basic concepts and techniques that may allow you to avoid frustrating and expensive calls to technical support departments.

▼▲▼

Pre-Installation Steps and Thoughts

Here are a few steps that you can take that will help to ensure that your sound card installation will be as trouble-free as careful attention and knowledge can make it.

In an ideal world, we'd be able to slap a new sound card into a free slot, screw it down, close the computer, plug the card's output into the speaker's input, and start making music. Unfortunately, in reality, we have to make decisions about Port Addresses and IRQs, change jumpers on cards (taking the risk of frying a chip either with static electricity or an incorrect change), let an installation program mess with our CONFIG.SYS and AUTOEXEC.BAT files, and restart our computers. And, if we use Windows, we must then let an install program modify our WIN.INI and SYSTEM.INI files, install and configure Windows drivers, and then restart Windows! In the process of all this, we are often faced with dialog boxes that we don't understand (so we just take the defaults, which are usually correct), installation instructions that read as if a computer has translated them from the Japanese or they apply to an earlier version of the product, and diagrams that are confusing, weirdly oriented or just plain inaccurate. I have personally experienced all of the above, plus weird error messages, hung computers, and mute sound cards.

Most of the time, blind faith will work, especially if you don't have any unusual options installed in your system. And many installation programs will actually test the setup for you to determine whether everything is working. Nonetheless, I know of one sophisticated software developer who has "never been able to get MIDI to work on my system" and many other individuals with problems of one sort or another. This chapter will help you to avoid such problems and to install, test, and enjoy your sound card quickly and easily.

None of the information in this chapter is intended to be a substitute for the installation instructions included with your sound card or multimedia upgrade kit. Instead, this should be viewed as supplementary information that gives you the perspective and background that the normally terse installation guides generally overlook. If you're lucky, you'll be able to skip this chapter and your installation will go smoothly and uneventfully. As Clint Eastwood said in *Dirty Harry*, "Do you feel lucky today? Do ya, punk?" I'd advise reading this chapter before proceeding; installation hassles are easier to prevent than to fix.

Important Warnings!

One instruction that is frequently omitted from manuals is the most important of all. It may be obvious to most people, but it still bears repeating because ignoring it can lead to catastrophic results:

Note!

Always turn off and unplug your computer before inserting or removing any cards.

There's a lot of electricity in there. It can fry a card or your motherboard. Practice safe installation.

In addition, make sure that you handle cards by the edges only—avoiding the edge connectors that plug into the slots on the motherboard—and that you touch a grounded device (such as the metal chassis of your computer) to discharge static electricity before touching a card.

Back It Up!

The most critical task before you install any kind of software or hardware in your computer is to back up at least your critical system files. Ideally, everything on your disk should be backed up at all times—disk crashes are rare, but the cost and effort of reconstructing your data can be massive—but I'll be pessimistic and assume that you don't do this. A new sound card or multimedia upgrade kit will make changes to AUTOEXEC.BAT and CONFIG.SYS (and WIN.INI and SYSTEM.INI if you're a Windows user). There's a small chance that these changes and the new hardware will prevent your computer from booting, in which case you will need backups of these files in order to restore order to your system. In fact, it's an excellent idea to have a backup startup diskette that you can boot from, with these files added to it, in the extremely unlikely event that an installation really messes up your system (see Disaster Recovery, below).

To create a bootable backup diskette:

1. Put a blank or erasable diskette in your A drive.

2. At a DOS prompt, enter the command FORMAT A:/S and follow the onscreen prompts.

3. Copy AUTOEXEC.BAT, CONFIG.SYS, WIN.INI, and SYSTEM.INI to the A drive.

4. Label the disk "System Backup" and put it in a safe place.

Interrupts, Port Addresses, and DMA Channels

These things are like your intestines—you know you need them but you wish you didn't have to think about them. Unfortunately, you don't always get your wish. A little knowledge about interrupts, port addresses, and DMA channels can be quite helpful in ensuring trouble-free installations. We'll try to keep it as painless as possible.

Sound cards use *interrupts* (also referred to as *IRQs,* which stands for "interrupt requests") to tap your CPU on the shoulder whenever they need attention, such as when a MIDI message is coming in and needs to be taken from the card and placed into memory. The CPU then reads that data from the *port address* corresponding to the interrupt. The process occurs in reverse whenever a program needs to send out data. Most sound cards use *Direct Memory Access* (*DMA*) channels to transfer digital audio data between the computer's hard disk and the card.

The critical point about this process is that *cards cannot share interrupts, port addresses, or DMA channels.* The DMA channel is not likely to be an issue (except on networks), but the port addresses and interrupts may well be. The PC only has 15 interrupts available, and a number of these are used by standard peripherals such as disk controllers, serial (COM) and parallel (LPT) ports, system timers, and the like. Sound cards come preconfigured to use the interrupts and addresses most likely to not conflict with other devices, but your system may differ enough from the typical one to make these settings inappropriate.

Unfortunately, there is no way for software to accurately determine which interrupts or port addresses are in use in your system. (This is one of the most important issues that will be addressed by the new Plug and Play specification.) You'll know there's a conflict when your system hangs or a peripheral doesn't work properly. (Usually, these symptoms won't appear unless you attempt to use the conflicting devices concurrently). On the other hand, you can actively try to avoid conflicts by logging your interrupts and ports, as we'll describe.

A Word About Setup Programs

Setup programs for sound cards will often ask you to specify an interrupt and port address or to accept the defaults. The dialog boxes that these programs present you with imply that you can choose any settings you like. Generally speaking, this is not so. The settings for most cards are not adjustable in software; you must actually move jumpers or set switches on the cards to change the settings. The dialog boxes that you see only give you the ability to inform the driver software of the changes that you've made to the card. If you don't make any changes on the card, then you must accept the defaults in the Setup program—nothing else will work. If you've made changes on the card, you must make the corresponding software changes with the Setup program to let the drivers know what you've done.

Logging IRQs and Port Addresses

One way to make your life easier any time you install new hardware is to create a log of your interrupts and port addresses. In fact, this is such a good idea that we've created a form for you to fill in, Figure 5-1. Just fill this in now and maintain it whenever you add a new card to your system, and you'll always know which interrupts and addresses are available.

▶ **FIGURE 5-1**

A handy table for recording interrupts and port addresses. The blank lines at the end are included for listing additional software drivers; for example, you may have multiple drivers in your system that reference a Sound Blaster card at address 220.

Device	Interrupt	Port Address
System Timer	0	
Keyboard	1	
	2	
COM2 or COM4	3	
COM1 or COM3	4	
LPT2	5	
Floppy Controller	6	
LPT1	7	
Clock	8	
Redirected IRQ2 (MPU 401)	9	
	10	
	11	
(PS/2 mouse)	12	
(Math coprocessor)	13	
Hard disk	14	
	15	

How do you go about filling in Figure 5-1? As we indicated, there's no single program that can give you all this information. However, Microsoft's MSD program, distributed as part of DOS versions 5.0 and above, can tell you which COM ports and printer (LPT) ports are installed in your system. Circle these on the chart, and note the addresses that they use. And, if you're using Windows, you can look at Control Panel Drivers to get more information. We'll take you though this process shortly. Finally, you can examine the manuals for any cards that you've installed beyond the standard ones that we've indicated in Figure 5-1.

Exploring Windows Drivers

You'll be able to tell quite a bit about the interrupts and addresses used by your cards by examining the state of the installed drivers with the Control Panel applet. Here's how to go about doing that:

1. Double-click on the Control Panel icon in the Program Manager's *Main* group.

2. When the Control Panel window opens, double-click on the icon labeled "Drivers."

3. You'll see a dialog box that shows a scrollable list of all installed drivers (see Figure 5-2). One by one, double-click each line in that list (or single-click the line and press the Setup button). If there are any parameters that you can view for that driver, they will be displayed in a new dialog box. Some of the drivers will display interrupt and port information, such as the following:

 FIGURE 5-2

The Drivers dialog box.

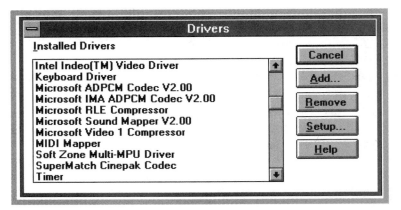

You can fill in many of the blanks in Figure 5-1 from the information that you find in these dialog boxes. As you go through them, don't make any changes. Remember, the drivers are usually set properly to reflect hardware settings, and changing a value in a driver dialog box can make it stop working.

After You Install a Sound Card

Congratulations! You've installed a sound card and its software without smoke pouring from your computer. With any luck, you'll be able to turn your computer on, boot up, launch Windows (if you use it), and use music programs without any trouble or weird error messages. However, a number of things may have gone wrong, and, if so, I'd like to help you fix them. Even if you don't have any problems, make sure to check out the section on Performance Tips—they are quite likely to apply to you.

Troubleshooting

These tips are meant to help you identify and fix problems that may occur during a sound card installation. Most problems can be fixed with a little care and effort, especially if you've taken the precautionary steps that we've discussed so far.

Disaster Recovery

Suppose the worst has happened—you've installed a new board and software, but there's some sort of conflict and your computer hangs somewhere during the startup process. Don't panic. Here are a few easy steps to a fully-functional system:

1. Shut off the computer.
2. Remove the card.
3. Put your System Backup disk in drive A.
4. Turn on the computer.
5. When the computer is finished booting, copy AUTOEXEC.BAT, CONFIG.SYS, WIN.INI, and SYSTEM.INI from the hard disk to a temporary subdirectory for use in Step 8.

6. To restore your system to its original condition, copy AUTOEXEC.BAT, CONFIG.SYS, WIN.INI, and SYSTEM.INI from the A drive to their original positions on the hard disk.

7. Remove the disk from drive A.

8. Call Technical Support for your sound card and try to figure out what happened.

It Won't Play When I...

It's possible that all your software and hardware is installed correctly and that you still get no sound from one or more sound sources. Most often, these problems are quite easy to fix. We'll cover some of the most common symptoms and solutions in this section. Some of the solutions will seem obvious, but the obvious is the first place to look when trying to solve a problem.

SYMPTOM: NO SOUND AT ALL.

Probable cause: Something is wrong with the output path.

Troubleshooting steps:

■ Set the master volume level in your mixer applet to its maximum value.

■ Set the output volume knob (if there is one) on your sound card to its maximum value.

■ Double check that the cord from your sound card to your powered speakers is plugged into an output jack and not into one of the sound card's inputs.

■ Confirm that your powered speakers are plugged in, turned on, and have their volume control turned up.

SYMPTOM: CAN'T HEAR CD AUDIO.

Probable causes: Either the CD slider in your mixer is set to 0 or the audio cable from the CD to the sound card is damaged or not connected properly.

Troubleshooting steps:

■ Make sure that you are testing the correct thing: even though the CD-ROM drive's light is on and it looks like your CD is trying to play CD audio, the CD-ROM program that you're using may instead be trying to play Wave or MIDI files from the CD-ROM. To test whether this is the case, put an ordinary audio CD into the CD-ROM drive and start playback with a Windows or DOS CD control application. See if the problem persists. If it does, then you truly have a problem hearing CD audio. Continue with the following steps:

■ Plug a set of headphones into the audio jack on the CD-ROM player to confirm that the device is producing sound.

■ Check your mixer to make sure that the CD audio input source is enabled and turned up.

SYMPTOM: CAN'T HEAR DIGITAL AUDIO.

Probable causes: Either the digital audio input slider in your mixer is set to its minimum setting, or you're trying to play a digital audio file format that isn't supported by your sound card (in which case, it's likely that you'll see an error message).

Troubleshooting steps:

■ Check that the digital audio input in your mixer is turned on and up. Sometimes this input is labeled VOC or WAV. If you're not sure, turn up *all* the sliders.

■ Test digital audio playback with a file that you know will work. An 8-bit mono file recorded at 22,050 Hz or slower should play back on any sound card. If you use Windows, the system sound files such as TADA.WAV (found in your WINDOWS directory) will do for this purpose. Any digital audio files supplied with your sound card should also work.

You're most likely to have a problem with digital audio files that you've downloaded from a BBS or obtained with a multimedia program or clip music package; files that you record yourself should play back flawlessly. Unless you have the Microsoft *Audio Compression Manager* (ACM) installed (see below for more information), 16-bit digital audio files will not play back on 8-bit cards. Compressed digital audio files will not play back on cards without decompression chips (and, furthermore, there are several "flavors" of ADPCM compression, and your card must have a chip that's compatible with the compression type used in the file). Files sampled in stereo at 44.1 kHz will not play back on cards that can't handle that data rate. This type of mismatch is the most likely source of your problem.

If you use Windows, there's a software solution. Microsoft's Audio Compression Manager, accessed via the *Sound Mapper* icon in the Control Panel, will automatically perform any necessary conversions (16- to 8-bit, high sample rate to low, or compressed to uncompressed) in real-time on your digital audio sounds before passing them on to your card. The current version (as of July, 1994) is stored in a file called ACM201.ZIP and is available on CompuServe, America Online, the Microsoft Download Service, and on other BBS systems. The ACM is also automatically installed with several other products, such as the Video for Windows runtime module (which a multimedia application may have installed on your disk for you), Windows NT, and the upcoming Chicago version of the Windows operating system.

SYMPTOM: CAN'T HEAR VIDEO SOUNDTRACKS.

This is really the same problem as the previous one. The soundtracks for video clips are played back through the digital audio playback hardware. If a video clip was digitized using a digital audio format that your sound card doesn't support, you won't be able to hear its soundtrack.

SYMPTOM: CAN'T HEAR MIDI FILES, OR MIDI FILES SOUND REALLY WEIRD.

Probable causes: Either the MIDI slider in your mixer is set to 0, the MIDI setup options in the program you're using for playback are set incorrectly, or the MIDI Mapper Setup is incorrect.

Troubleshooting steps:

- Check that the MIDI input in your mixer is turned on and up.

- Turn to Chapter 10 for instructions on listening to MIDI files in both DOS and Windows.

Performance Tips

There are a couple of changes that Setup programs typically make to your system files that are likely to slow down your computer. Here's how to regain lost horsepower.

Optimize Your Memory Usage

Most sound card installation programs add lines to your system's CON-FIG.SYS and/or AUTOEXEC.BAT files to load device drivers and initialization programs automatically when the system is powered on. These will naturally use up some memory. If you're using version 6.0 or later of DOS, run a program called MEMMAKER, located in your DOS directory, after the installation. This will alter your AUTOEXEC.BAT file, changing the way that programs are loaded into high memory and making the best usage of all installed memory. You should run this program every time you make changes to CONFIG.SYS or AUTOEXEC.BAT, or if you add memory to your system.

You may be using a third-party memory manager such as QEMM. In this case, use whatever utilities the vendor has provided to reoptimize your memory usage after you install your sound card. Your system will love you for it.

Eliminate Extra Files

Is your hard disk nearly full? Of course it is. Do you really need 3MB of sample sequences, wave files, and miscellaneous utilities floating around on your hard disk? Not likely. Get rid of some of them, exercising due caution. The best form of caution is to back up your hard disk on a daily basis! Remember that if you blow it and trash a program file that you really need, you can always reinstall the software using the Setup disks.

Of course, before you go on a major disk purge, it's a good idea to identify the programs that you want to keep. Take a few days (or minutes, or hours) and experiment with the programs that came with your sound card to see if any are fun or useful. Then trash the rest (remember: in Windows, you can identify the filename associated with any icon in the Program Manager by highlighting the icon and then pressing Alt-Enter).

If you're not sure whether a file (or files) that you'd like to delete is actually necessary, you can always create a temporary subdirectory and move it there. Then, if your system doesn't complain after a few days of usage, go back and delete the subdirectory and everything in it.

Chapter **6**

Your Computer and Your Sound System

There are many advantages to integrating your computer's sound system with your stereo system and/or musical equipment rack. The greatest of these advantages is the consistent enjoyment of truly gorgeous sound, whether using the computer or not. The PC speakers give you perfect separation and, if you have a subwoofer, exceptionally tight and powerful bass response. Your larger stereo speakers give you added volume and presence.

Other advantages of integrating your PC and stereo sound systems are the ability to record your computer-based music onto tape and the ability to sample from the radio (subject to copyright restrictions, of course, discussed at length in Chapter 8).

There are many ways to interconnect your PC and home stereo. We'll diagram a few useful examples and list their pros and cons in this chapter. First, though, take care that your physical setup doesn't place you so close to one or the other of your stereo speakers that you can't enjoy a good balance. I've diagrammed my physical setup in Figure 6-1. Notice that my usual work position is not ideal with respect to balance from the two stereo speakers, but it's more than good enough for excellent sound.

Connectors and Cables

Just in case you don't know the standard terminology for the connectors that are commonly used in audio components, here's a quick review of the basics.

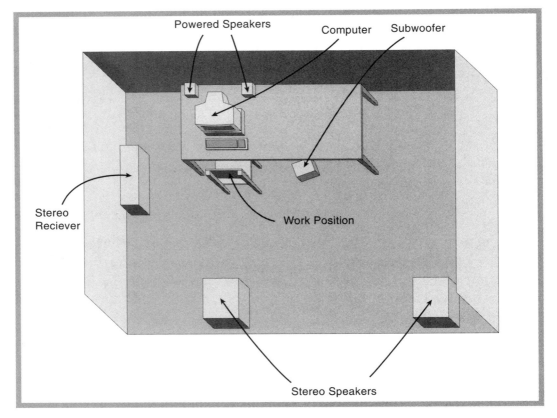

▶ **FIGURE 6-1**

The physical layout of stereo speakers and powered computer speakers.

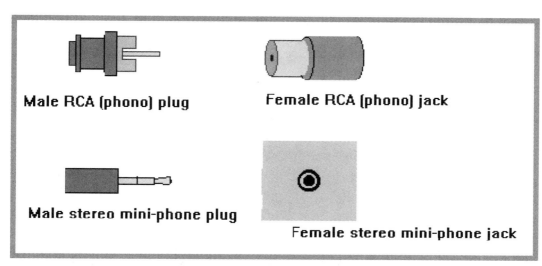

Male RCA (phono) plug

Female RCA (phono) jack

Male stereo mini-phone plug

Female stereo mini-phone jack

▶ **FIGURE 6-2**

Common connectors.

First, audio connectors come in complementary pairs. A *plug* (or *male* connector) is plugged into a *jack* (or *female* connector) of the same type. You're most likely to use both RCA connectors and stereo mini-phone connectors, as shown in Figure 5-2. The terminology associated with these connectors is potentially confusing: RCA connectors are also called *phono* connectors (because phonographs have traditionally been connected to receivers with them), which are not to be confused with *phone* connectors. Phone connectors (which have nothing to do with telephones today but were used in old plug-in telephone switchboards) are available in both stereo and mono versions and in both the mini (1/8 inch) size that your computer gear uses and in the standard 1/4 inch size used in guitar cords and many headphones.

Most audio connections in conventional stereo systems are made with stereo RCA cables. These consist of a pair of cables (one for each channel) molded together, with a pair of male phone plugs on each end. Your receiver undoubtedly has several sets of female RCA jacks on its rear panel to accommodate this type of cable.

On the other hand, most PC audio connectors are made with stereo mini-phone cables. A single cable carries the signals for both halves of the stereo signal, and stereo mini-phone plugs on each end connect with corresponding jacks on your sound cards and speakers.

If you want to meld these two systems together, you need to use *adapter* cables. If your computer is very close to your receiver, you can use Y-cables such as the one pictured in Figure 6-3, with a male stereo mini-phone plug on one end and a pair of male RCAs on the other. Unfortunately, these cables are often not long enough to span the required distance, so you may have to resort to using two cables, as shown in Figure 6-4: a standard stereo RCA cable coupled with a Y-adapter with a stereo mini-phone plug on one end and a pair of female RCA jacks on the other. All these cables are available at your local electronics store.

Basic Setup for Speakers With Multiple Inputs

If your speakers have multiple inputs, it's a simple matter to listen to your stereo system—your radio, CDs, tapes, and records—through your computer speakers in addition to through your stereo speakers. Simply connect a Tape or Video output from your receiver to the second input of your speakers, as shown in Figure 6-5.

The virtue of this simple setup is that it enhances your everyday listening without any complications. You can even listen to enhanced sound when your computer is turned off. The limitations are that you can't sample or record sounds onto tape without changing configurations.

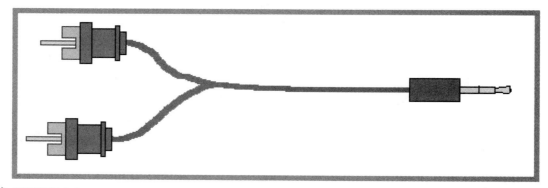

▶ **FIGURE 6-3**

A male-RCA to stereo mini-phone Y cord.

You can expand this setup by connecting another Y cord from your CD-ROM player's headphone jack to any available input on your receiver. Then you can play audio CDs in your CD-ROM drive and listen to sound through all four speakers.

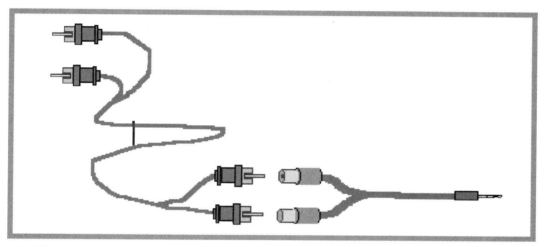

▶ **FIGURE 6-4**

Use a short Y cord with female RCA jacks and stereo RCA cable to make the connection from your sound receiver.

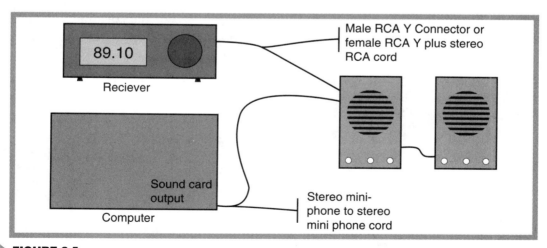

▶ **FIGURE 6-5**

Connecting your computer and receiver to a pair of powered speakers with at least two inputs.

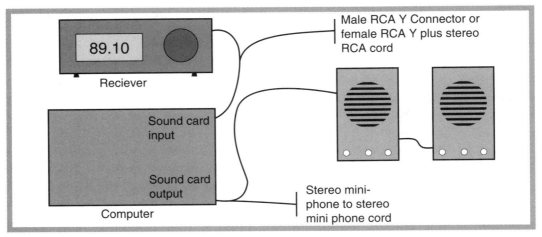

▶ **FIGURE 6-6**

Setup for sampling.

Sampling Setup

Figure 6-6 shows a variant of the previous setup. In this case, a Tape output from your receiver is sent to your sound card's input jack instead of to a speaker. This enables you to record sounds from your stereo onto your hard disk as digital audio files. It also has the advantage of working with any powered speakers, whether or not they have extra inputs. In addition, you can control the volume of the receiver's output (as heard through the computer speakers) with your sound card's mixer applet.

The main disadvantage of this setup is that you can't hear sound through the powered speakers unless your computer is turned on. Also, the output of the receiver is passed through your sound card before going to the speakers, which adds a small amount of distortion and noise. And, as in the previous setup, you can't record your PC's output, and sounds from your PC will not be played over your stereo speakers.

Recording Setup

If you've created music on your PC that you want to transfer to a non-digital medium (a cassette, for instance) or even to a digital audio tape

▶ **FIGURE 6-7**

Setup for recording.

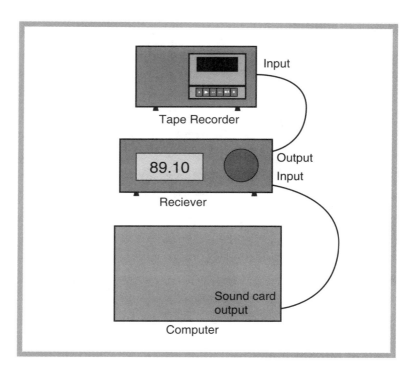

(DAT), you'll want to route the output of your sound card to an input on your receiver. Figure 6-7 shows the simplest way of accomplishing this. This setup will let you listen to the output of your sound card through your stereo speakers. Add a cord from one of your receiver's outputs to your PC speakers to enjoy all your speakers at once.

The disadvantage of this system is that you can't listen to your radio and your system sounds at the same time.

Chapter **7**

Sound Quality

The best equipment can sound terrible if you don't have it set up correctly. The worst equipment can sound decent if you treat it right. This chapter is a primer on noise control. Learn to practice good audio hygiene—your ears will thank you for it.

The Signal Chain

You may find it hard to believe, but every audio signal is altered numerous times on the tortuous path from the source to your ear. This path is called the signal chain. Let's take the example of audio from your CD-ROM. Figure 7-1 shows the various stages of amplification and alteration that music recorded on a CD must undergo before it actually reaches your ear. (Note: the diagram is fairly general and may not reflect exactly what goes on in any particular system). None of these stages is perfect: under normal operating conditions, each adds a tiny bit of unintended distortion to any signal passing though it. This is perfectly acceptable. But, as we'll see, when these stages are improperly adjusted, excessive, unpleasant distortion may result. After a leisurely stroll though the signal chain, we'll pause to rest, reflect, and discuss The Golden Rule of Signal Hygiene.

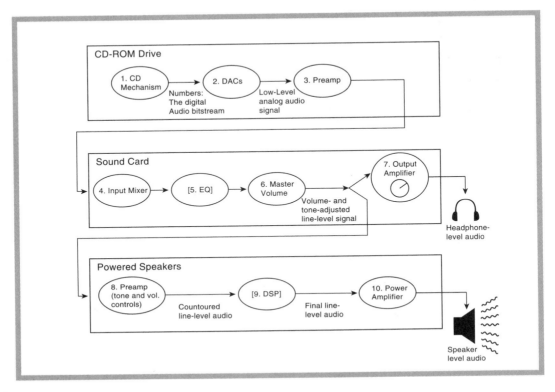

▶ **FIGURE 7-1**

The many links in the signal chain.

About Amplifiers and Preamplifiers

When we take a close look inside audio components, such as receivers, sound cards, powered speaker systems, or whatever, we'll run into chips or circuits that boost, attenuate (weaken), or modify the signal in some other way. The final stage is responsible for the biggest boost, from a *line level* signal (a standard signal strength expected at connections between electronic components) to one strong enough to move large speaker cones thousands of times each second. This is called the *power amplifier* stage. The earlier stages often boost or attenuate line level or low-level (weaker than line level) signals, but not as dramatically. Sometimes these other stages also shape the signal with equalization (tone controls). These circuits, with varying capabilities, are called *preamplifiers,* or simply preamps.

Inside the CD-ROM Player

At stage one in Figure 7-1, the CD mechanism reads the digital data from the disc and sends it to the CD-ROM player's DACs (one for each channel in most players). These DACs (stage two) convert the number stream into a weak electrical current with voltage fluctuations that represent the music. A not-very-powerful preamp in the player (stage three) amplifies this signal to line level.

Inside Your Sound Card

The audio signal received from the CD-ROM is mixed with all other sound sources (stage four). The signal may be amplified (which can mean either strengthened or weakened) in the mixer section. On some sound cards, the mixed signal is then passed through an equalization (tone control), or EQ, section (stage five). After the EQ, the signal is passed through another preamp stage, under control of the "Master" sliders in your software mixer, to adjust the final volume passed to the powered speakers or headphones (stage six).

Once the sound passes through the Master Volume, it can take one (or both) of two paths, depending on your sound card. Some sound cards feature headphone outputs, some have line outputs, some have both, and some (such as the Sound Blaster 16) have a single output that is switchable between the two types.

The difference between these outputs is that the headphone output produces a stronger signal. A line level output is ideal for passing on to a pair of powered speakers, where it will be amplified further, whereas a headphone output is designed to be the last stage of amplification. It must be strong enough to drive a pair of headphone speakers. To this end, signals sent to the headphone output first pass through a volume control (the knob on your sound card) and then through a weak-powered amplifier—one just strong enough (four watts or so per channel) to drive the small speakers in a pair of headphones (stage seven).

If your sound card has a switchable output, then set it for line level if you use powered speakers, and set it for headphones if they will be your main "listening interface." As we'll discuss in more detail shortly, the wrong setting here is one of the most common causes of bad sound. If you put a headphone-level output into a pair of powered speakers, you can overload the speakers' input circuits and get ugly distortion. If your sound card only has a single, headphone-level output, keep the volume knob on the card at a low-to-middle setting when using powered speakers. You can determine a good value for this by playing the loudest music that you can through your sound card, and setting the sound card volume control to the highest setting that doesn't cause distortion.

Inside Your Powered Speakers

Once the line-level signal reaches your powered speaker inputs, its long path is still not quite over. First it passes through yet another pre-amp (stage eight), where it can be molded by tone, volume, and balance controls. Then the signal passes through a DSP section (stage nine), if there is one, where additional processing may occur to tailor the output for close or more distant listening. Finally, the signal is fed to a power amplifier (stage 10), where it is boosted to the strength necessary to drive the speakers.

In systems with subwoofers, the sum of the left and right channels is also sent to the subwoofer unit, where an even more powerful amplifier boosts the signal to drive those punchy bass speakers.

Sources of Noise

You may have noticed that there is a lot of redundant processing in a typical signal chain. There are, for instance, three separate places to set the volume of your audio CD signal: with the "CD" slider in the mixer, with the "Master Volume" slider, and with the volume control on your speakers. The cleanest possible system would eliminate at least one of these stages. Still, this arrangement gives you lots of flexibility, along with lots of power to make the wrong decisions!

It's not hard to tune a PC sound system so that noise is at a minimum for your sound card. There's not much that you can do about the electrical interference inside your computer chassis, other than to purchase a better-shielded sound card if yours is noisy. You can try to move cards to different slots, but that's not likely to do much for you. However, you can control your levels in the signal chain, and this is very significant. Just remember:

The Golden Rule of Signal Hygiene

A single principle can guide you infallibly to sonic satisfaction:

Keep each output as hot as possible without overloading the next stage's input.

Most input sections can be overloaded by feeding them signals that are too loud, which will cause them to distort. We've already mentioned the common mistake of feeding a headphone-level signal to a powered speaker input. It's also possible that turning a sound source's level too high in the mixer will create levels that will overpower a later stage. You can also boost a level too much by pushing the tone controls, especially the bass, all the way to the top of the scale.

This principle also applies to the output of the final amplifier, which can overload the speakers if the amp is turned up too high, causing both distortion and physical damage to the speakers.

The first thing to do if your sounds are distorted is to turn down the volume at your speakers. If the distortion goes away, then it stems from overdriving the speakers. The solution is to not turn the volume up that high. If the distortion persists at low or moderate volumes, then the signal is already distorted by the time it reaches the amplifier and is being properly amplified and reproduced by the speakers.

This means that you should move one step back in the signal chain and see if the input to your speakers' preamp is overloading it. Try turning down the volume knob on your sound card, if it has one. If there's no volume knob, turn down the Master Volume in the mixer applet. If these measures don't solve your problem, then go one step back and turn down the individual inputs. Eventually you will identify the source of the overload. Once you turn that down, you can turn it and every level past it (except your final listening level at the speakers) up to the maximum level that doesn't cause distortion. You'll be able to turn the volume up at the final stage to reach your desired listening level without undue distortion.

While we're on the subject of headphone-level signals, let me add a tip if you want to make a digital audio recording from a cassette player. Don't connect the player's headphone jack to a line input on your sound card; instead, use the tape player's line out jack if there is one. If the headphone jack is all you have, keep the volume knob on the tape player in a low-to-middle position.

I've been harping on the second half of the Golden Rule of Signal Hygiene because it's the more important one, but let's not ignore the first half. We want to keep our signals as hot (turned up) as we can without causing an overload. The drawings in Figure 7-2 demonstrate why.

Figure 7-2a shows two stages in the processing of a quiet signal, while Figure 7-2b shows the same two stages as applied to a louder signal. The results, as shown in the right side of the figure, are more noise in the first case. Let's examine how that comes about.

When a signal goes from the output of one component to the input of another (stage one), a small, usually imperceptible, amount of noise is inevitably added. Nothing in life or audio is ever perfect. The amount of noise is the same regardless of the strength of the desired signal. This means that the noise will be a smaller component of the total signal when it combines with the louder source than when it combines with the weaker one.

The amount of noise added at that stage may be imperceptible, but if amplification is applied later to boost the signal (stage two), the noise will be boosted too. This results in the kind of signal shown at the right in Figure 7-2a, where the noise level is visibly more prominent than it was before amplification. If the amplification is high enough, the imperceptible can become not only perceptible but annoying.

In contrast, take a look at Figure 7-2b. In this case, we start out with a stronger signal than before. The same amount of residual noise is added to the signal, but since the combined signal is already strong,

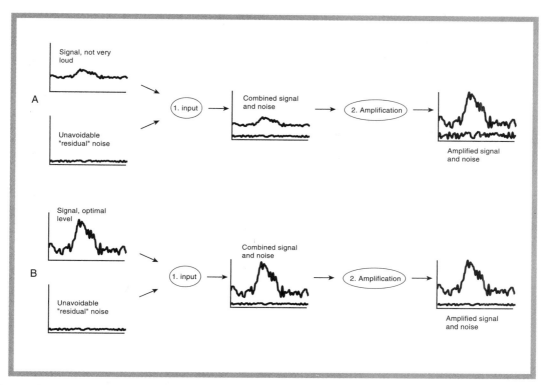

▶ **FIGURE 7-2**

These diagrams show why an original signal at a high level (Signal B) will result
in less apparent noise than one that starts at a lower level (Signal A).

it doesn't need amplification at stage two. You can see the results of
the process on the right. The noise component is less pronounced
than in the diagram above it and will remain so through any further
processing of the combined signal.

In contrast with the problems caused by too-high levels, which
make themselves apparent when they cause distortion during loud
passages in the music, problems caused by too-low levels show up as
an excessive amount of background noise and a need to turn up the
volume control on your speakers unusually high.

Unused Mixer Inputs

There's one noise source that isn't addressed by The Golden Rule of
Audio Hygiene. If you have mixer levels turned up for sound sources

that you're not using, you are adding noise to the mix for no good reason.

Run your sound card's mixer software. Is the microphone input turned up, even though you never (or hardly ever) use a microphone? Turn it all the way down, and then save your mixer settings. Do the same for any other inputs that you don't ordinarily use.

It's especially important to keep noise levels low during the recording process. Any extra noise that you record into digital audio files will plague you every time you listen to them, no matter how much you clean up your audio act. It's important to use your mixer to disable recording of all unnecessary sources and to keep your levels as high as possible without overloading. We'll discuss this in much greater detail in the following chapter.

Follow these few simple rules, and you will enjoy the best audio quality that your system can deliver.

Chapter **8**

Recording and Editing Digital Audio

If you want to record yourself singing or playing the saxophone, create a narration for a presentation or digital video clip, record a news bite from the radio, or add sound effects to common system events (under Windows), then digital audio—stored in .VOC and .WAV files—is your medium.

A sound card and sound recording program (included with every sound card) transform your computer into a digital audio "tape" recorder, except that your hard disk is used for storing the music instead of tape. You can overdub (record additional tracks while listening to existing ones), mix, and otherwise transform audio tracks in lots of useful and/or bizarre ways, create sound collages and environments, slow down music clips to half-speed so you can play along with them, create new wavetable samples (for some sound cards), and generally have a lot of fun with digital audio.

You'll find the keys to the playground in the rest of this chapter. We'll start off by talking about what makes digital hard disk recording unique and then move on to the topics of listening to and recording digital audio files. If you want to record vocals, acoustic instruments, or other sounds from the air, pay close attention to the section called "Using Microphones"—it contains tips that none of the manuals will tell you. After that, we'll talk about the various editing and mixing tricks that make this medium so much fun. We'll talk a bit about "Dream Systems" and also give you the copyright information you need in order to avoid improper use of someone else's material.

Digital Recording on Disk vs. Tape

In order to get a grasp of just what you can and cannot accomplish with digital audio, let's contrast your digital audio recording system (which we can also call a "hard disk recording system") with a true digital audio tape (DAT) recorder. Your system can, in fact, edit audio—a task impossible with DAT recorders alone. However, the DAT is likely to provide better sound quality than your system, although the gap between high-end sound cards and DATs is not vast.

Both your system and a DAT recorder use analog-to-digital (A/D) converters to change incoming audio signals into a stream of digital data, as we've discussed in Chapter 3. However, there are differences in quality. DAT recorders cost at least $550, and the professional models cost over $1,000. The better DAT recorders use high-quality A/D converters specifically designed for professional recording applications. These sample more accurately than the more economical ones in your sound card. And the big bucks recording studios often go a step further, adding external units to their DAT recorders whose only function is to provide the highest quality A/D converters that money can buy. Realistically speaking, though, you and I might be hard-pressed to tell the difference in audio quality between the best converters and the ones in our sound cards, especially with the computer fan running.

Still, DAT recorders are likely to make lower-noise recordings than your computer. No piece of equipment is perfectly noise-free, but many DAT recorders come quite close to achieving this ideal. As we've already discussed, only the high-end sound cards have shielding capable of producing really quiet recordings, and even these are not likely to match DAT specifications.

Don't take this too hard. Just because TAFKAP (the artist formerly known as Prince) or U2 wouldn't record with your sound card doesn't mean that there's anything wrong with it. In fact, you can make recordings whose sound quality will amaze you and your friends using your own equipment. These are perfectly suited for your own entertainment, for soundtracks to digital video movies, and for demo tapes. Besides, pristine audio quality isn't everything. Several (but not many) best-selling records have been produced from masters created on four-track cassette-based ministudios, which don't even approach the quality that you can achieve with an inexpensive 16-bit sound card. And, if you are an aspiring professional recording artist, you can enter the realm of professional systems by checking out the "Dream Systems" section at the end of this chapter.

Hard disk recording has one extremely significant advantage over tape recording—editability. Because disks are a random-access medium as opposed to the continuous, linear medium of tape, you can extract sections of any recording that you've made and manipulate them in a variety of ways. You can cut and paste verses, eliminate bad sections, mix multiple takes, reverse, bend, and stretch sections of music, and just generally go nuts. None of this is possible with tape-based systems.

Listening to Digital Audio Files

Listening to digital audio files is quite simple, either from DOS or Windows. You must simply pay attention to the format of the files that you're using. If a format isn't compatible with your sound card or environment, you can use a simple utility to transform it into something more appropriate. You can also play back digital audio files from within digital audio editing programs, but we'll get to that in due time. In this section we'll cover all that you need to know for simple playback.

Playing Back Digital Audio Files in Windows

Wave files are the coin of the realm when it comes to digital audio in Windows. If the file that you want to hear doesn't have a .WAV extension, use one of the methods described in the "File Conversion" section below to transform it into a wave file.

The fastest way to play back wave files in Windows is to use the Media Player applet that comes with Windows 3.1. When you double-click on its icon in the Program Manager's Accessories group, you'll see a screen such as that shown in Figure 8-1. Pick the "Open..." choice from the File menu and select the wave file that you wish to hear. Then press the button in the lower left corner of the Media Player window (this is the Play button). You should hear your digital audio file play back.

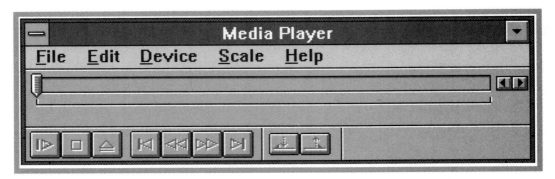

▶ **FIGURE 8-1**
The Microsoft Media Player.

If you hear nothing, then suspect one of two likely problems. The first is that the volume may be turned down, either at your speakers or in your mixer applet. Open up your mixer applet and take a look. The slider that controls the volume of digital audio will be marked either "Wave" or "VOC" (it's a needlessly confusing interface design to label a slider "VOC" in a mixer meant exclusively for Windows, but old habits die hard)! The other problem that might prevent you from hearing a digital audio file applies if you have an 8-bit sound card. Eight-bit cards cannot play back 16-bit sound files. If you suspect that this is the case, make a copy of the audio file and convert it to an 8-bit file using the methods described in the "File Conversion" section below. Then try to play it again. It should work.

Playing Back Digital Audio Files in DOS

This is generally quite a simple process. Your sound card undoubtedly came with a DOS utility (or utilities) for playing back .VOC files, .WAV files, or both. Creative Labs' Sound Blasters, for instance, come with VPLAY for .VOC files and WPLAY for .WAV files. You invoke either of these programs from the command line. Here's an example:

```
\sb16\vplay c:\soundfx\carcrash.voc
```

You can use statements such as these in batch files to add startup sounds or narrated instructions to installation routines, if you like.

File Conversion

There are several reasons that you might want to convert the format of existing digital audio files. You might want to convert a voice file to a wave file for easier use in a Windows environment, or you might want to go in the other direction to create a voice file that can be used by an older program. If you have an 8-bit sound card or are developing a product for a market that must cater to 8-bit sound cards, you may need to convert a 16-bit file to 8 bits (you'll suffer a loss in sound quality if you do this, of course). You may want to convert a file compressed with the ADPCM method (see Chapter 3) to an uncompressed file, or vice versa. There are several reasons *not* to convert an 8-bit file to a 16-bit file—you can't gain sound quality that isn't in the original recording, the files will get bigger, and they will play on fewer cards—although utilities exist to perform this task. However, you may want to perform this conversion if you want to process the sounds in the file with 16-bit resolution or if you want to use the file for some purpose that requires 16-bits. Finally, you may have a desire to change a sampling rate (usually downward) or to convert a stereo file to mono in order to conserve disk space.

Your sound card may or may not come with utilities to perform some of these transformations. The Sound Blaster 16, for instance, comes with WAVE2VOC and VOC2WAVE, which interchange wave and voice files. It also includes VOCO2N and VOCN2O (think of these as "old to new" and "new to old," respectively), which convert files from the "old" 8-bit voice file format to the "new" 16-bit format or vice versa. You can combine these utilities: To convert a 16-bit wave file to an 8-bit wave file, for example, first apply WAVE2VOC, then VOCN2O, then VOC2WAVE. Or, you can use a digital audio editing package that will perform these and other tricks.

Digital audio editors, which we'll cover in an upcoming section, are necessary for performing some of the more elaborate conversions that we've mentioned. These editors are useful, fun, and interesting in their own right. But there's an added bonus—if you have an 8-bit sound card or one without ADPCM compression, some digital audio editors can actually convert the files that you can't hear to ones that you can.

Recording Digital Audio

There are several steps involved in recording digital audio. In this section, we'll take you through the process, step-by-step.

1. **Load a recording program.** There are a number of programs for both DOS and Windows that can record digital audio. Your sound card probably came with one or more of these. If you don't have a program dedicated to recording and playback, you probably have a digital audio editor, which provides these functions and more.

2. **Choose a data file format.** This requires evaluating your needs and how they relate to the tradeoff between sound quality and file size. As we've discussed, CD-quality stereo digital audio requires 10MB of disk space for every minute of sound. The consequences of huge disk files (assuming that you have the space on your disk for them in the first place) are cumbersome backup procedures (if you back up to floppies rather than tape) and slower editing. Also, editing programs often create a temporary disk file as large as the original, so plan on extra disk space for that.

Sixteen-bit sound files sampled at 22kHz provide very high-quality music. You can cut file size in half by halving the sampling rate, going from 16 bits to 8, or sacrificing stereo and using mono instead. This last choice is often the best because it doesn't degrade the essential sound quality of the music. In most cases, cutting the sampling rate to 11kHz produces better results than cutting the "bit width" to 8; in other words, a 16-bit, 11kHz file will sound better than an 8-bit, 22kHz file, all other things being equal.

Speech and some sound effects can be safely sampled at 11kHz or lower. They don't contain as much critical high-frequency information as music.

3. **Select a sound source.** You can record wave files from a line-level input, from a microphone-level input, or from an audio CD in your CD-ROM drive. Most DOS recording programs include a menu choice or command-line option for choosing an input. Windows programs often omit this because you can use your mixer applet (which you can run simultaneously with the recorder) to choose your inputs (see Figure 8-2).

▶ **FIGURE 8-2**

The Recording Control portion of the Sound Blaster 16 Mixer applet is set to record from the card's MIDI synthesizer.

Note that the multi-tasking abilities of Windows gives you a lot of flexibility while recording. You can run the Media Player (or another program) to start and stop the playback of MIDI files or CD audio while your recording application is busy recording in a separate window. Some DOS recorders and editors combine these functions into a single program.

4. **Check recording levels.** Unfortunately, not all recording programs come with level meters (see Figure 8-3). These meters tell you how strong the input signal is. Generally speaking, you'll get the cleanest recordings if these meters stay as close as possible to the top of the scale without ever lighting up the Clip light. If the levels are too low, your signal won't be much louder than any background noise or hiss in your system—you'll need to boost the signal substantially during playback in order to listen to it comfortably, and you'll also be boosting the hiss. That's why the signal should be recorded as "hot" as possible. On the other hand, if you ever light up the Clip indicator, it's all over. You will get ugly

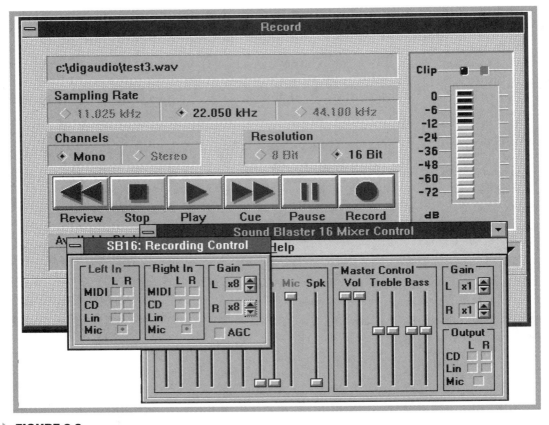

▶ **FIGURE 8-3**

Using a mixer applet and editor simultaneously under Windows.

digital distortion where the clip occurs. (This is much more critical with digital recording than with analog tape, which distorts in a softer, more forgiving manner.)

In some recording applications, the level meters aren't automatically active. I've seen some programs that make you press Pause to activate them, while others make you actually start recording (and then let you hit Pause) before you can read the meters. If you can't figure out how to activate the meters, check the manual or the help files.

If you're working in Windows, you can adjust recording levels in your mixer applet while watching their effect on meters in your recorder, as shown in Figure 8-3.

The mixer shown contains a control labeled AGC. This stands for Automatic Gain Control and is intended to help boost the microphone input level so that it can be recorded well. This is sufficient for making some recordings with microphones, especially for narration or other speech applications. However, I have found that other methods for recording with microphones work much better for music and other applications where sound quality is a serious concern, and we'll discuss those methods.

5. **Make your recording.** When your levels are set, it's time to press the red Record button. Of course, if you're a musician recording yourself, you will immediately freeze up and forget everything you ever knew about playing or singing, but that's a subject for a different book. In any event, it's always a good idea to make a short test recording to check that everything is working as it should before committing your energy to an all-out performance. Record for a short time and then press the Stop button.

6. **Listen to the results.** Hit the Play button to listen to your test recording (you may have to press a Rewind button first). Does it sound cool? Then go back to Step 5 and record the real thing.

7. **Trim it.** Usually when you make a recording, you wind up with extra space at the beginning and end that you don't want. If you're using a bare-bones recording program, there's not much you can do about this, but if you have access to any editing program, you

can easily delete the unwanted portions. This will make the results more like what you intended and also free up some disk space.

8. **Normalize it.** This function is only available in some digital audio editors, but you can simulate it in nearly all of them. The goal is to make your recording as loud as possible without adding any distortion. When you activate you program's normalization function, if it has one, it will look at all the samples in your recording and take note of the highest value (actually, highest absolute value, since samples are both positive and negative) it finds. It will then figure out a multiplier which will make that sample reach the limits of the sample range and multiply all the samples by that value. This scales the recording so that it just reaches, but never exceeds, the limits of the sampling range (see Figure 8-4). In effect, this is digital amplification—it increases the volume of your recording without adding any noise.

If your editing program doesn't have a Normalize function, you can get really close by amplifying the wave until it almost fills the

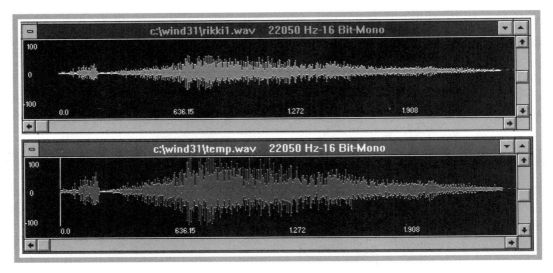

▶ **FIGURE 8-4**

An unnormalized wave file [top] is amplified to the maximum limits with normalization [bottom].

vertical range of the display. If you do this, make sure that your editor has an Undo function or that you work with a copy of your recording. It's easy to go too far and amplify the recording to the point of clipping (see Figure 8-5).

Microphone Tips

Digital recording with most sound cards and microphones is a tricky proposition and is best approached by indirection. If you're recording speech, then you can get away with just plugging a microphone into the input and recording as above (although I did discover that, at least on a Sound Blaster board, recording with AGC turned off and then normalizing produces substantially less hiss than using AGC. The moral: the officially-recommended course of action isn't always the best. Whenever you can, test alternative approaches yourself). In general, though, you're better off recording miked instruments and vocals onto tape (if you have a good cassette deck or a DAT recorder) and then digitally recording the results onto your hard disk through your sound card's Line input.

There are several reasons why this gives better results than plugging into the microphone input on your sound card. The main one is that special preamplifiers are necessary to boost wimpy microphone output levels to something that can be recorded decently. It's a fact of life that most tape decks of moderate-to-good quality (this includes cassette tape decks costing around $150 or more and emphatically includes all DAT recorders) have better preamps than most sound

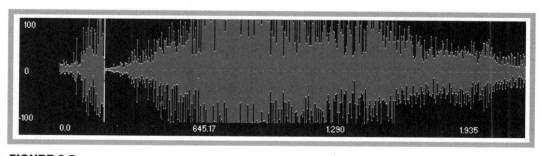

▶ **FIGURE 8-5**

Amplifying a waveform too much results in clipping distortion, which can be seen in the squared-off portions of this wave.

cards and don't have to deal with the noisy interior of your computer's chassis. The second reason, which is more minor, is that computers create noise from their fans and their disk drives which can leak into your microphone to be recorded along with your intended signal. If you shut off your computer's power and record into a tape deck, you will have substantially less background noise polluting your recording.

Microphone Types

Your choice of microphone will affect the quality of your recording. The microphones that are built into some cassette recorders are barely acceptable for speech and completely unusable for music. It is possible to make good recordings with microphones costing less than $100, and it seems like overkill to pay much more for a microphone intended for PC recording usage. At the high end, if you're a vocalist and want to record the master for a hit CD, you'd be best off bringing your MIDI backing tracks (Chapters 9 and 10 will teach you how to create these) to a professional recording studio where you can record you vocals from an isolation booth using super-expensive microphones.

If you simply want to record speech, the microphones included with several multimedia packages (such as the Microsoft Sound System) are perfectly adequate. Otherwise, most consumer electronics stores sell microphones designed to work well with portable cassette recorders and/or DATs.

If you're a performing vocalist, you probably have (or should have) a dynamic microphone to bring to jam sessions, rehearsals and gigs. Dynamic microphones work like speakers in reverse—the sound waves produced by your voice move a lightweight element in the microphone called a *diaphragm*. The movement of the diaphragm through a magnetic field causes a small electrical current to be generated and sent through a microphone cable to the mixer or preamplifier. Dynamic microphones are very popular for the stage because of their durability and good sound quality. (Other types of microphones, such as *condenser* microphones, are more sensitive but also more delicate and are primarily used in recording studios.)

Decent dynamic microphones are available for under $100 through any musical equipment supplier, although you may find it worth your while to invest more—you'll get superior resistance to feedback (that awful howling noise that occurs when sounds from speakers leak into a microphone and are amplified and played back through the same speakers and enter the microphone again, and on and on) and suppression of *microphone handling noise* (rumbles that occur when you shift a microphone in your hand) and *popping plosives* (overloads that can be caused by the wind from "P" and "B" sounds sung too close to the microphone). If you get a stage microphone, you may need to obtain a transformer (inexpensive) or other adapter in order to make it suitable for direct recording.

When recording with a microphone, a stand is highly recommended. It eliminates microphone handling noise and is a major convenience. Solo vocalists can use a simple microphone stand. Other acoustic instrumentalists may find that a stand with a *boom* attachment will give them more flexibility in positioning the microphone so that it captures the fullest sound from their instruments.

When using a microphone, be careful to avoid overloading it. Don't (if you're a vocalist or narrator) put your lips right on top of it, and avoid blowing into it. Make a special effort to move your head away from the microphone when plosives come up.

Editing and Mixing Digital Audio

This is where the fun comes in, but it does require patience. Because digital audio files are so large, some of the operations involved in editing them are rather time-consuming, involving minutes of staring at that annoying hourglass cursor. Still, many of them are quite fun and/or useful and are worth the wait.

In order to edit digital audio files, you'll need a digital audio editing program. It's quite possible that one of these came with your sound card; however, these programs are fairly complex and you may want to upgrade to a more capable program in the future.

A digital audio editor will generally be designed to edit either voice or wave files, and many can import or export both these formats in addition to several others. These days, most of the prominent digital audio editors use wave files as their primary format. For convenience, we'll call all digital audio editors "wave editors" henceforth, unless we are explicitly referring to a program designed for voice files. Similarly, unless we're specifically talking about digital audio files in Windows (which are always "wave files"), we'll use the term "wave file" to refer to any kind of digital audio file.

One note: Throughout this chapter, I'll be using two or three digital audio editing programs to illustrate many of my points. This does not mean that these are the only editing programs that you should consider for your own use—only that they are the most popular ones. So many of these programs have been released recently that it is simply impossible to use all of them. When and if the time comes for you to purchase one, know which features you want the most (you'll figure this out from experience with your bundled editor) and examine the buyer's guides in magazines such as *Multimedia World* and *New Media* for details on the current crop.

The Importance of Backups

Because digital audio files are so large, it's generally not possible for editing programs to keep the entire file in your system's memory. Instead, they edit the files in place on your hard disk. This sometimes means that there's no going back—in some programs, edits may not be undoable, and you may not have an option of either reverting to the last-saved version of a file or closing a file without saving changes.

Some programs get around this by maintaining an Undo storage area for some operations and by warning you whenever you're about to attempt an operation that can't be undone. These Undo areas are sometimes in memory and sometimes temporary files on disk. Other programs make a full backup of whatever file you're about to edit, which, in effect, gives you the option not to save changes when you exit the program or close the file. However, there are many programs which provide neither of these safety nets. If your editor is one of these (or if you're not sure) and if you care about your recorded files (in other words, if it would be a pain in the neck to recreate them), then you ought to make a backup copy, either on disk or tape, before you start to edit them.

Zooming Through Wave Displays

The most common task in editing audio files, and one which we've already mentioned in our discussion of recording, is trimming extraneous sound from the beginning and end. In order to accomplish this, you need to be able to read a waveform display and precisely select audio segments. Since these skills are the basis for just about all editing operations, they're worth examining in depth.

Figure 8-6 shows a short wave file that I recorded from a classical guitar CD with Turtle Beach's *Wave 2.0* program, one of the most powerful wave editors available. I chose to illustrate these operations with this type of recording because it's easier to isolate individual notes in a solo performance than in a group setting. Narration is also easy to edit because it's essentially a "solo performance," using words instead of notes. Once you're comfortable editing solo segments, you can easily move on to complex ensembles.

My first action after recording the guitar performance was to normalize the recording. This is easy in Wave. First choose Select All from the edit menu, and then choose Normalize from the tools menu. Not only does this optimize the audio level of the recording for the cleanest playback, but it also makes the graph easier to edit because the plot spans the full vertical range of the display window (although in many programs you can control the vertical zoom amount independently of the audio level).

Interpreting the Wave Display

The graph in Figure 8-6 plots the amplitude, or value, of each sample on the vertical axis, and time on the horizontal axis. You'll notice that the graph is roughly symmetrical around the horizontal axis. That's because sound waves alternate between positive and negative values. They alternate so rapidly that, for viewing convenience, the program displays the graph with a solidly filled-in area. Figure 8-7 is another view of the same file, shown as a pure graph without a solid fill, with only the positive values displayed. This shot is taken from another excellent wave editing program, Sound Impression for Windows, which can also display the wave in the solid-filled, positive-and-negative format that I prefer.

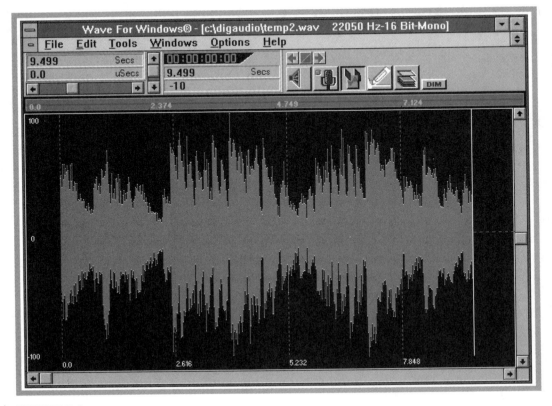

▶ **FIGURE 8-6**

An excerpt from a classical guitar recording, shown in Turtle Beach's Wave
program.

Loud portions of the music correspond to higher values on the plot. Looking again at Figure 8-7, notice that the section of music that begins near the 2.579 second marker seems louder than the section before it. In fact, listening to the music reveals a new, prominent melodic phrase entering at that point (you'll have to take my word for it).

A typical musical note has a sharp *attack phase* (lasting only a few dozen milliseconds), followed by a rapid decay to a slightly–softer level, where it very gradually dies out. You can identify individual notes or chords by that profile, especially when you look a little more closely. Figure 8-8 shows a single note highlighted in a close-up view.

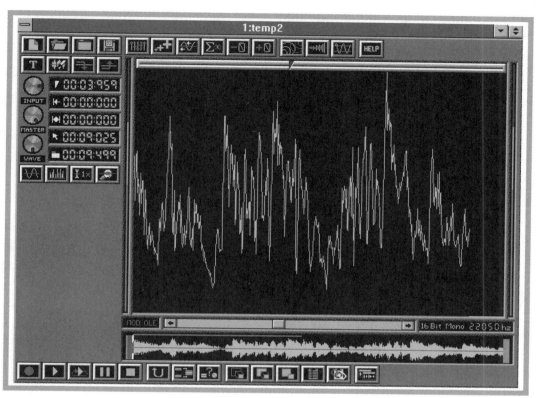

FIGURE 8-7

A line-only display of a waveform, shown in Sound Impression *(which can display the waveform in several formats).*

Playing a Highlighted Area

In order to extract a phrase from a recording for later use, you must first select it. I usually start by selecting an area that's slightly larger than the area I really want and then zooming in to adjust the endpoints, as you'll see. Figure 8-9 shows my first rough cut at extracting a phrase.

In most programs, selection is simple—you just click in the graph area and drag over the portion of the plot that you want to highlight. Once you've selected an area, you'll probably want to listen to only the selected area to verify that you've selected correctly. In Wave this is easy—clicking the speaker icon will play the selected area if one is selected, or the currently-visible portion of the wave if there is no current selection. Most wave editors have a way of playing the current

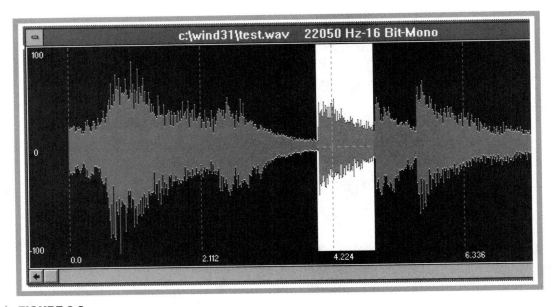

▶ **FIGURE 8-8**

The highlit region shows the characteristic shape of a single note or chord.

selection only, and you ought to investigate this (either in a help file or the manual) and make at least a mental note of it. Often, all it takes is clicking the Play button or pressing the Space bar.

Zooming and Tweaking

Most wave editors can zoom to a very detailed level in order to perform precision editing. In Wave, zooming is particularly easy—you just hold down the right mouse button and drag over the area that you want to fill the screen.

I've started out by zooming to the front of my selected area. Once there, I can shift-click at any location on the screen to either extend or trim my selection. Figure 8-10 shows how I've trimmed it, by starting my selection just before the attack of the first note in the phrase. Once I've done that, the next steps are to zoom out in order to view the entire segment and then to zoom in on the right side of the selection, adjusting the endpoint to be just before the first note that's *not* in the phrase. This lets the last note in the phrase sustain for as long as possible before it's cut off.

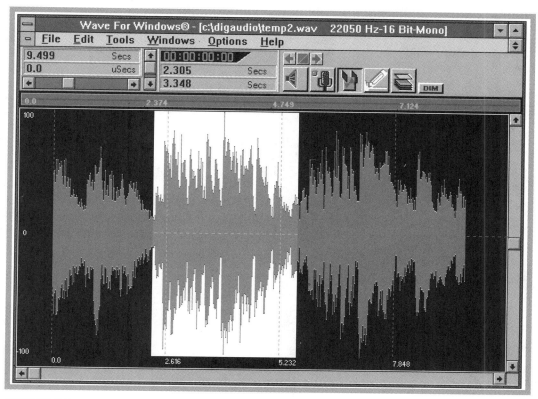

▶ **FIGURE 8-9**

The first step in trimming is to roughly select the region that you'd like to keep.

Zooming out is usually accomplished with a wave overview display. In Sound Impression, it's the display under the main editing window, which has draggable vertical bars on each end that bracket the portion of the wave displayed in detail above in the main window. In Wave, it's the numbered bar just above the editing window, which you drag over to highlight the portion of the recording you wish to display.

Trimming

Once you have the exact area selected that you want, then you can trim off the excess. Some editors have a Trim command that will delete everything that's not currently selected. In other editors, you'll need to copy the selected area, create a new file, and paste the selection into

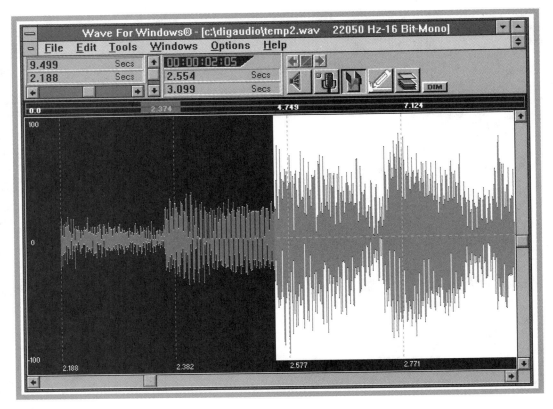

▶ **FIGURE 8-10**
Select the precise beginning of a phrase by shift-clicking just before the sharp attack of its first note.

it. Still other programs will save only the selected area when you issue the Save As... command.

Fades and Transitions

When you cut a musical phrase off at the end, it's quite possible that the last note will seem to stop abruptly and unnaturally. Sometimes you can make this effect less pronounced by *fading out* the last note or phrase, making it decrease in volume over time, so that the recording is already silent by the time of the abrupt stop.

Different programs have different means for accomplishing fades (either fade-outs or their reverse, *fade-ins*). Most programs have a button or menu choice for fades, although some stash this effect under the more general category of "Gain Adjustment" or "Volume Adjustment." Often, you'll be able to use sliders to set the starting and ending volumes of the fades. This allows you to fade to a non-zero level, which can be useful if you're fading down some music in preparation for mixing it with a narrated voice-over.

Fade-ins and fade-outs are useful for many sorts of transitions. Fade-ins are typically used more for *sound design* (the use of sound effects, dialogue, and music for dramatic purposes) than for music. While it's rare for a song on an audio CD to begin with a fade-in, it's perfectly appropriate to fade-in the sounds of an environment in order to establish a scene. Just describing the sounds of a bar, for instance—half-heard conversations, tinkling glasses, and a piano in the background playing "Misty"—conjures up a vivid mental image.

It's possible to use sound design to conjure up visual images in the listener's head, even if he or she isn't actually looking at any scenes. If, on the other hand, you're creating sounds to accompany images, your transitions will need to take into account the type of visual transitions that are being used. When the video editor (which may also be you!) uses abrupt transitions (*cuts*, in the lingo), then fades in, the music won't do. Instead, you'll either want to cut abruptly, in sync with the video, or you'll want to keep a continuous music track going in order to provide a sense of continuity to counterbalance the visuals. If the video has a lot of quick, evenly-timed cuts in it, you can arrange your score so that the cuts happen right on the beat! Or, if you do the music first, the video editor can cut to the beat. That way, your music both contrasts and complements the images.

For slower transitions, whether in the mind's eye of the listener or on a video screen, audio *cross-fades* are an excellent device. It's a simple concept—one recording fades out while another fades in. The correct amount of overlap between the two is a highly subjective judgment and depends on the pacing of your sound design. Study the section on Mixing before attempting cross-fades, because the technique involves operations on two wave files at once.

Effects

When we spoke of purchasing a sound card in Chapter 3, we discussed the effects that are sometimes built into the card's synthesizer chips. In most (if not all) cases, however, these effects only apply to synthesized sounds and cannot change the playback of digital audio files. However, with a wave editor creating effects right in your wave files, you can make echoes, reverbs, choruses, and stranger effects that will play back perfectly on any sound card, regardless of whether or not it has an effects processor onboard.

The main drawback of adding digital effects to wave files is that the process is time-consuming. In one instance, it took 48 seconds for my computer to add reverb to a wave file slightly over one second in length! This does not encourage experimentation and fine-tuning of parameters. In fact, if you're really serious about going nuts with effects such as reverbs, delays, equalization, and the like, then you'd be well-advised to purchase an external multi-effects processor at a music store. These boxes use custom-designed, dedicated effects chips to perform amazing tricks and let you change parameters in real time. Of course, if you feed your computer's output through one of these, you need a good tape recorder (ideally, a DAT) to capture the results. This is clearly not a solution for everyone.

Still, computer-based effects have their place. If you're not ultra-picky about fine-tuning parameters and only want to add a sense of spaciousness, then just about any reverb settings will do—and it probably won't take you more than two or three tries before you find the ones that are right for your purposes. Also, although digital EQ is considerably less usable than a dedicated *graphic equalizer* (a box with sliders on it to control many different frequency ranges, which lets you "dial in" just the sound you're looking for), the digital version is still excellent for removing conspicuous problems such as hums or too much high end in your recording. It just requires patience and an Undo function in your edit menu.

We've already defined, in our discussion of sound cards, some of the more common effects that you can use. In the remainder of this section we'll confine our discussion to the effects we haven't yet covered.

Reverse

This is a fun effect, particularly useful for embedding and/or deciphering backwards messages in rock songs. It simply moves the samples around in the file or selected area so that the last shall be first and the first shall be last. It's a great effect to add to speech, distorted electric guitars, or just about any other instrument. If you have a wavetable sound card capable of accepting samples (see Chapter 3), try loading some reversed samples—they make great MIDI instruments.

Digital Delay

We've already mentioned this in Chapter 3, but it's instructive here to look at some of the options that the different wave editing programs give you for customizing your delays. Figure 8-11 shows *Sound Impression's* flexible options. This dialog box lets you set up three independent delays (called *taps*), each with its own speed and *decay* percentage. The decay parameter is designed to mimic real-life echoes—each echo is softer than the one before it, until the overall volume eventually decays below the threshold of audibility. The decay

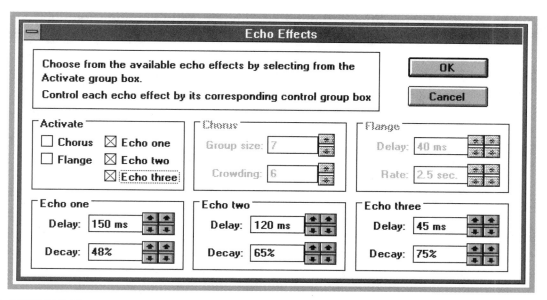

▶ **FIGURE 8-11**

Sound Impression *allows you to set delay times and decays for three delay taps.*

percentage parameter is used one of two ways, depending upon whether the program's designers were drinking from half-full or half-empty glasses of Jolt Cola. In Sound Impression, higher percentages produce softer echoes. In other programs, higher percentages produce louder echoes; the parameter is then likely to be called *feedback*.

Each tap in a delay is capable of creating a (theoretically infinite) series of ever-quieter echoes. In practice, the programs usually stop creating echoes once they've filled up the original file length. You might want to try adding a long chunk of silence at the end of a file if you want your echoes to last for a while.

A single delay tap will take an individual note—for example, a drum hit—and turn it into a pulse. If you have several taps, you can create more complex rhythms by relating the delay times in simple mathematical proportions. Make your second delay time one and a half or one and a third times the first one, for instance. If you use delay times shorter than 40 milliseconds or so, you're likely to perceive the effect as a thickening of the original sound rather than as a separate echo.

You can create complex rhythmic effects even if you only have a single delay tap. Try starting with a single source file (perhaps with just a single note in it). Apply delay and use Save As... to save the file under a different name. Then revert to the original file, apply delay with different parameters, and use Save As... again. Then move to the section on Mixing to combine these files. You can create a lot of interesting percussion beds with this approach.

Changing Playback Speed, Sample Rate, and Pitch

Changing the playback speed of a recording not only slows it down or speeds it up, but it also changes the pitch. Recordings sound radically different at different speeds. A fun way to create sound effects is to record a note or drum hit from your synthesizer and then slow it down to one-half or one-third of its original speed.

Changing the playback speed doesn't change the original sample. If you save the file, quit your edit session, and then play back the sound, you'll hear it at its original pitch. If you want to change the pitch permanently, change the sample rate instead. Sometimes this function is accomplished through a menu command, sometimes through a button, and sometimes it's only available as an option when you Export the current file to another format.

Time Compress/Expand

This can be a handy function if you're trying to fill an exact amount of time. If you've recorded a piece that's 32 seconds long for a 30-second commercial, you can either increase the sampling or playback rate slightly and accept a small pitch increase, or you can use time compression (only available in some editors) to shrink the time without changing the pitch. The price you pay for this, though, is a fairly long processing time while the file is being shrunk, and slightly degraded audio quality.

Other Effects

There are many possibilities for altering digital audio files in a variety of bizarre ways. Turtle Beach, for instance, has included a number of effects under the "Auto Stutter" category in its Wave product. These effects, with names such as "Standard Stutter," "Long Cyborg Voice," "Underwater Voice," and "Music Delay Stutter," among others, work by chopping up your file into little pieces and inserting short blank spaces between them. Some programs, Wave among them, also offer distortion effects.

Mixing

Mixing simply means combining different sounds in measured proportions. In a recording studio, the mixing stage is where all audio tracks that are recorded on tape (commonly up to 48 tracks for a single song!) are combined into a final stereo master. Each of the individual tracks usually contains a recording of a single instrument or vocalist, and each is monophonic (although some pairs of tracks represent the right and left channels of an instrument recorded in stereo). During the mix, the amount of each track that will make it into the final mix is controlled by a volume slider. A pan control (one for each track) on the mixing board sends some of the signal to the left channel of the board's output and some to the right channel. Often, while the master is being recorded, the engineer (and possibly one or two assistants or artists) will change levels, mute individual tracks, and occasionally rotate a pan knob, all in the interests of producing a sound that's alive and that serves the artistic purposes of the song.

This kind of mixing is a bit beyond our capabilities with a single PC and a basic sound card, as you'll see in the next section (check the "Dream Systems" section for information on how to expand those capabilities). However, we can easily accomplish more limited mixing goals, both for music and for sound design purposes. Suppose you're interested in creating a soundscape of a beach—waves crashing on the shore, birds calling, a quiet guitar strumming in the distance, people laughing and playing volleyball. You can do it all on your computer by mixing a number of different wave files (possibly including some "clip sounds" for elements that you can't record or fake yourself) into one. In this section, we'll tell you about the different approaches to mixing that are found in Wave editing software. Before we do, however, it may be a good idea to align our infinite expectations with the useful but less-than-infinite capabilities of mixing on your PC.

Wave Mixing Limitations

The main barrier to real-time mixing on the PC is that most sound cards can only play back two channels (one stereo pair) at once. Therefore, in order to play back a mix that consists of three or four files, your software must first combine the wave files to a single, stereo file (usually written to disk) and then play that back. Because this process can take a few minutes with long files, it isn't conducive to interactive fine-tuning. Instead, you make a few guesses at relative volume levels, try it a few times, and stop when you've got something you can live with or your patience is exhausted.

Another limitation is that mixes aren't dynamic. Although you can set relative volume levels for the different components of a mix, you can't change those levels mid-mix (other than by adjusting the gain of different portions of each file prior to mixing) as you would if you were sitting at a mixing board in a recording studio.

Now you know that a computer isn't as capable as a full recording studio. But that shouldn't come as a surprise—professional studios cost hundreds of thousands of dollars (although a home studio costing only a few thousand can make professional recordings of certain types of music—see Dream Systems). Use the tools that you have in the best and most fun ways possible and you'll have a running start on understanding and using a professional studio if and when you have the opportunity to work in one.

Paste Mixing

Most wave editors allow you to copy a digital audio segment into the clipboard and paste it into another file or elsewhere in the same file—usually wherever you position an "insertion point." A simple Paste will generally replace the sound in the target file with the sound in the clipboard, while a Paste Insert will make room in the target file to insert the clipboard without overlaying any part of the existing recording. Paste Mix, on the other hand, will mix the samples in the clipboard with the samples in the current file at the insertion point. In some programs, a dialog box will pop up asking you whether you want to boost or lower the volume of the segment in the clipboard during the mix.

Multiple-File Mixing—One Approach

Several programs allow you to mix multiple digital audio files at once. The dialog box shown in Figure 8-12 shows you how this is done in Wave. Since Wave allows four files to be open at once, you can mix any three files into the fourth file window. This box shows that different volumes and start times (the position in the target file where the source will start) can be chosen for each file. It also shows that entire source files or just selected portions can be mixed together.

Multiple-File Mixing—Another Approach

One approach to multiple-file mixing that I find particularly effective is that used in Sound Impression, as shown in Figure 8-13. Up to 16 different audio files can be laid out in a "composition" grid and mixed together. The approach isn't perfect—you can't specify different levels for the individual files, and (as in other methods) you can't audition the mix without going through a time-consuming "build" process. Still, it's great for sound design and for simply experimenting and having a good time by layering a bunch of wave files together and seeing what happens.

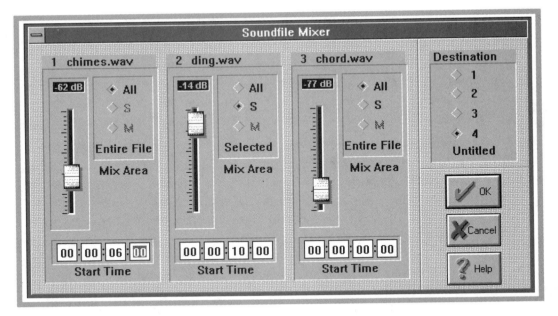

▶ **FIGURE 8-12**

Wave *allows you to adjust volumes and start points as you mix up to three Wave files into a fourth.*

Dream Systems

There are a variety of systems, most of them rather expensive, that can add professional digital multitrack recording and mixing to your PC. Just to give you a taste of the possibilities, we'll briefly describe some of the high-end systems that are available today.

Digital Multitrack Tape Recorders

The most pragmatic additions to your PC for true studio-like capabilities are digital multitrack tape recorders. These recorders can be synchronized to your MIDI sequencer (giving you 16 channels of MIDI sound in addition to your digital audio) and also chained together to give you as many channels of digital recording capability as you need. Because they record onto tape instead of hard disks, they work well with all computers, regardless of processor speed or hard disk capacity, and can record longer pieces than disk-based systems. They offer

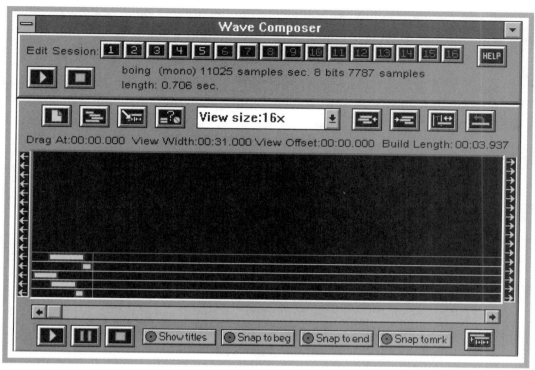

▶ **FIGURE 8-13**

Sound Impresssion's Wave Composer *allows you to mix up to 16 wave files arranged in a grid, with time as the horizontal axis.*

you precise control of all recording functions but will not let you edit your tracks on a computer screen.

The most popular recording product in recent years is probably the ADAT 8-track digital tape recorder, released by Alesis. Competing with the ADAT are the Tascam DA-88 and a number of other recorders. These devices typically cost from $2,000 to $5,000, depending on the options that you purchase, and require the addition of at least a small mixing board and an ordinary DAT recorder in order to create stereo master tapes.

Hard Disk Multitrack Recording Systems

The ultimate recording tool for me would be a well-designed multi-track hard disk recording system with a hard disk array as big as Brazil and enough processor power to forecast the weather on Venus. Here on Earth, we can make some great music with relatively modest systems, but the bottom line is still that a hard disk recording system is only as useful as your disk is big. If a stereo recording at CD sampling rates consumes 10MB per minute of sound, then an 8-track recording consumes 40MB per minute, and a three-minute song would take up about 120MB. Even assuming that you can free up that much hard disk space, you have to consider how to back it all up. Diskettes will not cut it—some form of tape or removable hard disk system is necessary.

Aside from disk capacity, there's the data transfer issue. Playing back four tracks from different wave files recorded at CD-quality requires the transfer of over 340KB per second from your hard drive. This in itself is not so daunting, but the fact that those bytes come from different files means that your disk head needs to do a lot of fast jumping around to collect data. That's why the Turtle Beach Quad system mentioned below uses the company's "Hurricane" data transfer architecture to get data from the disk instead of the DMA (direct memory access) system used by most other cards, and why the Digidesign system bypasses your hard disk entirely and requires an external SCSI drive in order to play back eight channels of digital audio simultaneously.

Turtle Beach Quad

This is a new system that brings multitrack digital audio recording and mixing under Windows to a new, low price. The Quad software is a four-track recorder that works with Turtle Beach digital audio cards to play back existing wave files while it records new ones. It can record and play back volume fader movements (through its "Turtle Recall" feature), allowing you to create, audition, and perfect a dynamic mix before you commit to writing that mix to a single stereo wave file. Once you've done that, you can load your stereo wave file into the first two tracks and mix in two more tracks of sound. You can repeat this as long as you'd like, enabling you to build up complex layered pieces.

Quad software will also send *MIDI Time Code* (MTC) through a driver, allowing sophisticated users to synchronize digital audio recordings with MIDI sequencers. MIDI Time Code is a stream of MIDI messages that contain time stamps that specify what time the "master" program (the one creating the MTC; in this case, Quad) thinks it is. All "slave" programs (the ones receiving the MTC, which are set to follow "external sync"; in this case, your sequencer) receive this MTC and play the part of the sequence that starts at the indicated time. Because MTC specifies times with a resolution from 1/25 to 1/30 of a second, depending upon your choice of format (you must choose the same format for the master and slave), the programs are synchronized with a very high degree of accuracy.

With a list price of $499 for the Quad Studio package, which includes both the Quad software and a Tahiti digital audio card, this puts some amazing capabilities in your hands at a remarkable price. Users who already own a Turtle Beach digital audio card can purchase the Quad software separately. The Tahiti card itself, by the way, can record and play digital audio and has a Wave Blaster-compatible connector for a synthesizer daughterboard (in other words, it can accomodate a Wave Blaster daughterboard or any daughterboard built to attach to the Wave Blaster connector on a card in the Sound Blaster 16 family), but it doesn't include a CD-ROM controller or a MIDI synthesizer.

Digital Audio Labs The CardD

The *CardD* (pronounced simply as "the card") is an excellent and economical hard-disk recording system that can be effectively used for professional purposes. I know of several recording studios that use it to produce soundtracks for commercials. A second card, the *I/O CardD*, adds digital input and output to The CardD so you can transfer wave files between your hard disk and a DAT recorder without any loss of fidelity. This means that the digital recording doesn't have to pass through a pair of digital-to-analog converters to go from the card into an audio cable and then through a pair of analog-to-digital converters in a DAT recorder in order to be recorded. Instead, it travels in digital form along a cable designed to transmit digital signals and is recorded byte for byte on DAT exactly as it was output.

Digital Audio Labs has just released a new product, the *Digital Only CardD*. This card comes with a Windows driver and will work with any digital audio recording or editing software. Because all its input and output is digital, you pretty much need a DAT recorder to take advantage of this card. If you have such a recorder, the combination of it with this card is a relatively inexpensive way to add true professional digital audio sound and editing to your computer.

Digidesign Session 8

This is a full 8-track digital recording studio, including real-time equalization and mixing. It uses your PC as a control interface, while all of the processing is done on its two cards and Audio Interface box. Two flavors of Audio Interface boxes are available. Both models include digital audio inputs and outputs, while the pro version includes the balanced XLR inputs and hotter signal levels favored in professional recording studios, along with top-notch A/D and D/A converters.

This deluxe package gives you a complete digital recording solution, including synchronization with Windows MIDI sequencers. The number and length of tracks that you can actually record will depend on the size of the external SCSI disk (a system requirement) that you connect to it, with a maximum of 250 tracks available.

Copyrights and Licensing

Digital recording gives you the ability to easily manipulate sound snippets from audio CDs, radio shows, commercial software packages, and other sources. If you do this just to entertain yourself and your friends, have a blast. If you release such sounds to the general public as part of an artistic or commercial (or both) endeavor, then you'd better pay some attention to the copyright laws.

We're in the legal section, so a disclaimer seems appropriate at this point. I am not a lawyer and am not qualified to give out legal advice, other than to tell you to consult a lawyer if you even suspect that a planned activity might violate copyright laws.

Every piece of media, be it sound, video, or text, that you don't produce yourself is likely to be owned by someone, some company, or some collection thereof. The vast bulk of the exceptions are works that have specifically been placed "in the public domain" by their creators or works whose copyrights have expired or which came into existence well before copyright laws were enacted. For instance, Beethoven's compositions are not copyrighted; however, most (if not all) recordings of his compositions are, as are the printed versions of them available from sheet music publishers. You could create a MIDI file of a Beethoven symphony and sell it to the public, but don't include graphics scanned from published scores or books, and don't include digital audio files recorded from commercial recordings (unless you obtain the rights first).

In order to use copyrighted pieces for anything other than "Fair Use" (a somewhat nebulous concept which includes making copies for personal use that won't be distributed to others, a limited amount of copying by educators and librarians, and certain other actions) as defined by the existing laws and court precedents, you must obtain written permission from everyone who has an ownership stake in them. If this is possible, it often involves paying a fee to the rights holders. There is no specific law governing the amount that should be paid—it's a matter of negotiation and will depend upon your intended use, the copyright holders' estimate of the value of their holdings, and many other factors.

There are often several different copyright holders for different aspects of a piece. For instance, the rights to a video clip of a musical performance might be split among performers, videographers, composers, lyricists, record companies, and management. If you want to use such a piece, you'll probably want to identify a primary rights holder, negotiate with her for the rights, and have her *indemnify* you against suits from other rights holders. This means that she claims that she has the right to license all the rights that you want, and that if others claim to have rights to the materials, it's her problem and not yours—unless, of course, she goes bankrupt, in which case you're probably responsible. As you see, this can get into some complex territory, so be sure to use a lawyer for this type of agreement.

There are even more possible complications. If a media clip is of, by, or about anyone famous, the celebrity may have a "right of publicity" stake in its usage, even if the celebrity had nothing to do with its production. For example, a celebrity could contest (under some circumstances) the publication of a candid photograph taken by a tourist at a restaurant.

On the other side of the coin, the Supreme Court of the United States has recently affirmed the right of 2 Live Crew to include excerpts from Roy Orbison's "Pretty Woman" in a song of theirs. The key point was that the song included the excerpt for purposes of parody, which is essentially First Amendment-protected speech. However, there were many contributing factors to the finding, and not everything that claims to be a parody would see that claim upheld in court.

The moral: Have all the fun you want to for yourself, and sample stuff from every record ever made if you just want to play your pieces for your buddies at parties, but talk to a copyright lawyer before taking any risks with publicly-distributed products.

Chapter 9

MIDI Concepts

MIDI music is the most flexible, malleable type of music that you can make with your PC. This is because MIDI deals with music at a conceptual level that is inherently musical. Digital audio editing is about manipulating samples, but MIDI is about manipulating notes (although there are areas where the two come together). Because MIDI is a well–designed, compact, symbolic representation of music, programs can manipulate MIDI files efficiently and effectively. These programs have been evolving since 1983 to meet the needs of musicians who can't afford to lose the inspiration of the moment to technical snafus and user–interface awkwardness. The result is some of the most sophisticated, graphically–oriented programs that exist in any area. I'm sure you'll find using them to be both a pleasure and a treat.

Before we get to the applications that manipulate MIDI, let's delve deeper into MIDI itself. Knowing the fundamentals of MIDI is a prerequisite to sequencing. If you're impatient to get started with an automatic composition or accompaniment program, you can skip ahead to the next chapter, referring back to this one when you need additional information.

What is MIDI?

As we mentioned in Chapter 1, MIDI started as an agreement among synthesizer manufacturers to let their keyboards and sound modules "talk" to one another. The acronym MIDI stands for the Musical Instrument Digital Interface. Its main purpose originally was to combat a fear of obsolescence among keyboardists, many of whom had been put into a position of investing thousands of dollars in a single company's products, only to see the company go out of business. This left their equipment in limbo, unable to advance without a major new investment in newer, better, and incompatible sound modules created by other companies.

MIDI succeeded beyond the wildest dreams of its creators. The synthesizer market exploded. Soon MIDI was talking to computers as well as sound modules, and sequencer programs were born.

MIDI is such an effective concept that you can't buy a new synthesizer today that doesn't include it (except for the least expensive units). Not only that, but many (if not most) effects devices (dedicated modules for reverberation, delay effects, and more) feature MIDI support. MIDI has been extended to control tape recorders, lighting systems, and several other classes of devices. In short, it has been one of the most successful inventions of modern times. As you can deduce from this broad range of applications, one of MIDI's key features is its remarkable expandability. Without any changes in the underlying hardware, and with full backward compatibility (a MIDI instrument from 1985 is still perfectly at home in a 1994 stage or recording setup), MIDI has embraced new synthesizer models, styles of synthesis, and even non–synthesizer applications. In this section, you'll learn about that expandability and the other elements that have contributed to MIDI's success.

MIDI Cables and Connectors

If you only plan to use a sound card and your computer for making music, without any external keyboards or sound modules, then you don't have to think about what a MIDI cord looks like. But the rest of us should know a few basic facts.

MIDI cables have a five–pin DIN (an international specification organization) connector on each end (see Figure 9–1). However, the cables themselves only have the three center pins wired; nothing is connected to the pins on the ends. This is one reason you should only use real MIDI cables (available from any musical equipment store or catalog) and not the five–pin DIN cables that you can find at electronics suppliers.

Most MIDI instruments have three MIDI ports (the five–hole jacks, or female connectors, that accept MIDI plugs) on their rear panels, labeled In, Out, and Thru. MIDI is a *unidirectional* system; that is, a

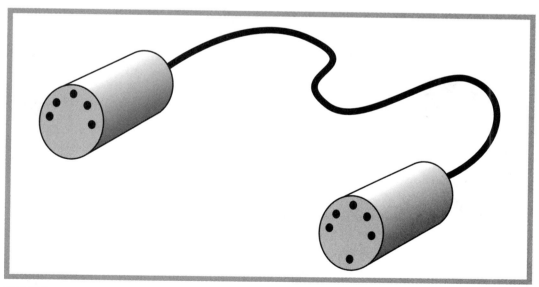

▶ **FIGURE 9-1**
A MIDI cable.

MIDI cable can only send data in one direction (from an Out or Thru port to an In port). The functions of the In and Out ports are obvious from their names—to receive and transmit MIDI data, respectively. The Thru port allows you to *daisy–chain* MIDI devices by relaying incoming MIDI messages to other devices further on down the line (see Figure 9–2). This is useful if you have several external MIDI modules or controllers. Normally, the Thru port only retransmits incoming messages and doesn't send messages originating with the controller (such as notes played on a keyboard), which go out the Out port. However, for convenience, many keyboards and controllers allow you to merge the Thru stream with the Out stream, sending the combined "river" out the Out port. This is often handy during sequencing.

Groundless Fears

Inside the instruments and MIDI interfaces, just behind the ports, are devices called *opto-isolators*. These are photocell–based circuits that guarantee that MIDI cables will never form electrical no-nos called *ground loops* that can create annoying hums in many musical systems. So, if your gear is ever plagued by a deep, steady hum (unlikely if you are a sound card–only user), you can rest assured that MIDI is not the culprit. This may not be the most significant feature for you personally,

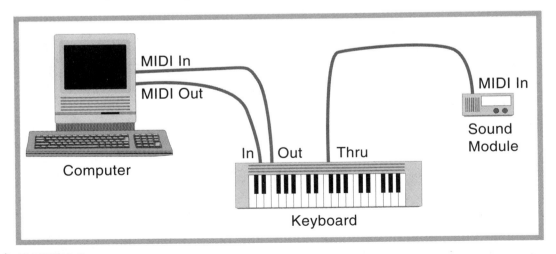

▶ **FIGURE 9-2**

A typical sequencing setup.

but tens of thousands of performing musicians would have nightmares on their hands if MIDI were a noisemaker.

MIDI Channels

MIDI synthesizers can play different timbres simultaneously on up to 16 MIDI *channels*. This concept of multiple channels is what allows you to create sequences with multiple parts—the bass might be on channel 1, the piano on channel 2, the guitar on channel 3, and so forth. A synthesizer with the capacity to respond simultaneously on more than one MIDI channel is said to be *polytimbral* (able to play many timbres). You can almost think of these devices as several independent synthesizers in one physical package. All sound cards and most currently–manufactured synthesizers are polytimbral, although some of the early pioneers (such as Yamaha's DX–7) are not.

As we'll see below, most MIDI messages are sent on a particular channel. There are some messages, however, that are meant to control the synthesizer as a whole and thus don't have a channel assigned to them.

MIDI Messages

There are many different types of MIDI messages (also called *events*), and we'll examine the most important ones in the following sections. They all consist of one or more bytes, which can travel over MIDI cables at speeds up to 31,250 bits per second. The first byte in each message is called a *Status Byte*—it determines the type of message and the channel it belongs to (if it's a message which applies to a single channel). The status byte may be followed by one or more *data bytes*. The actual number of data bytes depends on the message type. Note events, as you'll see, have two data bytes, while Program Change events have only one. System Exclusive messages, on the other hand, have a variable number of data bytes—the end of the message is signaled by a special "End of System Exclusive" message.

Status bytes all have their highest bit set to 1, while data bytes have them set to 0. This means that data bytes effectively have 7 bits for representing data, which gives them a range of 0–127.

It's very common in music for a number of successive messages of the same type to occur. For instance, many music tracks consist almost entirely of Note On and Note Off (which can be a variant of Note On, as you'll see) messages. In a case such as this, it would be redundant for a keyboard or computer to send a status byte with each message. Instead, both the transmitter and receiver devices use a convention called *running status.* The status byte for any new message in a MIDI channel is assumed to be the same as the previous one until a new status byte comes in. This adds efficiency—a stream of MIDI messages that uses running status can be up to 33 percent leaner than one which uses a status byte for each message. Although the efficiency of MIDI is not often an issue, very dense multi–channel sequences with lots of pitch bends and volume changes can sometimes overtax MIDI's transmission speed. This is where running status has the most significance.

Now that you know how MIDI messages are constructed, it's time to have some fun and delve into the messages themselves.

Note On

These are the most important messages; without them there would be no sound. The Note On message consists of three bytes:

1. **Status Byte** says that this is a Note On message and names the channel that it should be played on.

2. **Note Number** tells the synthesizer which note to turn on. This note can be anything from 0 to 127, although the ends of the range are not very useful (a piano, with the largest range of any acoustic instrument, only has 88 notes). Middle C, the C in the middle of the piano keyboard, corresponds to note number 60.

   There are two quirks that you should be aware of regarding note numbers. The first involves the extremes of the range. Since many synthesizer sounds are pretty awful when transposed down to four or five octaves below middle C, many synthesizers will automatically bounce really low (or really high) note numbers into a playable range. For instance, if you use a sequencer to send a Note On message for note number 0, the synthesizer will probably transpose it up three octaves and play a note number 36. Or the synthesizer may simply play nothing.

The other note number quirk concerns the labeling of octaves. When, as you'll do later, you edit sequences with a sequencer program, you'll see that notes are not labeled with their note numbers; instead, they are labeled with a note name and octave number (such as "A6"). This is much more musically useful than just a number. Unfortunately, two different conventions exist for octave numbering. Some sequencers and synthesizers refer to middle C (note number 60) as C3, while others use C4 to represent the same note. The day may come when you look at instructions that tell you to "play A#2 and such–and–such will happen," yet, when you do it, the wrong sound emerges. In such a case, it's most likely that you'll get the desired result if you play a note either an octave below or above the note that you think of as A#2. It's ugly, but the truth often is.

3. **Velocity**   is represented by the second data byte of the Note On message and measures how fast the key (if you're playing a keyboard controller) was moving when it triggered the Note On event. Normally, though, you think of this as reflecting how hard, rather than how fast, you hit the note. Like the note number and most other MIDI parameters, velocity has a value in the range of 0 to 127.

Most synthesizers use velocity to affect the volume of the note, with velocities of 127 triggering the loudest notes and velocities of 1 triggering the softest. (A velocity of 0 has a special meaning, which we'll see in a moment.) The best synthesizers also use the velocity to affect the timbre of the note, commonly by using internal filters to make louder notes brighter, or sometimes even by triggering entirely different samples. This corresponds to the behavior of acoustic instruments, when louder playing changes not only the volume but also the character of the sound (think of a sax player moving from lovely, smooth playing to raucous squealing as he blows harder). At its most basic level, velocity is simply a piece of incoming data, and professional synthesizers let you "map" it to affect nearly any aspect of the sound.

Think of velocity as corresponding to volume and you'll do fine. But be aware of the difference between it and the Volume Continuous Controller that we'll get to in a few moments. The Continuous Controller will affect the volume of all the notes in a given channel, while velocity is a property that belongs to each individual note. The Volume Continuous Controller is used to balance the different channels with respect to one another (bass vs. piano vs. drums, for instance), while velocity is used to control the *dynamics* (differences between soft and loud sounds) within a single track.

Note Off

What goes up must come down, and what is turned on must be turned off. If you could only turn notes on but not off, you'd get an amorphous mush pretty quickly, no matter what you played, as note after infinitely–sustaining note is piled upon the sonic slag heap.

The MIDI specification defines a Note Off message that is similar to the Note On, with its own status byte, note number, and *release velocity*. However, few keyboards actually use this method. Instead, most keyboards have adopted the other way of turning notes off, which is to send a Note On message with a velocity of 0. This has the disadvantage of not providing for the expressive release of notes, but it has the advantage of allowing a stream of Note Ons to turn notes on and off without switching running status back and forth between Note On and Note Off modes. This contributes to the thinning of the MIDI stream, which can be a good thing.

For convenience, in the rest of this book we'll use the term "Note Off" to refer to either of these methods for turning a note off.

Program Change

One important MIDI message is called *Program Change,* which is used to switch timbres in the sound module. When a synthesizer receives a Program Change 1 message, for example, it changes the timbre to whatever you've programmed into the first area in memory, called either *Program 1* or *Patch 1.* In General MIDI synthesizers this is standardized (as you'll see in more detail below), but that is not the case in every synthesizer.

The Program Change message consists of one status byte which indicates that the message is a Program Change and the channel it's destined for, and one data byte which gives the patch number to switch to. Being a data byte, the patch number is in the range of 0–127; however, since many people prefer to start counting at 1, it is usually displayed as having a range of 1–128.

Control Change

Control Change messages alter important aspects of sound such as volume and pan position (how much to the left or right of center a sound is placed). The original MIDI specification defined 121 different Control Numbers, from 0 to 120. Uses for some of these were recommended, but not required. Most synthesizers use Control Number 7 to affect volume and Control Number 10 to affect pan position. The full set of recommendations is listed in Appendix C. General MIDI synthesizers must respond to a few of these messages in a standardized way. These requirements are also indicated in Appendix C.

Control Change messages are often sent by *Continuous Controllers*, which are usually physical devices capable of continuous variation. Volume pedals attached to synthesizer keyboards are common Continuous Controllers, as are *mod wheels*, which are levers on keyboards that are most often used to control vibrato in synthesized sounds, as we'll see in the next section.

Control Change messages don't have to emanate from a Continuous Controller, however. They can also be created in many sequencer programs by either drawing curves in a window or by dragging on–screen sliders. We'll discuss this at greater length in Chapter 10.

A Control Change message has three bytes, as follows:

1. **Status Byte**—says that this is a Control Change message and indicates its channel.

2. **Control Number**—a number from 0 to 127 indicating which control function the next byte applies to; for instance, under General MIDI, Control Number 7 will affect Volume, while Control Number 10 will affect Pan.

3. **Controller Value**—a number from 0 to 127 indicating the value for the Controller. The function (volume, pan, or what–have–you) will immediately take this value when this byte is received, completing the Control Change message.

Control Change Examples

Control Change messages usually come in streams. For instance, a fade-out in a solo piano part would consist of a stream of Control Change 7 messages starting at the current volume (often set at the beginning of a sequencer track) and decreasing to 0. Figures 9–3 through 9–5 show three views of this; the first is an *event list* in which all the MIDI events are listed in order of their start times, the second is a *piano roll* showing the notes in graphical notation, and the third is a *Control Change graph* which shows the Volume messages in a form that is more convenient to understand and manipulate. Control Changes can be drawn and erased in sequences with pencil–like tools, or recorded from any device that sends them, such as a volume slider on a synthesizer or a MIDI footpedal (a pedal that sends out MIDI Control Change messages).

A fade-out in a multi–channel arrangement would require descending Control Change values in each active channel. If you have all sixteen of these channels occupied with notes and Control Changes, you can start to see how MIDI's bandwidth might be taxed. Some synthesizers combat exactly this situation by allowing you to designate one

▶ **FIGURE 9-3**

The Recording Control portion of the Sound Blaster 16 Mixer applet is set to record from the card's MIDI synthesizer.

channel as a *Global Channel*, and they will apply any Control Changes sent on this channel to all channels in the synthesizer.

Control Changes don't have to be used continuously. It's common to place a single Pan (Control Change 10) and Volume message in the beginning of each track to place each instrument in the stereo spectrum and to set its basic level.

Modulation, associated with Control Number 1, is a useful tool for adding expression to sustained notes and is often recognized by even non–General MIDI synthesizers (it is defined in the original MIDI specification but required for General MIDI certification). When you

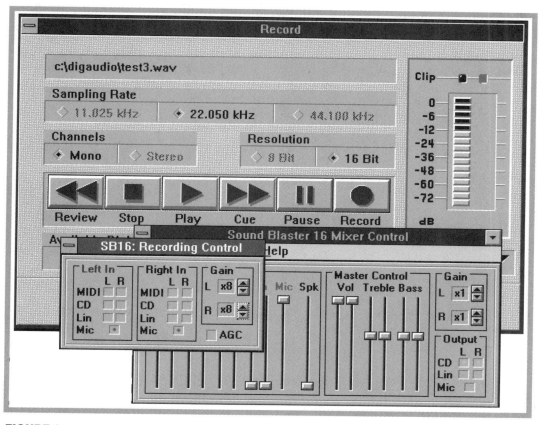

▶ **FIGURE 9-4**

Using a mixer applet and editor simultaneously under Windows.

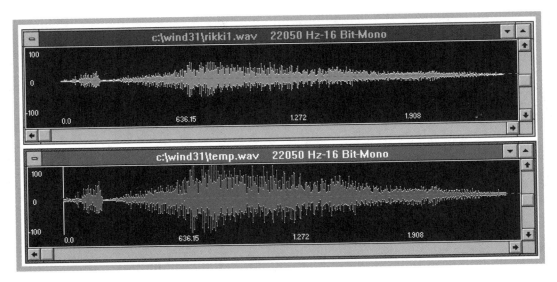

▶ **FIGURE 9-5**

The Volume messages in a long fade-out, shown in Passport's Master Tracks Pro For Windows.

increase the value of this control, a warble is applied to the pitch of any notes in the channel. This simulates the *vibrato* effect that is often used by string and wind players. In order to change the speed of the vibrato, however, you may have to learn to program the synthesizer's sounds (see "Patch Programming" at the end of Chapter 10). Or, your sound module may use a separate Control Number to affect the modulation speed, as do the GS units mentioned below.

Certain control functions are not meant to be used continuously. For instance, the *Sustain* function is commonly associated with Control Number 64. This function emulates the behavior of the damper pedal on a piano. When Sustain is on, all notes that are played will be sustained indefinitely—the sound module will postpone acting on any Note Off messages that it receives until Sustain is turned off. At that time, it will act on all the postponed Note Offs and return to normal handling of new Note Offs.

The Sustain function can only be on or off, so it is (logically speaking) a switch, not a continuously–variable knob or slider. Synthesizers handle Control Change 64 messages by interpreting values from 0 to 63 as off and values from 64 to 127 as on. All Control Numbers in the range from 64 to 95 are supposed to be interpreted similarly, as switches.

Control Changes are often used to control other parameters such as reverb and chorus depth, filter frequencies, and the like; however, these uses are not standardized, and you'll have to consult your manual to learn which controllers are supported by your sound card or module.

You may have wondered why the Control Numbers used by Control Change messages only extend up to 120, instead of all the way up to 127 like most of the other parameters in MIDI. The answer is that messages that would otherwise be interpreted as Control Numbers 121 to 127 are reserved for special purposes and called Channel Mode Messages. You won't often have occasion to deal with these messages, but if you ever need to enter or edit them in a sequencer, you'll usually simply treat them as Control Change messages with high Control Numbers.

Most of the uses of Channel Mode messages are beyond the scope of this book, and most readers are unlikely to need them. The most significant exception is Channel Mode message 122, Local Control Off, which can be handy during sequencing and is discussed in Chapter 10.

Pitch Bend

Pitch bending is an important part of some forms of instrumental expression. Guitar players use it extensively and pianists not at all. In between these extremes are wind players, who alter their pitches subtly by the intensity of their blowing and *embouchure* (position of their lips). MIDI provides a mechanism for emulating these effects, called *Pitch Bend* messages. If you want to create realistic–sounding guitar tracks, you'll need to use Pitch Bend—not only for bends, but also for *hammer-ons* and *pull-offs*, which guitarists use to sound new notes without picking them. These effects add continuity and phrasing to melodic passages.

MIDI guitars usually send Pitch Bend messages with each note, while keyboards rely on a joystick–like device called a *pitch wheel* mounted on the left side of the keyboard. Usually, the keyboardist manipulates the pitch wheel with her left hand while playing solos with her right. These wheels are spring–loaded to return to the zero position when you release them. If you have no controller, you can draw Pitch Bend curves with a pencil–like tool in your sequencer package, although it is difficult to get these to come out sounding natural.

Pitch Bend messages are similar to Control Changes in that they apply to all notes in a given channel and tend to come in streams. Unlike the data bytes in Control Change messages, however, the two data bytes in Pitch Bend messages are both dedicated to expressing the amount of pitch bend. Since each contains seven bits of data, the two together contain 14 bits, enabling them to represent numbers in a range from -8,192 to +8,191. The range of −64 to +63 that a single data byte would allow is not fine enough to create smooth pitch bends in some cases (especially when the Pitch Bend Range, described below, is large)—you'd hear the intermediate pitches in any bend individually, creating a kind of staircase effect. Unfortunately, most synthesizer pitch benders send data with less than the full resolution—7- to 9–bit resolution is common. Also, some sequencers (e.g. *MasterTracks Pro*) only record and play back seven bits of Pitch Bend data.

Okay, so a Pitch Bend message can have a value between −8,192 and +8,191. You're probably wondering what that means in musical terms. The answer is subtle and depends on the *Pitch Bend Range*.

Pitch Bend Range is a parameter that is set in both the controller and receiving sound module—if they are set differently, the results can be ludicrous (or entertaining, if your tastes are a little strange). Pitch Bend Range can be set to different values in each channel, although there is seldom a reason to do so. With a Pitch Bend Range of 2 (or, more precisely, ±2), the highest Pitch Bend value will raise the pitch of sounding notes by two semitones (half-notes), while the lowest Pitch Bend value will lower the pitch by the same amount.

The General MIDI default value for Pitch Bend Range is ±2 semitones. This is fine for most purposes, although MIDI guitarists may well find that a range of ±4 works better for them. If you want to emulate slide guitars, you'll want to use a larger range—±12 or more.

It's usually possible to change the Pitch Bend Range of a sound module from its front panel; however, sound cards don't have front panels. If you ever need to change the Pitch Bend Range of a sound card, you can use a sequencer to do so (for all General MIDI sound cards, at least). Insert the following messages at the beginning of a sequence:

```
Control Change 100, Value 0
Control Change 101, Value 0
Control Change 6, Value: desired Pitch Bend range
```

Most MIDI controllers will transmit a sequence like this if you change their Pitch Bend Range. These messages convey something from an obscure corner of the original MIDI specification that has become more common since the advent of General MIDI—a MIDI *registered parameter*. These registered parameters are a back door to the expansion of the MIDI standard. They define up to 128 additional messages that synthesizers can recognize along with the base set. As we'll see in the next section, System Exclusive messages provide another avenue of expansion.

System Exclusive Messages

These mysterious messages provide a way for synthesizers to transmit data that is longer than the standard messages and that no other synthesizer may understand. They are primarily used for sending *bulk dumps* of the synthesizer's memory to a computer for editing, storage, and backup. This isn't too important for casual MIDI usage, but if you customize the sounds in your sound card, you'll be using these messages to do so (although you may not know it, because a *patch editing program* will hide the details from you). System exclusive dumps are also sometimes included in sequences to set up the sound module for the song.

Unlike other MIDI messages, System Exclusive (also called *Sys–Ex*) messages both begin and end with a status byte. After the initial status byte comes an identification code. Although there are several extended codes available, this is mostly used to identify the manufacturer of the synthesizer sending the message. After this comes an arbitrary number of bytes that can mean anything that the manufacturer chooses, followed by a closing status byte. Any device receiving a Sys–Ex message coded for a different manufacturer will ignore it.

Other Messages

There are a number of additional MIDI messages used for synchronizing sequences with analog tape decks or videos, for shutting off all notes, for changing the tuning of a synthesizer, for sending sample data, and many other purposes. However, the set that we've described above will take you a long way. If you want the full specification, you can order it from the International MIDI Association (address in Appendix D).

General MIDI

General MIDI is a standard that was issued by the MIDI Manufacturer's Association in 1991 to solve a serious problem for game and interactive title developers. The MIDI specification standardized messages such as "Note On," "Note Off," and the others that we've discussed. It accomplished its original purpose of allowing keyboards and sound modules from different manufacturers to be connected admirably, and it even engendered an entire new way of creating music, sequencing. However, there was no standardization of sounds from one synthesizer to another. New synthesizers were constantly coming out with interesting and unique sounds, but many musicians simply wanted a clarinet or a slap bass or a piano to be easily accessible without painstaking sound programming. Sending out a Program Change message with a value of 1 could call up patches with names as varied as Heavenly, Obese, Winds 'n' Wood, and Star Brass on different sound modules. Each new sound module came with a substantial learning and reprogramming task in order to meet the most common musical needs. On one sound module that I owned, I had to spend several days reprogramming all the sounds to respond to Control Change 10 so that I could pan them properly in my sequences. It was not fun.

Furthermore, as farsighted multimedia development companies such as Warner New Media (which proposed the idea of General MIDI specification) looked at the implications of the growing popularity and sophistication of computer games, they could see that a way was needed to ensure that MIDI music created for one sound module would sound good on others. This sentiment was echoed by a number of vendors and purchasers of MIDI clip music. The customers often had to spend hours laboriously remapping Program Changes in song files in order to get them to sound good on their own setups. General MIDI was the solution that the MIDI Manufacturing Association hammered out, and it has proven to be an excellent one in many ways.

There have been, and continue to be, instrument designers and musicians who claim that General MIDI is a straightjacket whose ultimate result will be to make all sound modules sound alike. This has not yet come to pass. Some sound modules have great piano sounds, others have superb winds, and still others have excellent strings. Some include extra features that go substantially beyond General MIDI and allow extra creative dimensions. Some have a General MIDI mode and a non–General MIDI mode that incorporates some of the manufacturer's more advanced ideas about how a synthesizer should work. And, finally, many professional synthesizers don't support General MIDI at all. Still, in the sound card market, and for the general–purpose music maker, General MIDI is a wonderful convenience that is extensively supported by music software and hardware.

The General MIDI Patch Map

As we've discussed, the most significant aspect of General MIDI is the standardization of the meaning of Program Change numbers. Under General MIDI, Program Change 1 always calls up an acoustic piano sound, Program Change 14 invokes a xylophone, and Program Change 49 sets up a string ensemble. This convention is known as the General MIDI Patch Map, which is shown in full in Appendix A.

The programs in the General MIDI Patch Map are grouped into sixteen sets of eight sounds each, as follows:

| 1-8 | **Pianos**—includes several varieties of electric and acoustic pianos, a harpsichord and a clavinet (a very funky–sounding keyboard instrument extensively used by Stevie Wonder) |

| 9-16 | **Chromatic Percussion**—instruments that work by striking tuned wood or metal objects, such as xylophones and marimbas |

| 17-24 | **Organs**—varieties of organs, accordions and harmonicas |

25-32	**Guitars**—both acoustic and electric, including distorted guitars
33-40	**Basses**—acoustic, electric, and synthesized
41-48	**Strings**—the violin family
49-56	**Ensemble**—you could easily use up all the voices of a sound module simulating an orchestral string section or a choir. These patches dodge that issue by giving you recreations of group sounds in a single voice.
57-64	**Brass**—trumpets, trombones and other horns
65-72	**Reeds**—saxes and more
73-80	**Pipes**—flutes, recorders, etc.
81-88	**Synthesizer Lead**—a collection of sounds that don't emulate any acoustic instruments but rather imitate often–used synthesizer sounds of the past; the ones in this group are all supposed to have a cutting, prominent sound that makes them suitable for lead parts.
89-96	**Synthesizer Pad**—these sounds are meant to be full, swelling, background sounds. General MIDI simply call them "Pad 1" to "Pad 8," and suggests qualities such as "new age," "warm," and "metallic," which results in quite a bit of variation from synthesizer to synthesizer.
97-104	**Synthesizer Effects**—meant for movie soundtracks and games; with names such as "Goblins," "Crystal," and "Brightness," you can expect no real standardization in these patches.
105-112	**Ethnic**—a useful collection of instrumental sounds from several cultures
113-120	**Percussive**—as we'll see below, most drums and percussion instruments are covered under a part of

General MIDI called the Drum Map. The eight sounds in this area, however, differ from the other drum sounds in that they can be played at any pitch, allowing you to create melodies with them or simply to custom-tune them to fit the rest of your arrangements like a glove. Drums in this group include Steel Drums, Agogo Bells, and Melodic Toms.

121-128 Sound Effects—unlike the synthesizer effects group, we have some fairly standard names here ("seashore," "bird tweet," etc.), although the realism of the actual sounds produced by different sound modules varies widely.

Sixteen–Channel Operation

The earliest MIDI synthesizers, such as Yamaha's DX–7 were *monotimbral*, meaning that they could only play a single timbre at a time. They were capable of playing many different patches, but not together. In order to create a multi–part arrangement, you'd either need multiple synthesizers or a multi–track tape recorder.

The situation changed rapidly, however, and many *polytimbral* synthesizers, capable of playing several timbres at once, emerged. Most of the second wave of MIDI synthesizers were polytimbral but not fully polytimbral. The famous Casio CZ–101, for instance, was an inexpensive synthesizer that could respond to sequences on four MIDI channels at once, while several early synthesizers from Ensoniq could play music simultaneously on any 12 MIDI channels. However, a synthesizer bearing the General MIDI designation must be able to play sounds simultaneously on all 16 channels.

The General MIDI Drum Map

General MIDI synthesizers reserve MIDI channel 10 exclusively for drums and percussive sounds. The choice of channel 10 (rather than, say, channel 16) doesn't have any intuitively obvious justification and has grown out of historical accident. Roland's MT–32 synthesizer was one of the first modules with a dedicated percussion channel (and a popular piece of equipment among serious gamers and musicians for several years), and it used channel 10. For some reason, that choice stuck.

Channel 10 is different than all the other channels in that each note triggers a different percussion sound. On channel 1, if you call up a piano sound, different notes will play that sound at different pitches. In contrast, on channel 10, middle C will play a high bongo sound, while the B just below it will play a ride cymbal.

As you see, in addition to a Patch Map for non–drum channels, an important component of General MIDI is its Drum Map, listed in Appendix B.

General MIDI Controllers

Before General MIDI, if you bought a new synthesizer, you couldn't even count on Controller 7 to change its volume. Instead, you might have had to program that response into hundreds of patches by hand. It was a nightmare. Under General MIDI, the most commonly–used Controllers are formalized so that you can rely on any General MIDI synthesizer to behave nicely with respect to the following Controllers:

1	**Modulation** (see Control Change)
7	**Volume** (see Control Change)
10	**Pan** (see Control Change)
11	**Expression**—a form of volume accent in addition to the main volume controller. It's recommended that people creating commercial sequences for distribution use this to control crescendi (volume swells) and diminuendi (fades) in order to achieve dynamics without disturbing the balance between different channels that the user may have set with Continuous Controller 7 messages.
64	**Sustain** (see Control Change)
121	**Reset All Controllers**—Control Change messages can cause bizarre effects in subsequent notes if they're not reset to zero after you're done using them. This message is used (with a value of 127) to let you start with a clean slate.

123   **All Notes Off**–Suppose you've sent a Note On message to a sound card and then your sequencer program crashes. Whoops! That sound card is still blasting away, and you're not sure which note is sounding, so you don't know which Note Off to send. It's an ugly (and, fortunately, rare) situation, but it happens. Do you want to reboot your computer just to shut the darn thing up? Take a knife to your speakers? Nahh...just send an All Notes Off command, and everything will return to the calm of a mountain lake serenely reflecting an amber sunset.

Polyphony

All sound modules bearing the General MIDI logo must have at least 24–voice polyphony. We've discussed just what this means in Chapter 3, but we'll touch on the main points here also. Twenty–four voice polyphony intuitively means that the sound module can produce 24 distinct notes at once; however, there are factors that often make the effective polyphony that you can achieve less than the published specification. In many cards, certain sounds (the richest ones) "eat up" two voices for each note, and in some cards (FM-based cards, in particular), panning a sound anywhere but dead center also consumes two voices per note. The net result is that the actual number of distinct notes that you can hear at once will often be less than the manufacturer's specification—sometimes as little as half the quoted value.

Some sound cards (again, notably the FM–based cards) conform to the General MIDI Patch and Drum maps but can't satisfy the General MIDI polyphony requirement. These cards are quite serviceable for most multimedia and for modest musical purposes (i.e., most three– or four–part arrangements), but their limitations will become apparent when you try to reproduce an eight–piece salsa band or a chamber orchestra.

What's Missing In General MIDI?

One could go a lot further than General MIDI in creating additional standardized elements—and, in fact, at least one company (Roland) has done so, with the creation of the GS specification described below. In that section, you'll get a taste of some of the additional ways that

General MIDI could be extended and the implications. However, there is one glaring omission in both the General MIDI and GS specifications: volume standardization.

Under General MIDI, a MIDI file scored for piano, bass, guitar, and drums will play back with exactly that instrumentation regardless of which General MIDI sound module is used; however, on some modules the piano will sound too loud, on some the bass will dominate, and on others the guitar will drown everything else out (just as in real life). In practice, the volume differences from module to module are not so dramatic as to be unusable, but it is still a good idea for any application that provides for playback of MIDI files to include a way for the user to set his own balance.

One interesting development in the area of volume standardization is the creation of The Fat Seal by George Alistair Sanger, aka *The Fat Man*. Sanger is a major composer in the world of PC gaming, having produced scores for *The Seventh Guest* and numerous other hit games. He has created "Fat Labs" and offered to test and certify cards from different manufacturers for a fee. Any card certified as "Recommended by The Fat Man for General MIDI music" will have standardized volume levels for different instruments and will also make minimal demands on the CPU while playing back music (so as not to interfere with the speed of the games that George loves). It remains to be seen how many manufacturers choose to pay the fee to have their cards certified, but it certainly is a good idea.

GS

The Roland Sound Canvas was the first General MIDI synthesizer on the market and, because of its immediate popularity, virtually defined General MIDI for the world. However, the MIDI implementation of the Sound Canvas actually goes well beyond General MIDI and is followed in all sound modules bearing the GS logo.

Because of the popularity of the Sound Canvas, there are a number of music programs that offer explicit GS support. This allows them to easily and/or automatically control aspects of the music, such as the amount of reverb to add to each track, that are not explicitly available on non–GS synthesizers (although they are sometimes available through non–standardized commands).

The GS logo belongs to Roland and has not yet been licensed to any other manufacturers. Still, some other units follow a number of GS conventions (some of which are simply guarantees that the ordinary MIDI Control Number conventions listed in Appendix C will be followed) without using a GS logo.

In the following sections, we'll expand on a few of the key aspects of GS. A complete copy of the GS specification can be obtained from Roland.

BANK SELECT. The General MIDI Patch Map provides for three distinct acoustic piano sounds—Acoustic Grand Piano (Program Change 1), Bright Acoustic Piano (Program Change 2), and Honky-tonk Piano (Program Change 4). What if a manufacturer wants to provide you with an alternate acoustic piano sound, or even several alternates? General MIDI offers no way of choosing such sounds, but GS does.

Under GS, a *pair* of Control Change messages, Controller 0 (value 0) followed by Controller 32, constitutes a *Bank Select* message. The value for Controller 32, in the range from 1 to 128, names the bank that the sound module should use. So, in answer to the above dilemma, a manufacturer can simply put the alternate piano sounds into banks 2 and 3 and have either of them be selected with a Program Change 1 once the proper bank has been selected.

These GS modules and others that support the Bank Select command (or, more properly, command sequence) must also implement a "fallback" strategy—no synthesizer is likely to fill up 128 banks with 128 different sounds in each (over 16,000 sounds)! So, if a Bank Select and Program Change combination comes in that the synthesizer can't support, it chooses a bank with a lower number (although not necessarily the bank with the next lowest number—the choosing method is actually fairly complex).

GS CONTROLLERS. Also, GS defines a number of new Controllers in addition to the ones defined by General MIDI. The most significant of these are:

---

66   **Sostenuto** is similar to the Sustain controller, number 64, described earlier in this chapter. The difference is that

Sostenuto only sustains notes that are already sounding when the controller arrives, whereas Sustain holds all notes. If Sostenuto is mapped to a footpedal, pressing the footpedal will allow you to hold a chord and play a solo over it, while Sustain would tend to turn any solo to mush (all notes, whether harmonious chord tones or somewhat dissonant passing tones, would be sustained). This can be a very useful feature; unfortunately, it is an optional part of the GS specification.

91	**Reverb Depth** allows you to set the amount of reverb independently on each channel.	
93	**Chorus Depth** allows you to set the amount of chorus independently on each channel.	

In addition, through a fairly complex series of messages, GS allows you to set the pitch, level, pan position, and reverb amount independently for each note in the drum channel.

General MIDI Compatibility in Sound Cards

Almost all 16–bit sound cards sold today are compatible with the General MIDI patch and drum maps, although many do not offer full 24–voice polyphony, as noted above. Older sound cards can be tricked into compliance with the patch and drum maps under Windows by using a special driver, although their polyphony will remain quite limited.

An East Coast software company called Voyetra has created drivers that will implement the General MIDI Patch and Drum maps on any FM synthesizer using Yamaha's OPL2 or OPL3 chipsets (which is just about all FM synthesizers). You can obtain these drivers from Creative Labs, or you can download an independently–produced shareware driver called FMSYN.ZIP from CompuServe or other sources.

File Types

There are a number of file types commonly used for MIDI sequences. This section will serve as your field guide to them.

Standard MIDI Files (.MID, .MFF)

In the first years following the announcement of the MIDI specification, sequencing programs started to proliferate like wildflowers. Each of these programs used its own file format, resulting in great inconvenience to musicians when they wanted to change programs or play their sequences on computers at recording studios or at their friends' houses. In response to this situation, the MMA created the *Standard MIDI File* (SMF), a uniform way of storing MIDI events in files. The structure of these files is platform–independent—it's easy to move them from Macintoshes to PCs and back (although it requires a software utility to enable one computer to read the other's diskettes and adjustment of the file type parameter if you go from PC to Mac). On the PC, SMFs generally have a .MID extension (the .MFF extension is also common for pre–MPC–specification SMFs) and are often simply called MIDI files.

The SMFs have been a tremendous success. Every current commercial sequencer program can read and write these files, in addition to its own proprietary ("native") format files.

During the development of the SMF specification, the designers realized that it wasn't enough to simply include MIDI events in a file. Also required was information about the musical structure of a piece, information that had been kept in the sequencers' proprietary format files. Sequencers use the traditional musical rhythmic forms of beats and measures to provide a musically-useful interface to the MIDI stream; a sequencer that was simply calibrated in milliseconds, for instance, could provide no easy way to select an exact number of measures for copying or other manipulation (one of the most common editing tasks in sequencing). A sequencer that provides a musical notation display must also know the key signature in order to display sharps and flats properly.

Since there is no MIDI "Set Key Signature" or "Set Meter and Tempo" event, these pieces of information are maintained by the sequencer program and stored in its proprietary format. SMFs include "meta-events" that specify this and other information more abstract than simple Note and Program Change events. In fact,

SMFs include an entire track dedicated to a *Tempo Map* (sometimes called a *conductor* track) which specifies playback speed variations on an instant-to-instant basis.

There are two formats of SMFs, called *Format 0* and *Format 1*. Format 0 is the older, simpler one, which contains all the MIDI data mixed together on a single, multi-channel track. When a sequencer imports such a file, it normally splits the data for separate channels into separate tracks. This procedure can result in a loss of information; if, for instance, you have your bass drum and snare drums on different tracks (but both on the drum channel, channel 10) and you export them as a Type 0 MIDI file, you'll find both those drums on a single track when you open or import the file. Format 1 MIDI files maintain the track structure of your sequences and are preferable in most instances.

Proprietary Sequencer Files

As all–encompassing as SMFs attempt to be, with a built-in flexibility and expandability that has characterized MIDI's development from the start, each sequencing program will inevitably add features that can't be reflected in SMFs. The situation is similar to that in word processing; although every word processor can save documents in ASCII (.TXT) file formats, you lose some aspects of the formatting when you do so. As programs develop, later versions add formatting features not supported by earlier versions, and you lose these features if you save a file in a format that is read by an old version.

The most common sequencer formats on the PC are the .WRK files used by Twelve Tone System's *Cakewalk* family of sequencers and the .MTS files used by Passport's *Trax* sequencer and *MasterTracks* family. Files with an extension of .CMF are Creative Music Format Files and include setup data for FM synthesizers along with MIDI sequences.

MIDI According to Microsoft

Now for something really confusing. When the MPC specification was first announced, Microsoft looked around and noticed that there weren't any sound cards on the market that even came close to General MIDI's polyphony requirements. At the same time, it was clear that the General MIDI Patch and Drum Maps were incredibly useful and that they could be implemented in software for existing sound cards. This led to the adoption of the Patch and Drum Map subset of General MIDI for MPCs, to the classification of sound cards into *Basic* and *Extended* devices, and to the Microsoft Authoring Guidelines for MIDI files.

The Basic device category was created to encompass the majority of the existing FM sound cards with limited polyphony, while Extended devices were the more–capable cards that were in the works (and are now on the market). A basic device music have six–note melodic polyphony, together with five–note polyphony on the drum channel, while extended devices need to support at least 16 melodic notes at once, together with eight percussive notes.

The Microsoft Authoring Guidelines for MIDI files provide a way of creating files that will play on both Basic and Extended devices. Unfortunately, it's not one of Microsoft's better attempts at a grand compromise and, in my opinion, causes more problems than it solves. Still, not everyone shares this opinion, and you may encounter files written to this specification and should know how to handle them, so we'll devote a little space to them here.

A MIDI file created in accordance with the Microsoft Authoring Guidelines is a SMF that contains two complete arrangements—one for Basic devices, in channels 11–16, and one for Extended devices, in channels 1–10. The Extended arrangement uses channel 10 as its drum channel, in accordance with General MIDI, but the Basic arrangement uses channel 16 for this purpose. The total polyphony requirement of each arrangement should fit within the capabilities of its target device.

If you encounter an arrangement written according to these guidelines, then the pair of arrangements in the file may actually consume more voices than you have available, while a single arrangement for either Basic or Extended devices would have played back without problems. Fix this by disabling the arrangement that's inappropriate for your sound card or module. You can accomplish this (in Windows) by using the MIDI Mapper, which we'll cover in the next chapter. If you're not in Windows, then use a sequencer program to cut and discard (or simply mute) the offending tracks.

Chapter **10**

Making Music With MIDI

In this chapter, you'll learn about all the ways that you can use MIDI to make music on your PC. These range from essentially passive (from a musical point of view) uses, such as exploring games that play MIDI sounds, to deeply creative uses such as creating multi-tracked sequences of your own musical compositions. There's a lot of territory in between, too, for people of all musical abilities.

Listening to MIDI files

Here's a basic question: Suppose you've obtained a MIDI file that you want to hear. You may have downloaded a favorite song from a bulletin board system, purchased a diskette of MIDI clip music, or received the file as a sample with a multimedia application or demo disk. How do you listen to it?

The answer to this question depends on whether you want to listen to it from a DOS or Windows environment. We'll cover each of these independently.

Playing Back MIDI Files in Windows

The fastest way to play back MIDI files in Windows is to use the Media Player applet that comes with Windows 3.1. When you double-click on its icon in the Program Manager's Accessories group, you'll see a screen like that shown in Figure 10-1. Pick the Open... choice from the File menu and select the MIDI file that you wish to hear. Then press the button in the lower left corner of the Media Player window (the Play button). You should hear your MIDI file play back. If you hear nothing, or if what you hear sounds so weird that something must be wrong, then skip ahead to the section on "Using the MIDI Mapper." The Media Player uses the output device specified in your current MIDI Mapper Setup to play back files; if this is set incorrectly, you'll hear nothing or strange sounds when you press Play.

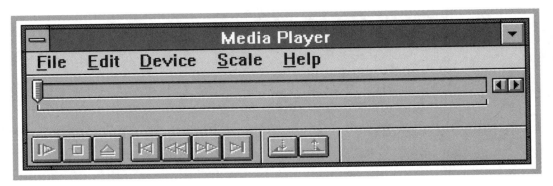

▶ **FIGURE 10-1**

The Windows Media Player.

Another way to listen to MIDI files in Windows is to use your sequencer to play them back, although a sequencer will typically take a few seconds longer to load than the Media Player. Sequencers usually offer you a choice of MIDI output devices. You can either choose to go through the MIDI Mapper or pick a sound card or MIDI output driver directly.

Playing Back MIDI Files in DOS

Most sound card packages include a utility that can play back MIDI files from DOS. Usually, as with the Sound Blaster family of cards, there's a three-step process involved in playback:

1. Load a DOS driver for the sound card.

2. Start the MIDI file player application and listen to your files.

3. Unload the DOS driver to free up memory for other applications.

Most sound cards sold today offer Sound Blaster compatibility by providing a driver that duplicates the functions of the official Sound Blaster driver. In light of that, we'll talk about the above steps in a little more detail, referring specifically to the software provided with Sound Blasters.

The DOS driver for the Sound Blaster is loaded by changing to the card's subdirectory and typing SBMIDI at the DOS prompt. There are a few software switches that you can set when you invoke this driver that will affect the way MIDI files are played, as follows:

■ Use SBMIDI /G if you know your file is in General MIDI format, with drums on channel 10.

■ Use SBMIDI /B if you know your file is in Microsoft's Basic MIDI file format, with sounds on channels 11-16 and drums on channel 16.

■ Use SBMIDI /E if you know your file is in Microsoft's Extended MIDI file format, with sounds on channels 1-10 and drums on channel 10.

■ Use SBMIDI /1 to ensure that sounds will play on the internal synthesizer.

■ Use SBMIDI /2 or SBMIDI /3 to ensure that MIDI messages will be sent out the MIDI Out port. The /3 parameter uses MPU-401 emulation and should be used in preparation for DOS sequencers that expect to talk to an MPU-401 MIDI interface. The /2 parameter can be used for other situations.

You can combine these switches if you like; for instance, SBMIDI /G /1 will set up your MIDI device to use the sound card's internal sounds configured for General MIDI, with drums on channel 10. It doesn't mean much, however, to combine the /G, /B or /E switches with each other, because they're contradictory, or to combine those switches with the /2 or /3 switches, because the Sound Blaster driver really can't do anything to set up external sound modules (not that

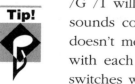

Tip!

they need any setup, generally). If you specify contradictory switches, you won't get an error message, and the later switches in your command line will take precedence over the earlier ones. The driver will inform you of the options that it puts into effect.

Once you've loaded the driver, you can either use a sequencer to play back your MIDI files, or you can use Creative Labs' PLAYMIDI application or its equivalent from another manufacturer.

When you're done playing with MIDI and want to use your computer for other tasks, you should unload the driver by typing "SBMIDI /U," or the equivalent command for your sound card, in order to free up memory for the next application.

Playing Back MIDI Files in Other Applications

Now that you've seen how to use a program to play back a MIDI file, it can be useful and instructive to learn how multimedia programs—games and edutainment programs, whether on disk or CD-ROM—use MIDI. In both DOS and Windows, these uses require drivers. A little more knowledge about drivers can help you troubleshoot any sound problems that you might run into using such programs (especially if you use Windows) and can spare you from a lengthy wait on "Hold" (on your dime) while an overloaded technical support staff slogs through the day's queue in order to reach you.

How DOS Applications Use MIDI

Other DOS applications use MIDI the same way that PLAYMIDI and DOS sequencers do—they assume that a Sound Blaster-compatible driver is loaded into memory, and they send it the same commands and messages that they would send to a Sound Blaster. Games and other applications that provide support for sound cards other than the Sound Blaster (when these cards are not in Sound Blaster emulation mode) do so either by talking to alternate drivers supplied by the sound card manufacturers or by using assembly-language calls to manipulate the memory registers of the card directly.

How Windows Applications Use MIDI

You've already seen examples of the two ways that Windows applications use MIDI devices. Most sequencer programs allow you to choose your MIDI output device directly or to choose the MIDI Mapper. Other programs, such as the Media Player, don't offer you a choice of MIDI output device. Whenever you are using a Windows program that doesn't offer a choice of MIDI output device, you can assume that the MIDI output is passing through the MIDI Mapper, and you can control it by opening the MIDI Mapper and changing various parameters.

By now, you're probably getting the idea that understanding the MIDI Mapper is pretty important to using MIDI in Windows. You also may have heard from friends that the MIDI Mapper isn't exactly the world's easiest piece of software to learn or use. Both of these statements are true. Fortunately, the vast majority of people will never have to tap into the deeper features of the MIDI Mapper, and learning the few aspects of it which you'll need is fairly easy, as you're about to discover.

Using the MIDI Mapper

The MIDI Mapper is a Windows Control Panel application that deals with Setups, Patch Maps, and Key Maps. These maps are used to help non-General MIDI synthesizers pretend that they're really General MIDI. Since most readers of this book will have a General MIDI synthesizer or sound card, or be able to convert their sound card to General MIDI operation with one of the drivers that we've mentioned in Chapter 10, we won't cover these in detail and will instead focus on MIDI Mapper Setups.

When you install a sound card in your system, the installation program generally creates a few MIDI Mapper Setups designed to work with the card. You can see these by taking the following steps:

1. Switch to the Program Manager.

2. Double-click on the Control Panel icon in the Main group.

3. Double-click on the MIDI Mapper icon to launch the MIDI Mapper.

4. When the MIDI Mapper displays its first dialog box, click on the Down Arrow next to the combo box labeled "Name."

You'll see several Setups. They may have names such as "Ext MIDI," "Basic," "Extended," "All FM," and so forth. Here's what you should know about these setups:

■ A Setup with the word "External" or "MIDI" in its name probably routes all the MIDI messages out the sound card's MIDI Out port, to whatever external sound module you may have connected. If this Setup is selected and no module is connected, you won't hear any sound when you attempt to play a sequence through the MIDI Mapper. This is the best Setup for sequencing with an external keyboard and using the keyboard's sounds instead of those in your sound card.

■ A Setup with the word "Basic" in its name probably has channels 11–16 activated and channels 1–10 shut off completely. If this Setup is selected, you won't hear any sound when you attempt to play a sequence that uses only channels 1–10 through the MIDI Mapper. This is usually the best Setup for playing back MIDI files created to Microsoft's specification if you have an FM synthesizer.

■ A Setup with the word "Extended" in its name probably has channels 1–10 activated and channels 11–16 shut off completely. If this Setup is selected, you won't hear any sound when you attempt to play a sequence that uses only channels 11–16 through the MIDI Mapper. This is usually the best Setup for playing back MIDI files created to Microsoft's specification if you have a high-polyphony sound card.

■ A Setup with the word "All" in its name probably has all channels activated and set to trigger the sound card's internal sounds. This is usually the best Setup for playing back sequences created by the automatic accompaniment programs that we'll discuss in the next section.

You can examine the details of any MIDI Mapper Setup by selecting it in the combo box and clicking on the Edit button. You'll see a screen such as that shown in Figure 10-2. The controls on this screen are capable of remapping data on one MIDI channel to another, but we're not concerned with that here. We're only interested in the column labeled Port Name. You can see from the figure that channels 1-10 are routed to the SB16 MIDI Out port, while the other channels are sent to the forlorn [None]. Clicking in any of the boxes in the Port Name column will bring up a list of all the available output drivers for MIDI messages. You can select a mix if you like, sending channels 1-5 and 10 to your sound card's internal synthesizer and sending the rest of the channels to an external keyboard.

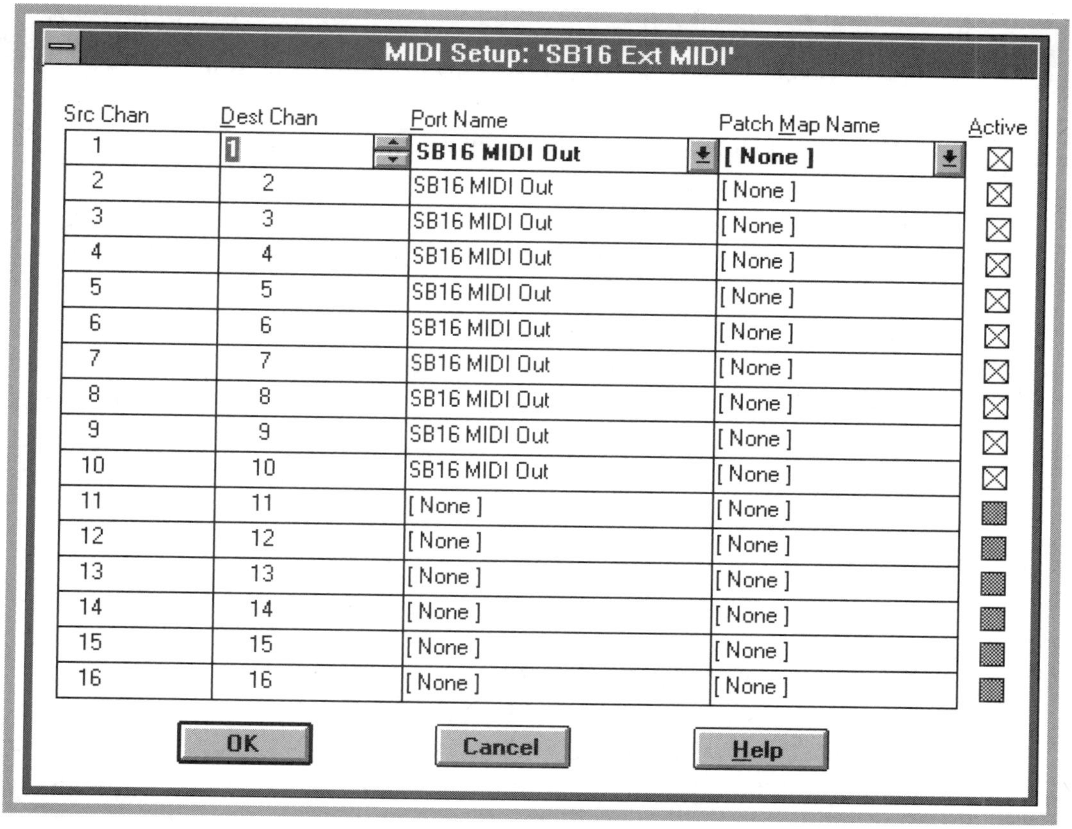

MIDI Setup: 'SB16 Ext MIDI'

Src Chan	Dest Chan	Port Name	Patch Map Name	Active
1	1	**SB16 MIDI Out**	**[None]**	☒
2	2	SB16 MIDI Out	[None]	☒
3	3	SB16 MIDI Out	[None]	☒
4	4	SB16 MIDI Out	[None]	☒
5	5	SB16 MIDI Out	[None]	☒
6	6	SB16 MIDI Out	[None]	☒
7	7	SB16 MIDI Out	[None]	☒
8	8	SB16 MIDI Out	[None]	☒
9	9	SB16 MIDI Out	[None]	☒
10	10	SB16 MIDI Out	[None]	☒
11	11	[None]	[None]	▣
12	12	[None]	[None]	▣
13	13	[None]	[None]	▣
14	14	[None]	[None]	▣
15	15	[None]	[None]	▣
16	16	[None]	[None]	▣

OK   Cancel   Help

▶ **FIGURE 10-2**

Editing a Midi Mapper Setup.

The Setup with its name visible when you exit the MIDI Mapper is the one that is active, and it will remain so until you select a different one.

Automatic Accompaniment and Music Generation Programs

There are a number of programs that are designed not only to provide a set of tools for recording and editing music (as sequencers do) but also to help you to quickly and easily create complete arrangements. You may, for instance, be able to create a pretty melody and nice chords but not have the faintest idea of how to create drum and bass parts to propel your song toward hit-dom, or at least demo-dom. Or you may know absolutely nothing about music but still want to build songs by selecting and recombining different snippets created for you on demand. The programs in these sections all provide you with unique, unprecedented ways of making music and innovative, composition-oriented interfaces to MIDI file creation.

None of these programs will create, at the click of a button, a full arrangement of a masterpiece that will endure for the ages; however, the tracks that they create are entirely suitable for practice backing tracks, for segues in multimedia presentations, for generating ideas that you can refine, and for a number of other uses. Many of the tracks produced with these programs can be exported as MIDI files and imported into a sequencer, where you can create or edit the melody using more traditional techniques. Regardless of how you use them, though, all of these programs are suitable for BIG FUN (and most are available in both DOS and Windows versions)!

Chord Changes and Styles

Most songs are built around a set of *chord changes* and a melody—in fact, these are what you get when you see a "lead sheet" (see Figure 10-3) The bass, piano, guitar, and all other accompanying instruments are expected to improvise parts that flesh out the chord structure. The song structure generally repeats a number of times, with each player creating variations on his or her basic part during each repetition. This

▶ **FIGURE 10-3**

The lead sheet for a short song shows the melody and the chord changes.

approach contrasts with European-derived classical music, with pieces built around the evolution of melodies and harmonies over time, with repetition used in a much more sparing manner, and with every note for every instrument predetermined by the composer. (There are some exceptions to this in the improvised harpsichord parts of the Baroque period and in 20th-century classical music.)

Most popular, rock, and jazz music is built around a repeating set of chord changes. Although each instrument is free to improvise in the context of those chord changes, certain other guidelines apply, depending upon the instrument's function in the ensemble. Drummers are expected to keep the beat moving, while bass players are expected to outline the chord structure by playing the roots (the letter names) of the chords on the strong beats. Guitar players and pianists, when they're not playing solos, are expected to play chordal embellishments that don't interfere with the singers, soloists, or each other.

The specific conventions for the types of beats a drummer may use vary from one style of music to the next, along with bass and chord patterns. The distinctive, off-beat rhythm guitar chords that characterize reggae would be completely out of place in a heavy metal tune, and heavy metal power chords would decimate a jazz tune. Melodies seem to be harder to classify according to style than percussion, bass, and chordal patterns.

The programs described in this section utilize styles and chord changes to help you create music. Each of the program authors has gone to great pains to analyze the melodic, accompaniment, and rhythmic patterns that make up various kinds of music, and each has succeeded in some areas. A number of styles come with each program. Some manufacturers sell additional style packs, and some encourage the creation of styles and distribution over computer networks.

Oddly enough, the most difficult style for these programs to capture seems to be good old rock-'n'-roll. Several varieties fare well, especially funk and pop, but hard rock and soul remain elusive and probably will continue to do so. This has a lot to do with the expressive nature of the distorted electric guitars and overblown saxes that give their character to these styles—both sounds that synthesizers don't reproduce well. In the case of guitar, this is because distortion is non-linear. If you sample each string playing through a distortion box and combine the samples, the results will not be nearly as gritty and grungy and just gloriously noisy as what you'll get if you play a full guitar chord through a fuzz. While this may be disappointing to synthesists, it's good news for guitarists.

Several of the salsa styles, while good, fall short of true Latin drive and feel because all these programs (with the exception of the latest version of Band-in-a-Box) insist on having all the instruments change chords at the same time. This is an appropriate assumption for many forms of music, but the Cuban styles often have a different approach—the bass part anticipates chord changes by a quarter note, and the piano anticipates them by an eighth note. In order to create an authentic Cuban groove (except with Band-in-a-Box), you'll have to take the output of one of these generators and surgically alter it in your sequencer.

On the positive side, these programs succeed well at jazz, pop, country, Brazilian, and many other forms. And, regardless of where on the quality scale the output of the programs falls, from mediocre to excellent, they all are excellent tools for creating instant, useful arrangements. Furthermore, if you dig down to the expert level and learn about how styles are created, you will get a fairly deep understanding of the strengths and limitations of the "analytical" view of music creation. In short, these are wonderful ways to get started making music on your computer.

The Jammer

This program literally had me laughing with how pleasant and easy it makes the creation of music (see Figure 10-4). Its basic metaphor is similar to Michaelangelo's technique for sculpting a horse: start out with a big block of stone, and then chip away everything that doesn't look like a horse. The Jammer is similar—you pick a style, tell it how many measures you want and in what key, and it generates everything for you. This includes chord changes, melodies, bass parts, and rhythm instruments. If you like some parts of what the Jammer did, you mark them as keepers and roll the dice again—everything except the marked tracks will change. You can proceed in this way until you have a complete piece of music.

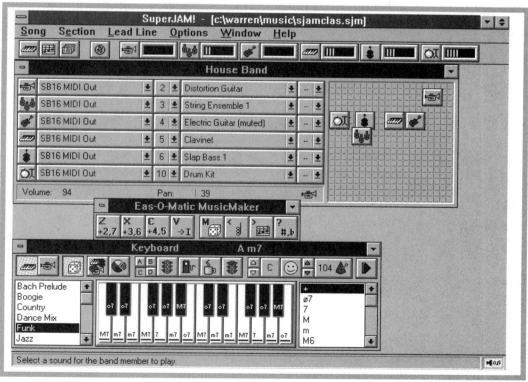

▶ **FIGURE 10-4**

The Jammer creates chord progresssions and melodies on demand.

The melody parts that The Jammer creates are often interesting but usually require editing to make them truly musical. I really enjoy using this tool as a source of inspiration. The chord changes that it generates are often refreshingly different and flow nicely, and the melody generator, while less successful, does comes up with good ideas now and again.

The Jammer comes in several versions. There are basic editions for both DOS and Windows and Pro editions for both environments. The Pro editions basically add the ability to edit styles, which lets you fine-tune the way the program creates music. This involves typing numbers for relative probabilities into a large number of boxes—not exactly an intuitive process—but it is well-documented and could provide hours of fun experimentation. And, after all, this is part of the "Pro" package, so it's fair for the programmers to expect a little work and thought from the user.

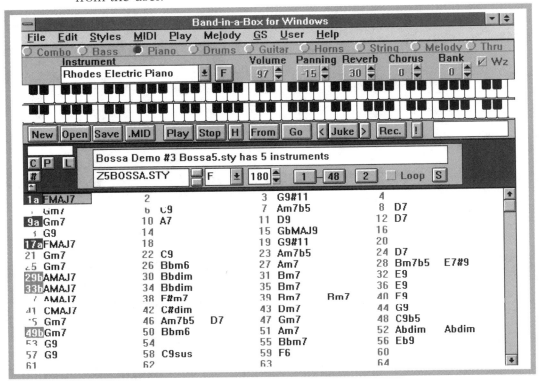

▶ **FIGURE 10-5**

Band-in-a-Box provides a lead-sheet-like interface that will be familiar to many musicians.

Band-in-a-Box

This was the first of the popular music generators (see Figure 10-5). It has achieved vast success by providing musicians with a low-cost backup band, available for rehearsal any time, day or night. It comes complete with several dozen styles (with many more available as options or from bulletin board systems) but excels at jazz.

You can make your own styles in Band-in-a-Box using the Style-maker application. As with style creation in the other programs, this requires a little hard thinking and some work, but the results can be rewarding.

Band-in-a-Box won't create melodies for you, but it will let you use a MIDI controller to record melodies along with your song and will also highlight lyrics that you type in on a measure-by-measure basis.

The publishers of Band-in-a-Box, PG Music, are pioneers in the area of low-cost music software. In addition to Band-in-a-Box, they sell a $29 Windows sequencer called Power Tracks Pro for Windows.

SuperJam

This is the most fun real-time music generator in the group. All the other programs present you with novel interfaces for constructing a song structure and then "compiling" a performance. SuperJam lets you create a song structure while it is actually playing. It lets you "mouse around" on a keyboard and change the chords or add melodies or drums, and it can record everything that you do.

This program is so easy to use that I've had parties at which complete musical novices have sat down and controlled a SuperJam backup band while others of us jammed along on percussion instruments. Take a look at the screen shot in Figure 10-6.

It demonstrates a number of unique and effective interface innovations. The top window in the figure is the Band Window, which allows you to adjust the volume and position of the instruments simply by dragging their icons around in a grid. The bottom window shows a keyboard, which functions as a home organ with "auto-accompaniment" keys—simply click on one, and the chords and bass line both change. This window also shows four different "grooves" (the buttons

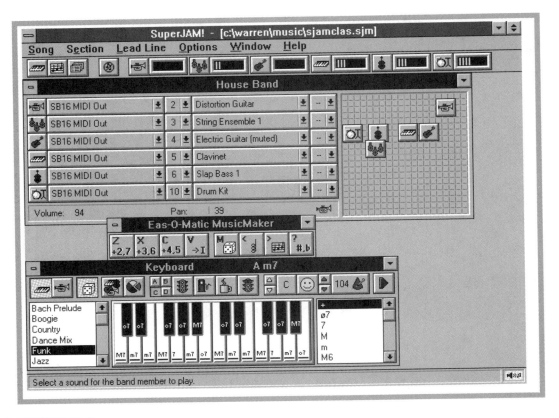

▶ **FIGURE 10-6**

SuperJam makes automatic music creation easy.

labeled A, B, C, and D) that are available for each style, and a smiley face that indicates that the current key is major. Click on it, and it turns to a frowning face for minor keys.

SuperJam's most effective innovation, at least for musical novices and children, is its Eas-O-Matic MusicMaker feature. This lets someone banging randomly on the bottom row of keys on a computer keyboard to create music (or a reasonable facsimile). The left-hand keys change the chord (within the song's key, as indicated in the Keyboard window), and the right-hand keys play melody notes, intelligently and automatically chosen to fit well with the chords that are playing.

Blue Ribbon Softworks, SuperJam's publishers, also publish a product called EasyKeys which incorporates many of SuperJam's capabilities into a package aimed at musical novices and children. Unfortunately for DOS users, both of these programs are only available for Windows.

Power Chords

This presents a rather different metaphor for sequencing, one aimed at guitar and stringed-instrument players. It allows you to combine chords and picking patterns together in a song to create accompaniments. You can pick the chords and patterns from libraries that the manufacturer supplies, or you can create your own by clicking on a fretboard. You can either use a standard six-string guitar fretboard, or you can design one of your own, with up to 12 strings tuned any way you like. You can even create chords with finger stretches that would be inconceivable on a physical guitar (see Figure 10-7).

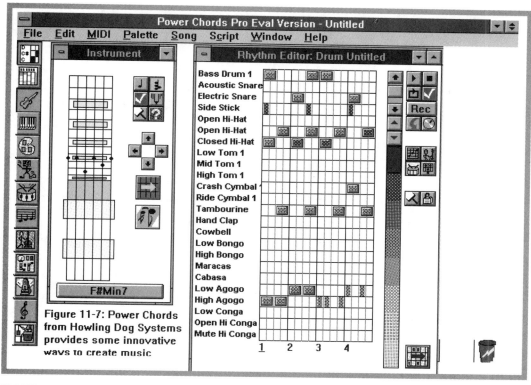

Figure 11-7: Power Chords from Howling Dog Systems provides some innovative ways to create music

▶ **FIGURE 10-7**

Power Chords from Howling Dog Systems provides some innovative ways to create music.

Power Chords is pattern-based. You create picking patterns, bass patterns, and drum patterns and then combine these with a set of chord changes and a melody that you create with the mouse. The result is a fun, graphic way of creating music. Power Chords' strongest feature is its rhythm generator, which makes the creation of percussion loops very intuitive and easy. A hidden bonus for guitarists is its ability to generate chord diagrams for any conceivable tuning.

Using Sequencers

Sequencers are the power tools of MIDI music creators. All sequencers can record and play back multiple MIDI tracks, but the most powerful present you with many ways of viewing and editing your data (yes, it's true—when talking about sequencers, your music becomes "data"). Editing capabilities range from the precise specification of individual notes—their start and end times can be set with millisecond precision—to bulk changes such as transposition and *quantization* (an important technique for tightening up rhythms which we'll discuss shortly). One sequencer even provides a programming language to allow advanced users to create custom transformations not dreamed of by commercial developers.

Sequencers vary greatly in their capabilities. You're almost certain to have received one bundled with your sound card. Instead of wondering what the best sequencer is and then saving for its purchase before making any music, try doing some actual sequencing with the tools at hand so that you can better understand which features you need or want that you don't already have. Then you can consult magazine buyers' guides or call up leading vendors such as Twelve Tone Systems, Passport Designs, Cubase, MidiSoft, and PG Music (see Appendix D for telephone numbers) to see whether their products will fulfill your needs. The next few scenarios will present a few case studies in sequencing to give you an idea of how it's done.

Creating Multi-Tracked Songs

Most people use sequencers to create multi-tracked performances. The term *multi-tracking* originally referred to the practice of recording different instruments on their own tracks on specially-designed tape recorders. This technique, invented by guitarist Les Paul in the 1940s, soon became a staple of the recording industry. Prior to multi-tracking, all performances were recorded live. If anyone made a mistake, everyone had to rerecord the take. What you got was what you were stuck with—it was impossible to rebalance the performance or to alter any of its components after the recording session.

Multi-track tape recording changed all that. Once the different tracks were laid down on the wide tape used for multi-track recording, each track could be rerecorded independently of the others. Additional tracks could be added at later dates to an existing recording, a technique called *overdubbing* (this, in fact, was a primary motivation for Les Paul's invention—he and his partner Mary Ford sold many millions of records created by overdubbing both Les' guitar and Mary's voice). After all the tracks were finished, a final *master tape* was made by running the tracks through a *mixing board*, where volume and tone adjustments could be made, and recording the results on a standard mono or stereo tape. This process became important in the record industry as soon as Les invented it; however, when the Beatles used these techniques to produce *Sgt. Pepper's Lonely Hearts Club Band* in the late 1960s, multi-tracking became an essential tool of pop record production and has remained so ever since.

MIDI Sequencing

MIDI sequencing is based on the concepts of multi-track recording, but it offers some significant advantages (and limitations). The biggest advantage is the ability to edit every aspect of a performance, down to each individual note. With a multi-track tape recorder, you can re-record a track or even a short phrase, but you can't drag a bad note to turn it into a good one or quantize a performance to tighten up the timing. Sequencers give you total control.

On the other hand, you can't use sequencers to record vocals or non-MIDI instruments, such as saxophones or guitars. The scope of sequencing is limited to controlling MIDI synthesizers. You can, however, use synchronization to combine acoustic sounds on tape with sequencer-controlled synthesizers; in fact, a large percentage of today's rock recordings are made using exactly this technique. Synthesizer backing tracks are created in a home studio or small "project" studio, where experimentation and composition are the rule and the hourly charges are small or nonexistent. Creativity can flourish in an atmosphere such as this. Once the backing tracks are completed, time is booked in a professional recording studio with expensive multi-track digital tape recorders, microphones, signal processing gear, isolation booths, and the rest. The singers and the charge-by-the-note professional studio musicians lay down their tracks over the backing tracks. Then the synthesizer tracks may be further tweaked and a final mix created sometime afterward.

The important point to note about this process is the way it allocates resources. Since the advent of MIDI, it is no longer necessary to book expensive studio time in order to develop multi-track musical concepts. These can be done in your home, at your leisure. Later, if you desire to add acoustic tracks, you can take your tracks to a large or small professional facility, depending upon your needs, goals, and budget. Or, for small projects, you can even consider recording your non-synthesizer tracks into a wave file and playing that back along with your sequence.

Recording Your First Track

This section basically applies to people who have a MIDI keyboard or other controller. If you aren't in this group, then you can still use sequencer step-entry, graphical note entry, or an automatic composition program to create your basic tracks and then move on to using the sequencer's editing features to fine-tune them. If this is your preference, skip the rest of this section and move on to "Editing Sequences."

Preliminary Steps

There are a few preliminary steps involved in setting up for your first recording. We'll explain them in detail, and it may seem quite complicated—but, in fact, these steps are easier to take than to explain. Furthermore, most of these procedures only have to be undertaken the very first time you record; after that, you'll be ready to simply fire up your sequencer and controller, hit Record, and start recording. Take it

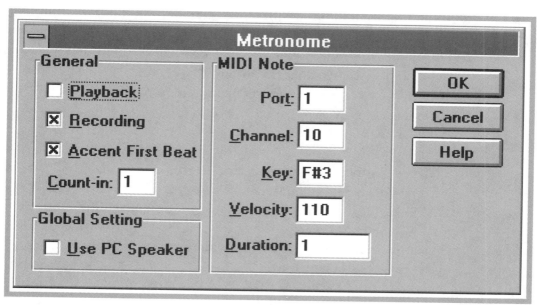

▶ **FIGURE 10-8**

You can set the metronome from the metronome options dialog box.

slow the first time through in the knowledge that the rewards will follow shortly.

SETTING THE METRONOME AND COUNT-IN OPTIONS. When you play basic tracks into a sequencer, it's best to play to a metronome. Sequencers can record free-tempo performances, but it's hard to match the tempo fluctuations in these when layering additional tracks. Also, free-tempo performances don't fall neatly into measure boundaries, making some kinds of editing difficult and quantization impossible. A metronome click will solve these potential problems for you.

Most sequencers are set up, by default, to produce a metronome click while recording. You can test whether this is true in your sequencer simply by clicking on Record. Do you hear a beat? If so, then you're home free. If not, search the menus and find a Metronome Setup or similarly-labeled choice. Figure 10-8 shows a typical metronome options dialog box. As you can see, there's an option to use the PC's speaker for a metronome click. Don't choose this—it's never loud enough. Instead, choose a MIDI note number on channel 10. This will produce a drum sound. I prefer to pick a "sharp" drum sound such as a clave (note number 75—D#5 or D#4, depending on your sequencer) or woodblocks (note numbers 76 and 77—E5 and F5 or E4 and F4) rather than a fuzzier sound such as a high-hat. Remember, your metronome sound will not appear in your final piece (unless you click the check box marked Playback). It's only meant to guide your rhythm.

The dialog box shown has a check box called Accent First Beat. This is a very useful option. When checked, the first beat of each measure will be played with a higher velocity (i.e., louder) than the other beats, which helps you keep track of where "1" is. Some sequencers offer, instead, the option of using a different note number for the first beat. This, too, is quite handy.

The dialog box also has a field for setting the number of measures to *count-in*. Metronome clicks are provided during a count-in to let you get used to the tempo and get ready to record. After the specified number of measures, recording begins.

I like to use two measures of count-in. You may prefer more, especially if you've got to dash over to a keyboard on the other side of the room after you hit the Record button on your computer. This parameter isn't critical when you record your first track, but it becomes more significant with later tracks. When you record your first track, you can always record a couple of measures of silence before you're ready to start playing and cut them out of the sequence when you're done recording. For later tracks, however, you'll want to start recording at the same time as existing tracks play, and a count-in is vital for this.

SETTING THE METER AND TEMPO: In order for the metronome to accent the first beat of each measure properly, the sequencer needs to know how many beats to play in each measure. This is expressed musically as the concept of *meter,* or *time signature*. A time signature consists of a pair of numbers, one above the other. The lower number indicates which note type gets a single beat. It's typically either 2, 4, or 8 (representing half notes, quarter notes, or eighth notes, respectively). The upper number is the number of beats in each measure.

The most common time signature is 4/4, followed by the 3/4 time used in waltzes. Some songs, such as "In The Still Of The Night," have the *compound meters* of 6/8, 9/8 or 12/8. They're called compound meters because they consist of two, three, or four major beats subdivided into groups of three. You can count along with songs in 12/8, for example, by repeating "One two three, two two three, three two three, four two three." Songs with less common meters include Dave Brubeck's jazz standard *Take Five* in 5/4 time, the Allman Brothers' *Whipping Post* with 11/8 in the verse and 9/8 in the chorus, and Sting's recent *Seven Days* in 5/4 and *Love is Stronger Than Justice* (The Munificent Seven) in 7/8 from *Ten Summoner's Tales*.

Your sequencer will have a way for you to set the meter of your song and most likely will also enable you to change it in the middle of the song if you so desire. Most likely, the default will be 4/4. If you want to change this setting, look for the term Meter in the program's menus. If you can't find it, search the online Help for the term Meter or, as a last resort, look it up in the manual.

Once you've set the meter, it's time to choose a tempo. This choice is strictly for your recording convenience—the tempo can be changed at any time, and you can even draw *ritardandi* (slow-downs) and *accelerandi* (speed-ups) into your tempo map later. For now, though, it's best to set a tempo that is somewhat slower than the actual final tempo of the song (unless the song is easy for you to play accurately at full speed). This will allow you to play carefully and accurately and to minimize the amount of editing and cleanup that you'll have to do after you record. When you play the sequence back at its intended speed, minor timing inaccuracies will be masked, and the whole song will sound smoother and more connected than the original performance. Don't choose a recording tempo so slow, though, that you lose the feel of the song.

You can check your tempo at any time by clicking on the Record button. You'll hear the metronome click in the meter and tempo that you've chosen. You can usually adjust the tempo by dragging a slider or typing the number of beats per minute that you want into a number box on the sequencer's main screen.

CONNECTING A CONTROLLER. In order to record, you need a controller. The controller's MIDI Out port connects to the computer's MIDI In with, as you'd expect, a MIDI cable. If you want to sequence using sounds in your keyboard or other controller, then you'll also want to connect the computer's MIDI Out to the controller's MIDI In; otherwise, you can forget about that connection and just listen to sounds played on your sound card.

Ideally, you can connect your controller right next to your computer so that you can easily move back and forth between the two. If this is not possible, however, it's no big deal. Many sequencers can be controlled from your keyboard, and you can also allow enough count-in time while recording to allow you to go back and forth between your controller and computer with time to spare.

SELECTING MIDI INPUT AND OUTPUT DEVICES. Your sequencer needs to know where to look for incoming MIDI data, and where to send the output. You tell it these things through a dialog box such as the one shown in Figure 10–9. (Don't let the complexity of this scare you—yours will be simpler than this. I regularly review products for magazines and have, I'm embarrassed to say, no fewer than three sound cards and a MIDI interface in my computer at the moment.) If you're in Windows, any drivers that have been installed through the Control Panel will show up in this dialog box. Some sequencers allow you to

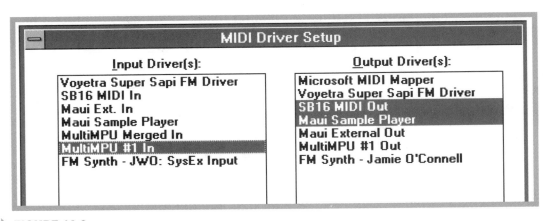

▶ **FIGURE 10-9**

Choosing MIDI Input and Output devices.

select multiple output devices for the song and then route individual tracks to different sound cards, while others limit you to a single output device (you can still play back your sequences on multiple devices by choosing the MIDI Mapper output route and then creating a MIDI Mapper Setup that uses multiple sound cards). If you want to listen to your sequence on your keyboard or external module, pick a "MIDI Out" output route; otherwise, pick a sound card.

SETTING LOCAL CONTROL OFF. If you're using a keyboard or other controller that makes sounds when you press a key or hit a pad, and if you want to use the keyboard as your sequence sound module, then, strange as it sounds, you'll want to disable the keyboard's direct control over its sounds. When you sequence, you want to achieve WYHIWYG—"what you hear is what you get." This is accomplished by listening only to sounds that are triggered from the computer; in other words, by logically disconnecting the physical keyboard from the sound module inside it (see Figure 10-10). This is referred to as turning Local Control off.

If you hunt through your controller's manual, you should be able to learn how to turn Local Control off from the front panel. If it's not obvious (or possible) to do this, try creating the following short

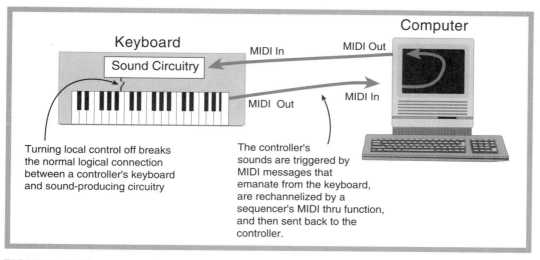

▶ **FIGURE 10-10**

A typical sequencing setup.

▶ **FIGURE 10-11**

A portion of a Track
Overview used in the text
to illustrate the concept
of rechannelization.

Name	Patch	Chn
Drums	-none-	10
Bass	**Fretless Bass**	1
Melody	**Alto Sax**	2
Chords	**Acoustic Guitar (steel)**	3

sequence (by inserting a message in your sequencer's Event List view) and playing it to your controller:

```
Continuous Controller 122, value 0
```

When you're done sequencing, you may want to turn Local Control on. Usually, the easiest way to do this is to turn off the power on the keyboard and then turn it on again. However, if you don't want to do this or it doesn't work, you can send the following message to your controller:

```
Continuous Controller 122, value 127
```

SETTING MIDI THRU. Most sequencers have a checkbox or menu choice that activates their MIDI Thru function. This takes the input from your controller and routes it to the output destination during recording. What's interesting and useful about this is that most sequencers will *rechannelize* your performance to the channel for the current track. This enables you to always play the appropriate sounds automatically.

To understand how this works, imagine that you've set up and named a few tracks as in Figure 10-11 and assigned channels and patches to each of them. In this case, simply selecting the Bass track with a single mouse click will enable you to play with a Fretless Bass sound, while selecting the Melody track will change your sound to an Alto Sax. It's the fastest and most convenient way to sequence.

SETTING THE RECORD FILTER. Sequencers can be configured to ignore or record certain types of data. The safest thing to do is to set your sequencer to record everything; otherwise, certain expressive aspects of your performance may be lost when you play them back. You can find these settings by looking for the sequencer's Record Filter command.

SELECTING A TRACK TO RECORD INTO. We're nearly ready to actually record something (you thought we'd never get there, didn't you?) All sequencers have a Track window, which is where you name your tracks and assign instruments and other characteristics to them. Click on a track, and select a sound for that track from a General MIDI patch list (usually by clicking or double-clicking into a column called Patch or Instrument). Play your controller—you should hear the desired sound.

STARTING TO RECORD. Now you're ready to get going. Hit the Record button (almost always the only red button on your screen), dash over to your controller during the count-in, and start wailing! When you're done, head on back to the computer and press Stop. Click on Rewind (it's nice how computers do this instantaneously, as opposed to tape recorders) and then Play, and you'll hear your performance played back for you.

MAKING THE KEEP/NO-KEEP DECISION. While you can fix almost anything that sounds bad in a sequence with your mouse, the process can be tedious (and can lose some musical flow) if you have massive mistakes to fix. If your first attempt was really awful, maybe the most merciful thing to do is to deep-six the track. Some sequencers will simply let you choose Undo to forget the take. With other sequencers, you'll need to select the track and look through the menus for a Kill Track command or its equivalent, or press the Delete key while the track is selected.

If only part of the track stinks, you have several options. If a couple of measures here and there are really good, you can mute the track for now, rerecord it, and then copy the excellent measures from the first take into the appropriate positions in the second. Or, if most of the track is good but a couple of sections are messed up, you can Punch In (as we'll discuss in the next section) and re-record only the selected sections.

In any case, it's always a good idea to save your work to disk every time you've finished a good take. You never know when a freak power outage or program bug is going to suddenly shut you down, wiping out the greatest recording of the past 50 years.

Punching In (and Out)

If you have a track that's perfect except for a few notes here and there, you can skip ahead to the "Editing" section and fix them there. However, if a whole measure or phrase (or longer section) is messed up, you'd probably be best off taking a second try at performing the offending parts. To do this, you set *Punch In* and *Punch Out* points in your sequence to be the start and end times of the passage that you want to replace. Now set the counter to a few measures before the punch-in point so that you'll have time to get in the groove before you're actually recording.

Note!

Note: you usually have several formats to choose from for your counter—the Measures:Beats:Ticks counter is usually the most useful. There are from 120 to 480 clock ticks per quarter note in most sequencers.

Now when you hit Record, you'll hear your old track play for a couple of measures, and then it will blank out at the point where you're supposed to supply new material. If you're playing a prepared part, you can play along with your prerecorded track (to capture the feel) and just keep playing when the track cuts out. Only the portion between the punch points will be recorded.

Quantizing

This is actually an editing technique and so would naturally come up for discussion a few sections down the road, but it's very important and can be useful before you lay down a second track. Quantizing is a way of automatically tightening up the rhythm of the notes that you've played. It's often a good idea to do this to your first track before layering additional tracks, especially if the first track is a bass or drum part, because the initial track serves as a guide for future tracks.

No musician is a robot. You'll never play a part consisting of quarter notes that fall *exactly* on the beat, and you'd never want to. The pulse is just a guideline—humans play parts that either anticipate the beat or lag behind it, and the result is expressive music. However, there's a difference between expression and sloppiness, and you'll know it when you hear it. And even true expression has its limits when you're sequencing, as track after track is built around a foundation that usually consists of bass and drums. In a live performance, everyone can be expressive within bounds, and a good ensemble will play tempos that breathe and flow. However, during overdubbing, the give-and-take that characterizes live playing is absent—when you over-dub chords on top of a bass track, you must adjust to fit the bass part, but the bass part can't reciprocate. This makes it more important that the most fundamental rhythm parts in a sequence be fairly metronomic (which doesn't mean that they can't be funky), leaving most of the expressive timing variations for later tracks. After the entire arrange-ment is put together, you can alter the timing of the initial tracks if you want.

Quantization is a tool for taking a human performance and making it more metronomic; however, it doesn't force you to go all the way to robotic playing. Most quantization tools in sequencers have a "strength" parameter which lets you partially quantize your tracks.

Quantization takes all the Note On events in a selected region (it could be an entire track, a few measures, three individual notes, or multiple tracks) and moves them to the nearest division of the beat—this division being one that you specify. You can quantize passages to the nearest quarter-note, eighth-note, sixteenth-note, eighth-note-triplet or to other divisions. You often have the option of quantizing note lengths as well as start times, which moves the Note Off events to the nearest division.

One tricky application of quantization occurs in jazz. Normally, jazz eighth notes should be quantized to eighth-note-triplets (swung eighths), but sixteenth notes should be quantized to "straight" six-teenths. Many sequencers can handle this, but with others you have to isolate the passages with sixteenth notes and quantize them separately from the ones with swung eighths. Look in the index of your sequencer manual for "swing quantize" to see how it can be done with your program.

Take care in quantizing. It can yield unexpected results. Save your unquantized performance before quantizing, and make sure to listen to the results before saving again. You may want to Undo the quantize and experiment with different parameters.

My personal experience may be different than yours with regard to quantizing, because I use a guitar controller to lay down tracks, and the timing of the instrument is fundamentally somewhat inaccurate. I have to rely on fairly severe quantization. When I create the most basic drum parts—bass and snare drums, and ride cymbals or high-hats—I quantize with 100 percent strength. I let the bass parts lie a little more loosely, usually quantized with about 85 percent strength, unless I'm going for a tight funk or hip-hop groove, which I quantize fully. The tracks still retain a human feel because of the velocity variations that are recorded from my playing, and because I avoid recording any two- or four-measure parts and looping them *ad nauseum*, a technique common among lazy musicians.

Overdubbing

You've recorded your first track, punched-in to fix any major mistakes, and possibly quantized it to tighten up the time. Now let's record a second part using a different timbre.

This part is quite similar to what you've already done, actually. You just select a different, empty track and pick a patch (of pickled peppers?) for it. Play your controller to make sure that you can hear the new sound. Then hit Record and, after the count-in, play along with your first track. Don't worry about the volume balance between the sounds for now—that's something you can adjust after all your tracks are recorded.

You can use the same techniques as before—punching in and quantizing—to tweak your new track. Then just continue creating additional tracks until you feel like you're done.

Editing Sequences

The basic data in your tracks consists of a time-stamped stream of MIDI messages. Your sequencer has a number of ways of presenting this data for your editing convenience, usually called *views*. A few standard views have emerged: track overview, piano-roll, event-list, controllers, and notation. Not every program offers all these views, and the way that each view is implemented also differs from program to program. You'll probably end up doing most of your work in one or two of these views, depending upon your own personal style.

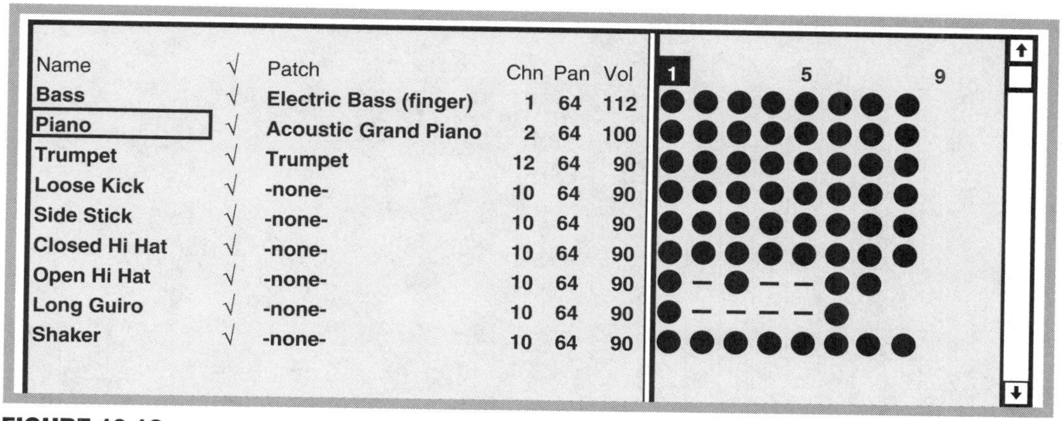

Name	√	Patch	Chn	Pan	Vol
Bass	√	Electric Bass (finger)	1	64	112
Piano	√	Acoustic Grand Piano	2	64	100
Trumpet	√	Trumpet	12	64	90
Loose Kick	√	-none-	10	64	90
Side Stick	√	-none-	10	64	90
Closed Hi Hat	√	-none-	10	64	90
Open Hi Hat	√	-none-	10	64	90
Long Guiro	√	-none-	10	64	90
Shaker	√	-none-	10	64	90

▶ **FIGURE 10-12**

The Track Overview gives you a bird's-eye view of your musical data.

TRACK OVERVIEW. The track overview is best for manipulating factors that apply to entire tracks, and for moving and copying measures. The overview shown in Figure 10-12 lets you assign a name and MIDI channel to each patch. The column labeled "P" lets you selectively enable or disable playback for each track. The Prg and Volume columns represent initial settings for the track; Continuous Controllers and Program Changes embedded within the track could change these during playback. The filled-in dots on the right side of the Figure show which measures have notes in them. You can drag these dots around on the screen to move or copy measures of music.

NOTATION VIEW. People who read music notation fluently may find this the most natural view to work in. Not only will this view display your recorded performances in musical notation, but it will also let you draw in additional notes with the mouse. It's a very handy view for some purposes, but it does have its limitations.

Whenever you view musical notation created from a performance, you're looking at an approximation of the data. In effect, the program must quantize a copy of your performance in order to display it on the screen. (It doesn't actually quantize the performance itself, which would change the way it plays back; instead it "rounds off" a copy of the performance in memory that is used for display purposes only.) If the sequencer didn't do this, your exactly-notated performance would be full of dotted 64th-notes and the 128th-note triplets because no one plays robotically (and, to further complicate the matter, the ends of notes don't often occur anywhere close to even divisions of the beat).

The limitations of the notation view stem from this inevitable approximation. First, you must choose a sequencer display resolution (like choosing a quantization value) that fits the music, or your sequencer must be smart enough to do that for you and do it well. Secondly, this view is not well-suited to fine-tuning the durations of individual notes or to sliding them slightly ahead of or behind the beat. Finally, most implementations of this view don't give you any graphic way of changing velocities.

What the notation view excels at, if you're fluent in musical notation, is note entry with the mouse and giving you the ability to spot clinkers (notes that are just plain wrong) and to correct them or delete them.

PIANO ROLL VIEW. This may be the most useful view for editing MIDI events, even though it may seem foreign to those used to traditional music notation. In this view, notes are represented in a two-dimensional grid showing exact start and end times, often with a bar graph called the *velocity pane* below the grid displaying the velocities of individual notes (see Figure 10-13). You can grab notes and slide, shrink, or stretch them until you've got what you want.

EVENT LIST. This is the most complete view in that it shows you every MIDI message in each sequence. For this very reason, however, it may be the least useful view for most editing purposes—there's too much information, presented in a very dry, non-musical format. Nonetheless, the Event List has its uses. In particular, this view is ideal for inserting Program Change messages into the middle of your tracks or for inserting Continuous Controllers (such as Bank Select messages). Some sequencers even allow you to insert commands in this view that will trigger Windows multimedia events, such as the playback of a wave file or a video clip.

The Event List view is also great for figuring out what *exactly* is going on in a sequence if it sounds weird or produces unexpected results.

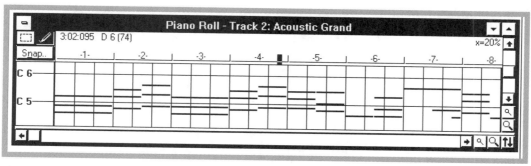

▶ **FIGURE 10-13**

A piano roll view showing just the notes in a B-measure fade.

CONTROLLERS. This view lets you edit Continuous Controllers in an intuitive and graphical manner. It's usually presented as a bar chart, such as the velocity pane in the piano roll view, and can be easily edited with a pencil-like tool.

FADERS. This provides a way of accessing volume and other Continuous Controllers that imitates the mixing consoles found in recording studios (see Figure 10–14). However, the fact that these are software faders instead of hardware faders gives them more capabilities than those in the average mixer.

In many sequencers, the faders are automated. In other words, they move in response to Continuous Controllers embedded in your tracks so that they always reflect the current values. Also, fader moves can be recorded in some sequencers, allowing you to overdub fader moves and create a mix that varies as the sequence progresses. The same applies to Pan Continuous Controllers, which are sometimes assigned to on-screen knobs instead of faders.

These features give you capabilities found (outside of MIDI-related software) only in automated mixing consoles costing $20,000 or more.

▶ **FIGURE 10-14**

Software faders can be used to control volume and other MIDI Continuous Controllers.

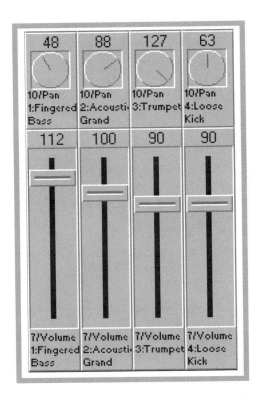

In most professional recording studios, mixes are performed in real-time by having one or more engineers act as an audio octopus, twisting knobs and moving faders as the final mix is recorded on a master tape. If someone blows a move, the whole mix has to be repeated. A complex mix can be an error-prone, time-consuming process. Fortunately, mixing MIDI sounds with a sequencer is much easier.

In some sequencers, faders can be assigned to any continuous controller. Figure 10-14 shows that the fourth fader is actually assigned to control modulation (vibrato) on the trumpet part.

LARGE-SCALE EDITING. So far, we've primarily been discussing editing operations that work with graphic editing views. There are also many larger-scale editing operations unconnected to specific views that can be quite useful. All sequencers allow cutting and pasting of musical sections, which in itself is handy for doubling parts and cutting out unwanted parts. Mostly, you'd do this in the track overview window. There are some other large-scale operations that are worth noting.

TRANSPOSITION. Any sequencer will let you change the pitch of all the notes in a sequence by a fixed number of half-steps, which is especially useful for matching sequences to a singer's range. Some, however, go further than that and allow *diatonic transposition*, which will transpose notes by amounts that vary by a half-step or two, forcing the result of the transposition into a fixed key. This is handy for creating harmony parts: copy the track you want to harmonize and paste it into an unused track. Transpose the new track up by a diatonic major third, for instance, and you have an instant harmony part. For a final bit of spice, change the instrument for the harmony part or randomize the timing of the Note Ons of both tracks slightly (see the next section) in order to give the harmonization a little bit of attractive human imprecision.

RANDOMIZATION. *Randomization* is the process of adding variation to some aspect of the music. If you record all your music from a controller, you'll probably never need to use a randomization function. On the other hand, if you quantize a track completely or if you create a two-measure drum pattern and then paste it into a song 50 times to create an incessant, unvarying percussion track, randomization can be just what you need to remove that mechanistic feel. Also, if you start with the output of an automatic composition program of some kind, you may feel the need to add more variation to one or more of the tracks.

Generally, you'll apply randomization to the start times of notes in order to "un-quantize" somewhat. Another ripe area for randomization is note velocity. A drum track created from multiple copies of the same track can gain a lot of interest if both of these transformations are applied in the right amounts.

EDIT FILTERS. With several high-end sequencers, it's possible to apply transformations to only certain subsets of the MIDI events in your tracks. For instance, if your downbeats aren't sounding powerful enough, it may be possible to increase the velocity of only those notes that occur within 30 clock ticks of the first beat of a measure, all with a single command. Or you can combine an edit filter with a Cut command to strip all Pitch Bend messages from a track. This is a powerful feature for the music professional.

PROGRAMMING. The ultimate power in sequence editing is to be able to program the transformations that you want to occur. Of course, this is also the ultimate in non-user-friendliness, requiring that you study a specialized programming language and go to the trouble of writing and debugging your programs. In other words, it's definitely not for everyone. Only one program, Cakewalk Pro, offers this feature. If you're both a musician and a programmer (as many people are, to one extent or another), this may be the way for you to tap into the deepest power of your sequencer. I personally have used this facility to automate some tedious, involved editing tasks that came up during the production of music for a CD-ROM and have been quite grateful for its existence.

Fine-Tuning Drum Parts

The easiest way to adjust the volumes of individual drum sounds is to alter their velocities, because MIDI Volume Continuous Controllers don't work. All the drums are on channel 10, and any volume messages on that channel will affect all notes equally. The same problem applies to the Pan Continuous Controller—it's not possible to use this to pan individual drum sounds without affecting them all. Still, there are solutions to both these dilemmas.

If you're using an external sound module or keyboard, then you may be able to program the volumes and pan positions of the individual drum sounds from the front panel. Similarly, you can use the patch editing software that is available for some sound cards (which we discuss under "Creating New Sounds") to adjust these parameters.

The best way to adjust note velocities is to begin by recording each drum sound into its own track. Then you can select the entire track (or part of it) and use a menu choice to alter the velocities. Alternatively, in some programs, the track overview window will provide a way to change the velocities during playback only, without altering any of the recorded velocities. (This provides a faster and easier way to experiment with drum mixes.)

Be cautious when you boost or lower velocities radically—you may inadvertently destroy volume variations within a track. For instance, if you have a snare drum track with velocities that range from 80 to 120 and you add 40 to all the velocities, the resultant velocities will range from 120 to 127 (since velocities can never exceed the maximum), and all the drum hits that used to take on a range of values from 87 to 120 will now have identical velocities.

There's no foolproof method for adjusting the panning of individual drum sounds, other than the front-panel and patch editing methods mentioned above. As a last, desperate measure, if you have a GS-compatible synthesizer, then you can send out the following sequence of Continuous Controllers to set the pan position of a percussive instrument:

```
Continuous Controller 99, value 28

Continuous Controller 98, value <note number of drum
sound>

Continuous Controller 6, value <pan position: 0=left,
64=center, 127=right>
```

This sequence is an example of the mysterious MIDI *Non-Registered Parameter Number* (NRPN). The process may, in fact, be even weirder than this, requiring you to send a System Exclusive string message to the card first to enable NRPN reception (this will involve studying your user manual and possibly calling your sound card manufacturer's technical support line). Most non-fanatics will simply live with the default panning assignments for the different drums and probably never even think about wanting to change them.

Maximizing Polyphony

It's possible to create a sequence that exceeds the polyphonic capabilities of any sound card, but your chances of doing this are especially good if you have an FM card. Not only can you exceed your card's polyphony with your own sequences, but you may also find this characteristic in sequences that you download or purchase. When you try to play a sequence that calls for more notes than a card can provide, the result is *voice stealing,* in which the card shuts off notes that are already sounding in order to play new ones. If many Note On commands arrive simultaneously, then the sound card will simply play as many as it can. This results in you not hearing all the music in a piece. This might bother you, particularly if it's your piece! Following are a few tricks for discovering whether a sequence has unheard music in it and for adjusting it so that you can hear all the music.

It's important to understand the way that voice stealing is implemented on most sound cards. Generally, drum tracks (i.e., anything on channel 10) can only steal voices from other drum tracks, and all the other channels will steal from each other in accordance with their channel number. In other words, sounds on lower channels will steal from those on higher channels. Thus, if you have a track assigned to channel 16, it is the most likely of the non-drum tracks to have stolen notes.

You can tell which tracks are losing notes by *soloing* each track. This function, provided in most sequencers, allows you to listen to one track in isolation, without the distraction—or the voice stealing—of any other tracks. By soloing a track, you can hear all the notes in it. If you hear the same notes when the track is soloed as when the entire piece is playing, then no notes are being stolen from that part. Put your sequencer in a loop so that you can listen repeatedly to a few measures at a time when you perform these listening tests.

When you've identified a track that is losing notes, mute all the unlike tracks (i.e., mute the drum channels if you're fixing a non-drum track, and vice versa). Then mute the other tracks, one at a time, until you mute one that causes your missing notes to suddenly start playing. This is the track that is doing most of the stealing. Unmute it while you try to fix the situation.

Sometimes, it's not possible to fix note stealing without cutting the least-important notes, but often a simpler remedy is available, especially for percussion tracks. Slide the two interfering tracks a fraction of a beat (10, 20, or 30 clock ticks, depending upon the timing resolution of your sequencer) in opposite directions so that one occurs before the beat and one after. In some sequencers, you can do this from the track overview in a way that alters the playback of the notes but not the underlying sequences. This is the easiest way to accomplish the sliding, but you can also do it by selecting a track and using a Move or Slide edit command.

As you slide the tracks, you'll often find that not only do the missing parts reappear, but the tracks become more human-sounding, fuller, and thicker. Note stealing is often the result of fully quantizing a large number of tracks so that everything lands squarely on the beat. Sliding things around a little not only gets those notes out of each other's way, but also is more similar to the way people play instruments. It's a win-win solution, and I highly recommend it. You'll be amazed how much sound you can squeeze out of a mere 11 notes of polyphony.

Creating New Sounds (Patches)

Synthesizers and sound cards are software-based, which means that there's a lot more power hiding under their surface than they present to you at first blush. Both FM synthesizers and many kinds of wavetable synthesizers allow you to customize their sounds and create new ones with the aid of the right software. This is an advanced area and one which even professional musicians rarely venture into. Manufacturers of professional synthesizers have found, time and time again, that their customers are more interested in creating music with the supplied sounds than in programming new ones—and who can blame them? Still, you may be a hardy soul with a strong interest in customizing your own instruments. This is to be commended, as you truly can create some fascinating and unique sounds through programming, and weird FM sounds are often more musical and interesting than FM simulations of acoustic instruments. If you have an FM synthesizer and want to program your own sounds, get a copy of *Patch View* from Voyetra Technologies.

Wavetable synthesizers have changeable sound parameters, too. Although these cards essentially play back short digital recordings of sound, options such as release times (how long it takes notes to die out), filter settings, and effects settings can sometimes be edited. Check with the manufacturer of your sound card to see if an editor is available. If not, be aware that with GS-compatible synthesizers and certain others, many of these parameters can be altered in your sequences simply by sending Continuous Controller messages to your card.

Chapter **11**

Educational Software

A remarkable thing is happening in the world of music education. Computers—or, more accurately, computer programs—have reached the point where they can teach us certain subjects as well as or better than most human beings. In fact, the best educational programs are like having an expert in the field at your beck and call, 24 hours a day with no hourly fee. A number of these programs are quite fascinating and valuable.

The increasing spread of multimedia-equipped computers has given educators a vehicle for teaching music theory, history, and performance skills that is light years beyond the printed page. Programs can integrate text, photographs, drawings, score excerpts, digital audio recordings, MIDI files, and video clips, and put them all under your control. They can synchronize on-screen text to performances on a compact disk. They can play back sound files while displaying notation, at the speed of your choice. They can listen to you sing or play the violin and warn you when your pitch is off. They can present you with exercises, grade them, and keep track of your progress.

Placing audio materials under the control of computer programs and accepting musical input from the student through a microphone, MIDI interface, or other means is an ideal way to teach many musical skills and much musical knowledge. However, you should be aware that, in the initial stages of vocal and instrumental practice, a human teacher is necessary to observe the student and to correct bad technique—no commercial computer program can analyze your playing posture, for instance. However, even at the early stages, a human teacher can be supplemented with computer-based training with good results.

The best programs go beyond technology and technique. They impart the knowledge, skills, or perspective of a master. Although many of the programs listed below fulfill their goals well, I can't help but single out two exceptional series. The series of composer-named CD-ROM titles (Multimedia Beethoven, Multimedia Stravinsky, Multimedia Mozart, etc.) that Dr. Robert Winter of UCLA produces, published by Microsoft, is simply stunning. It combines erudition and wit, resulting in titles that are fascinating for both casual and serious students of classical music.

The second great series is The Music Lab Series by Temporal Acuity. These programs constitute a full, progressive course in basic musicianship. It's not just a collection of random exercises—it's a method.

There is still a lot of music education software that hasn't been written. Full-blown courses in harmony, counterpoint, and orchestration, complete with computer-graded exercises, could open those areas to amateur musicians who don't have the time or money to enroll in college courses. Unfortunately, we haven't seen these arrive yet, perhaps because the cost of development at present would overwhelm the expected profits.

Still, there is already an impressive variety of effective music education available to you. Although we can't cover every program in existence, we will describe the major ones and point out their virtues and flaws.

Music History

Music history is the study and analysis of what's been done in music. Interpreted in a broad sense (which is certainly what I intend to do), it is the study of musical pieces, styles, and artists, along with their cultural and historical contexts. Unlike music theory, which is intended for musicians, music history can be enjoyed by anyone. It can deepen your appreciation and enjoyment of pieces that you already know and introduce you to music that is unfamiliar.

Most music history software is designed for CD-ROM. That's because this medium allows a combination of music recordings, text, images, and notation that is ideal for the presentation of this topic.

Microsoft Multimedia Composers

As I mentioned at the top of this chapter, I love this series of CD-ROMs. It has been produced by Dr. Robert Winter, a music professor at UCLA. Each of the volumes contains a complete, top-notch performance of a great piece of classical music and an in-depth interactive exploration of the music, the composer, and the times. What distinguishes these discs are the quality of the scholarship, the human and engaging way that it's presented, and the structure (allowing both novices and experts to partake of this fount of knowledge at their own levels).

These discs are not glamorous—believe it or not, they have no digital video, no animations, no futuristic virtual universes, and some don't even have full-color photographs (Multimedia Stravinsky, for instance, uses tinted monochrome drawings with a sepia-like feel). Yet they're full of expert information, appealingly organized, and thus will stand up to hours upon hours of use.

The choice of pieces for analysis is outstanding. The first volumes in the set include some of the most interesting pieces of Western classical music. Multimedia Beethoven is centered around Beethoven's ninth and final symphony, arguably the greatest piece of orchestral music ever written. Beethoven was already deaf when he wrote this piece, and fully immersed in the vast spaces of his own musical universe. The result is one of the most massive, exuberant, and complex works Western concertgoers have ever enjoyed.

Multimedia Stravinsky presents the only orchestral work of the twentieth century that is certain to take a place in history beside Beethoven's best work, Igor Stravinsky's *The Rite of Spring*. This piece's disturbing rhythms, violent chords, and sheer sensuality caused a riot at its premiere in Paris in 1913. Multimedia Mozart covers Mozart's "Dissonant" string quartet, and several more titles are being released each year.

The heart of each title is a section called "A Close Reading" (see Figure 11-1). In this section, the entire piece is played, while comments about each passage appear on the screen. At any point, you can delve even deeper into the music by pressing the button labeled "A Closer Look." Another button toggles the level of the outline at the screen's left from the detailed view shown to a bird's-eye perspective.

Other sections include descriptions of the composer's life and times, a multimedia glossary with audio examples, a guide to the instruments used in the recording, an intriguing game that tests your knowledge of the composer and the piece, and additional sections which vary from title to title.

The only thing missing from these multimedia masterworks, which would provide the icing on the cake, is a scrolling version of the full

▶ **FIGURE 11-1**

"A Close Reading" from Multimedia Stravinsky *provides an informative play-by-play description for the piece.*

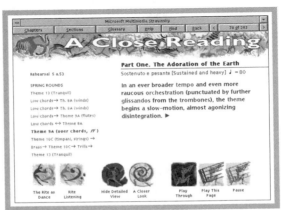

score. But the technical and design problems involved in presenting this are formidable (a computer screen can only provide a tiny viewport into a full orchestral score). It's a small complaint in the context of big benefits—the biggest of which is the substantial chunk of Dr. Winter's experience and insight that each volume delivers to you, in a format that will keep you coming back for more. ▪ *Published by Microsoft*

World Beat

I must confess that I'm prejudiced in favor of this program—I created the basic design and edited much of the content. In view of that, I will keep my description free of glowing superlatives. World Beat is an introduction to the music of the world. There are video clips of music from 40 countries, many additional audio clips, and original articles describing over 165 musical styles from all corners of the Earth. The video clips include the music of remote African villages, Chinese temple bells, American country blues, a samba in the streets of Rio de Janeiro, and many more musical styles, both traditional and modern.

The "Music Studio" section of World Beat has MIDI files and notation for 35 musical traditions (Figure 11-2). You can change the balance and speed of these pieces and play along with them as you watch the notation. You can also export them to your hard disk and build your own pieces around them.

World Beat collects more information and examples from diverse musical styles than have ever before been assembled in one work, if I do say so myself. It requires a 486SX/25 or faster computer, a CD-ROM drive, and Windows 3.1 or higher. ▪ *Published by Medio Multimedia*

Composer Quest

This entertaining disc was one of the first multimedia CD-ROMs to take advantage of Windows 3.1. There are two sides to this program— "Learn" and "Play." In Learn mode, you browse a timeline that puts the key composers of each period in a cultural and political context (see Figure 11-3). The program covers both classical composers and jazz artists, although the treatment of jazz is rather cursory, with few recordings and no artists after Duke Ellington. Classical music fares much better.

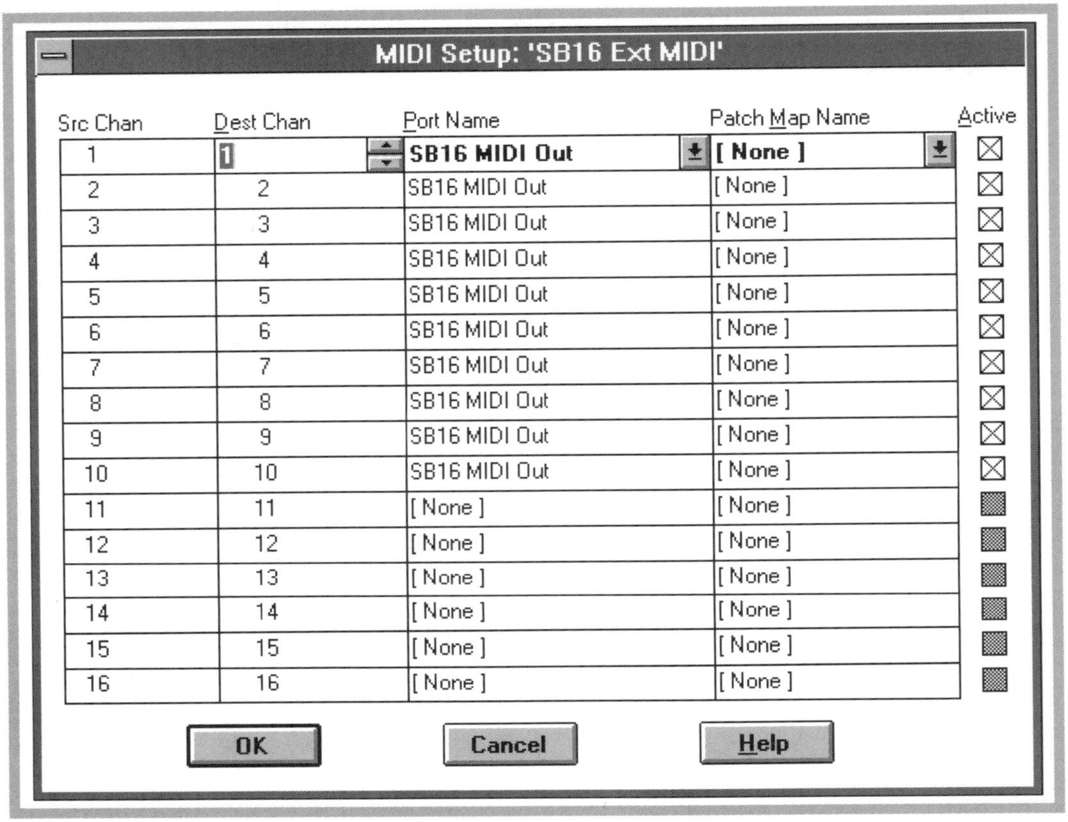

Src Chan	Dest Chan	Port Name	Patch Map Name	Active
1	1	**SB16 MIDI Out**	[None]	☒
2	2	SB16 MIDI Out	[None]	☒
3	3	SB16 MIDI Out	[None]	☒
4	4	SB16 MIDI Out	[None]	☒
5	5	SB16 MIDI Out	[None]	☒
6	6	SB16 MIDI Out	[None]	☒
7	7	SB16 MIDI Out	[None]	☒
8	8	SB16 MIDI Out	[None]	☒
9	9	SB16 MIDI Out	[None]	☒
10	10	SB16 MIDI Out	[None]	☒
11	11	[None]	[None]	■
12	12	[None]	[None]	■
13	13	[None]	[None]	■
14	14	[None]	[None]	■
15	15	[None]	[None]	■
16	16	[None]	[None]	■

MIDI Setup: 'SB16 Ext MIDI'

OK   Cancel   Help

▶ **FIGURE 11-2**

World Beatís Music Studio shows how different styles of music are put together.

When you pick a musical era to explore, you'll read about the main composers of the period along with selected information about the arts, sciences, ideas, politics, and society of the time. A biographical article about each composer is supplemented with two or three short excerpts from his works.

The game side of Composer Quest stems from a humorous premise. I quote: "You are in the 20th century. The planet Earth's natural resources are rapidly being exhausted. The IEDD (Intergalactic Environment Defense Department) is recycling all paper back into trees! All written material (including written music) is at great risk! Your mission: save a great musical work to your Digital Gizmotron." You

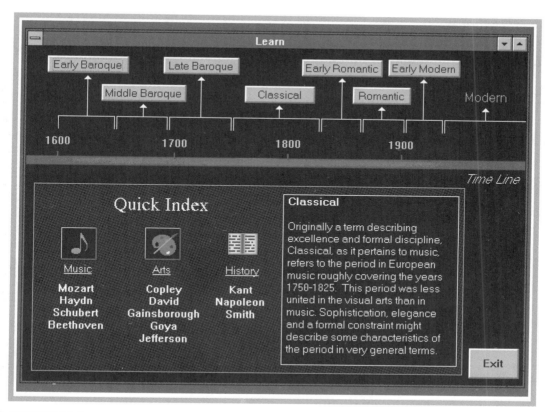

Composer Quest's Learn module displays a unified view of music and the culture that surrounds it.

click on an ear to hear part of a piece, and then it's up to you to locate the composer and the piece. First, you have to guess a date to travel to, then a composer, then a piece. If you pick the wrong composer, he'll give you a hint. The faster you find the piece, the better your score.

I like both the game and the learning mode. The game is a good test of general musical knowledge—if you can identify a composer by ear and know roughly in what years he lived, you've acquired an important and gratifying body of knowledge and listening skills. The learning section is an excellent and ambitious concept, although reading the text can be a little dry. Still, I've come back to this CD-ROM a number of times over the course of several years, and it has always rewarded the effort. ■ *Published by Dr. T's Music Software*

Music Mentor and Session

Music Mentor is an engaging introduction to the concepts of classical music that maintains a folksy, easy-to-understand tone without being simplistic (see Figure 11-4). It covers classical music styles from early music through modern. Within each style, melody, rhythm, harmony, timbre, texture and form are discussed.

Music Mentor uses MIDI files for its musical examples, which means that the sound quality of the examples depends on your sound card. It also means that you can take advantage of hot links to Session, a sequencer that is included with Music Mentor, to examine the notation for any example, listen to it at different speeds, or alter it in other ways. It's a nice touch.

▶ **FIGURE 11-4**

Music Mentor presents a good selection of musical concepts in an easily-digestible form, with an appealing mix of graphics, text, and MIDI.

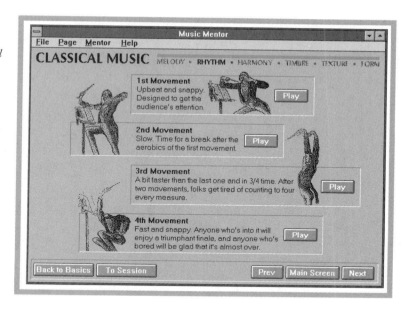

With a list price of $149 (in mid-1994), the package of Music Mentor and Midisoft Session is a good buy if you need a sequencer and Session meets those needs; however, it strikes me as expensive for Music Mentor alone. I hope that someday Midisoft chooses to unbundle the two programs and make Music Mentor available at a lower price. ■ *Published by Midisoft*

Musical Skills

The programs listed in this section are meant to help musicians at all levels develop musical skills and knowledge.

General Musicianship

These programs teach the types of skills typically taught in high school and college music theory courses—music theory, sight-singing (the ability to read pitches in standard notation and sing them), and ear training (the ability to recognize notes and chords).

The Music Lab Series

This is a truly impressive DOS-based program that actually accomplishes what the others profess—it gives you the equivalent of a full year of intensive training in essential musical skills. And it's delightfully progressive—the eight exercises all have 20 levels that are consistent with one another in the difficulty of the note sets that they're drawn from. Its basic teaching tool is the *solfeggio* system (associating sylla- bles sych as "Do, Re, Mi" to scale notes) used by singers and musicians for hundreds of years to master musical skills.

Originally designed for use by music teachers at levels from ele- mentary school through college, the program is starting to see increased sales to individual musicians who are serious about improv- ing their skills. It doesn't require a powerful computer, but it does require the installation of a custom card, which does the job of recog- nizing pitch (required for the Sing and Read exercises).

The current version of the Music Lab Series produces sounds only through the PC speaker or a MIDI interface compatible with Roland's MPU-401 model. A new version is in the works that will also support Sound Blasters and other cards.

Because I've found them so valuable, I'll describe the exercises provided in the Music Lab Series:

- **NAMES** —— The computer plays notes, and you guess which notes they are. At the easiest level, there are only four notes to choose from. At the most complex level, pairs of notes are played, chosen from a complete two-octave chromatic scale.

- **NOTES** — Notes are displayed in a staff. Your job is to pick the solfege syllable that corresponds to each note.

- **SING** – The computer highlights a note; you have to sing it. The computer tells you whether you're sharp or flat. It won't accept sliding into the pitch, a bad habit of many novice singers. This is a great way to improve pitch accuracy for singers.

- **ECHO** — The computer plays phrases and then asks you to tap out the rhythm of the notes on your computer keyboard—an excellent way to improve musical memory.

- **PLAY** — The computer displays a phrase in notation. Your task is to tap out the rhythm of the phrase on the computer keyboard, which develops rhythm reading skills.

- **NOTATE** — A phrase is played. You must remember the phrase and create the rhythmic notation for it.

- **WRITE** — This combines all the recognition skills used thus far. A phrase is played. First, you notate the rhythm (as in the Notate module), and then you assign pitches to the notes.

- **READ** — A phrase is displayed on the staff. Your job is to sing it. The computer then displays a graph showing your pitch and rhythm accuracy (see Figure 11-5). ■ *Published by Temporal Acuity Products*

Play It By Ear

This DOS-based program from Ibis offers the most comprehensive control over ear training that you could ever wish for. You can control

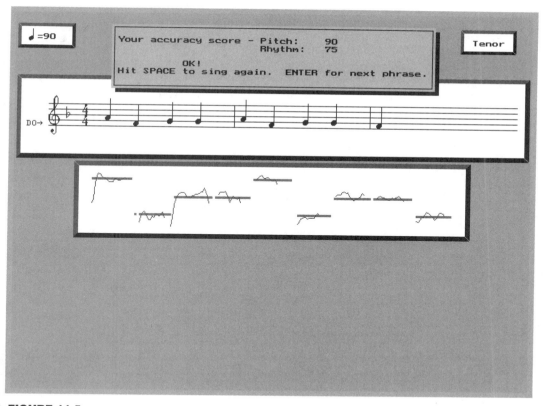

▶ **FIGURE 11-5**

The Music Lab Series Read exercise displays a graph showing how well you've tracked the pitch in sight-singing drills.

the types of intervals or chords that are presented to you, what inversions they can take, whether they're presented simultaneously or as arpeggios, and many other parameters. If you know the specifics of your ear training problems, you can benefit from this program. My major reservation is an unusual one for me—there's *too much* control given to the user. You have to decide what you want to be quizzed on, instead of using a preplanned, progressive program. This calls for better pedagogical judgment than many users of the program are likely to possess. ■ *Published by Ibis*

Soloist

This is an appealing game that asks you to read progressively more difficult melodies. Two measures of music at a time are displayed on a screen, and you are supposed to sing or play the music into a microphone. A pitch indicator shows whether you're sharp or flat—go too far off and you get an "X." Four correct answers in a row can erase the last X, and you keep ascending through the levels until you accumulate eight Xs. It's a fun game, especially for singers and players of instruments with continuous pitch (as opposed to pianos or fretted instruments) who must work on their intonation. ■ *Published by Ibis*

MiBAC Music Lessons

This is a set of music lessons that teach a number of basic musical and keyboard skills. I enjoyed the scale recognition exercises the most. I would have enjoyed several of the playing exercises if I were a keyboardist, but this program (and almost all others that accept MIDI input from an external controller) doesn't work well with a guitar controller such as I play—the unintentional low-velocity and low-duration notes that the controller produces are interpreted as answers, which messes up the process rather severely. But that's more a criticism of the controller than of the program.

Here are the drills, along with my comments on them:

- **NOTE NAMES**—The computer displays four notes, and you either play them on your MIDI keyboard or click them on the on-screen piano keyboard.

- **CIRCLE OF FIFTHS**—Six exercises test whether you can name the notes in the circle of fifths.

- **KEY SIGNATURES**—The computer presents you with various key signatures—you have to name them.

- **MAJOR/MINOR SCALES, MODES, JAZZ SCALES**—Different scales and modes are named, and you're expected to play them. You can do it with an external MIDI controller or with the on-screen keyboard. These are good exercises.

- **SCALE DEGREES**—I've never thought that learning which note in the scale is the "submediant" helped me to understand anything about the structure of music, but you may encounter terms such as this in your reading. If so, this drill is one way to learn which is which.

- **INTERVALS**—The computer shows the notation for an interval and plays it, and you're supposed to come up with its name. This prepares the novice for interval recognition exercises.

- **NOTE/REST DURATIONS**—This shows you various notes and rests, along with time signatures, and asks you how many beats they represent, a good exercise for beginners.

- **SCALE RECOGNITION**—My favorite exercise of the group, this plays a scale and asks you to guess which one it is.

- **INTERVAL EAR TRAINING**—This presents different pairs of notes to you and asks you to guess the interval. This is the most advanced exercise in the group. It has three levels but could benefit from many more—there are far too many possible intervals to choose from at the Beginning level.

    ■ *Published by MiBAC Music Software*

Play-Along Software

An excellent way to sharpen your instrumental skills is to play along with recordings. Over the last forty or fifty years, many cassette- and video-based instructional programs have been developed for musicians. However, none of these provides the convenience and utility of computer-based programs for learning music. Programs that combine MIDI files and notation give you the ability to play along at any speed without changing the pitch. Also, they give you instant access to the songs you want, instead of making you hunt around on a cassette for them.

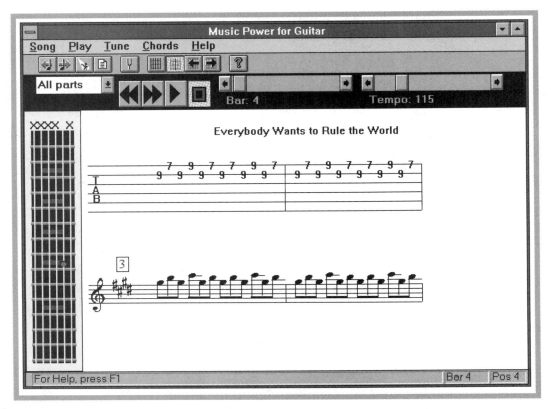

▶ **FIGURE 11-6**

MusicPower displays notation, tablature, and a fretboard diagram as a MIDI file of a full band plays at your choice of speed.

Not all the programs in this section work the same way—some display notation on-screen, some make use of an accompanying booklet, and some have no notation at all. Some of the guitar products provide tablature. And one product—this author's own Learn It From CD—doesn't use MIDI at all.

MusicPower for Guitar

This is an entertaining, fun, and effective program for learning rock guitar. You learn by playing along with MIDI files of some very hip songs, including the Talking Heads' "Burning Down the House," Tears for Fears' "Everybody Wants to Rule The World," Elvis Costello's "Everyday I Write the Book," and seven others (additional songs are available in add-on packages).

You get a full arrangement of each song, complete with drums, bass, multiple keyboard tracks, and all the trimmings. As the songs play back at the speed of your choosing, the guitar parts are displayed on the screen three ways: in standard musical notation, guitar tablature, and as dots on a guitar fretboard (see Figure 11-6). It's a good presentation, and an exciting way to learn to play some cool guitar parts. Players of all levels, whether they can read music or not, will learn to play a fun selection of songs.

I do have a couple of reservations about the first release of this product. MusicPower only displays two measures on each screen, with no overlap between screens. This makes it difficult to play the first measure of each pair, because the notation doesn't appear until slightly after the measure starts. It would be nicer if the program put three measures on-screen, but only moved forward two measures at a time. This would allow you to read ahead, which is the right way to read notation, anyway (it's like looking far ahead of you while you're driving). I'd also like to see the notation include chord names, a conspicuous absence in the first release. ■ *Published by MPower*

Solo Assimilator—Masters of the Blues

This product, from Lil' Johnny Enterprises, is a collection of MIDI files of 11 smoking guitar solos by B.B. King, Muddy Waters, Buddy Guy, and others. The files include a full backup band, and the package includes a booklet with transcriptions of all the solos in standard notation and guitar tablature.

The files are also provided in Band-in-a-Box format, which gives owners of that product the ability to change keys easily and apply different backing styles if they wish.

Generally, I enjoy this product, but it would be more helpful if it included digital audio files of the original solos. The MIDI files don't capture the nuances of guitar tone, and they don't include pitch bend, so they miss the subtleties of string bending, an important component of blues solos. ■ *Published by Lil' Johnny Enterprises*

Riffs

Riffs is the software engine that administers music lessons from a growing roster of star guitarists such as Steve Morse, Adrian Legg, and

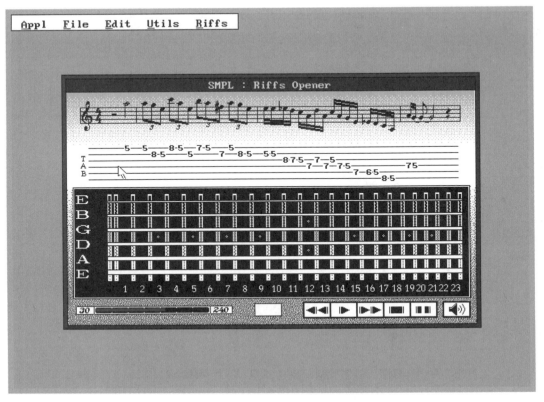

▶ **FIGURE 11-7**

Riffs teaches the guitar licks of the pros.

other well-known players. Each lesson includes 25 riffs (short solos) such as the one shown in Figure 11-7. Notation is displayed, and you can listen to a recording of the original solo played by the artist (at full speed) or to a MIDI version, the speed of which you can vary. Each riff is accompanied by lessons explaining how to practice and use the melody. If you have the G-VOX hardware from Lyrrus, you can see the notes that you play on your guitar appear as dots on the on-board fingerboard; however, the hardware is not necessary to benefit from these lessons.

This combination of a digital audio recording of a real-life guitar solo with a MIDI file that can be played back at any speed and text is a good meld of the computer's teaching capabilities. The artists chosen

▶ **FIGURE 11-8**

Learn It From CD makes it easier to play along with your favorite songs.

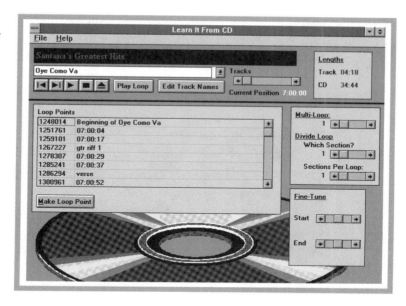

so far are among the best guitarists on the planet, and each library is inexpensive. If Lyrrus keeps up the pace of releasing libraries, this tool will grow in popularity rapidly. ▪ **Published by Lyrrus, Inc.**

The Guitarist, The Pianist, and The Jazz Pianist

These products from PG Music show dots moving across a fretboard or keyboard while a talented instrumentalist plays jazz standards (in the jazz titles) or classical music pieces (in the Pianist). You can play back these excellent performances at any tempo or listen to them in juke-box mode, but there's no notation provided (except for the Windows version of The Jazz Pianist), either on-screen or printed. For me, that is a serious drawback. Classical pianists will, of course, be able to purchase the printed music separately for the pieces by Beethoven, Chopin, and others and may then find The Pianist to be quite a valuable tool. ▪ **Published by PG Music**

Learn It From CD

Magazine interviews with many great musicians reveal that they learned how to play by playing along with the radio. For non-classical music, learning to play the songs that you love from recordings is an excellent way to learn—it bypasses the limitations of any particular formal method and aligns your playing with your musical passions.

Until now, learning from recordings has been cumbersome. It has generally involved recording your song onto a cassette, finding a phrase that you want to learn, playing it, and then rewinding to find the beginning of the phrase again. Each cycle through, there's a fair amount of awkwardness and trial and error as you spend three-quarters of your time working the tape recorder and one-quarter actually playing.

I became frustrated with this process and wrote a program to help me (and you) learn songs from audio CDs (see Figure 11-8). It's a Windows program that makes it easy for you to play along with audio CDs in your CD-ROM drive. It allows you to create loop points anywhere you like on the CD—usually at the start and end of a phrase or a set of chord changes that you want to learn. Then, by pressing the Loop button, you can hear your phrase played back over and over again.

You can easily subdivide a loop so that you can listen to the first half, the third quarter, or the eleventh sixteenth of the phrase. This lets you narrow in on a single note or chord if you wish! It's easy to adjust, add, or delete loop points. Each loop point can be labeled—I label mine with descriptions ("beginning of guitar solo," etc.), with the chords, or with the lyrics from the phrase)—and all the information is saved and instantly recalled the next time you pop your CD into the drive.

Learn It From CD has other features that make listening to CDs in your CD-ROM player a pleasure, but those are incidental to its main function, and we won't go into them right now.

At the time of this writing, distribution plans for Learn It From CD have not been firmly established. You can find out the current status by sending e-mail to me at 76545,1527 on CompuServe or 76545.1527@compuserve.com on the Internet.

Piano Instruction

There are several products available to teach keyboard skills. Although I highly recommend that piano novices obtain the services of a human instructor (especially to establish the proper hand position and to cor-rect bad physical habits), these programs may supplement those lessons and give the student additional incentive to practice. Or, once the motivated student has taken a few lessons, these programs may carry him or her through a few months of acquiring basic skills. The programs all require an external MIDI keyboard (although one config-uration of the Miracle system includes one).

The Miracle Piano Teaching System

This system has garnered good reviews. You can get a keyboard syn-thesizer and software together, or you can purchase the software alone for use with any MIDI keyboard. It contains several hundred lessons which teach you to play progressively more difficult songs, along with several arcade-style games to sharpen your skills. Many piano novices have enjoyed this program and learned the basics of piano playing. The lessons stop at the elementary level.

■ *Published by The Software Toolworks*

Piano Works and Piano

Essentially two versions of the same program, Temporal Acuity's Piano Works runs under DOS, and Musicware's Piano is designed for Win-dows. Both of these provide a large number of progressive drills that will teach the student to read and play notes in several positions with both hands. The system is heavier on theory than the Miracle and may be a better choice for some.

■ *Piano Works is published by Termporal Acuity Products,*
Piano is published by Musicware

For The Children

In this category the goal is not so much to teach specific musical skills as to engage the child and involve him or her in musical activities.

Dr. T's Sing-A-Long

This program will get kids involved in singing 25 nursery rhymes while they watch cute animations. There are two modes—"normal" and "kid" mode. In kid mode, the program has a child-proof interface that

Musicus is a Tetris-like game that uses blocks with widths that reflect the durations of the notes printed on them.

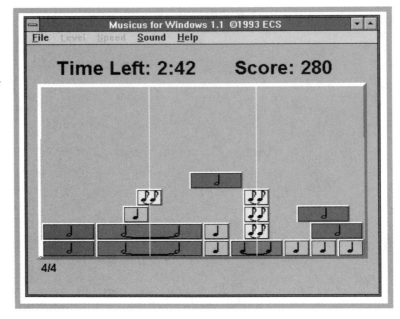

youngsters 4–7 should be able to operate easily. In normal mode, you get to see a bouncing ball and lyrics so that you and your child can sing the songs together.

Mr. Drumstix Music Studio

This is a music construction kit for youngsters from Howling Dog Systems. It comes with 20 children's tunes built-in, but it has an open-ended interface that allows kids to drag patterns to Mr. Drumstix or Ms. Florida Keys and watch the animated characters move as they play them. They can also scramble segments of music and reorchestrate them. I'd judge this program as intriguing for 6–10 year olds.

Musicus

This is a Tetris-like game played with musical blocks (see Figure 11-9). Blocks containing musical symbols appear at the top of the game board. Their width is proportional to the symbols on them. You must maneuver them into positions to form complete lines.

Ear Challenger

The name of this game should really be "Memory Challenger." When the game begins, the first note of a musical phrase is played, while a key on the on-screen keyboard is pressed and colored. The player clicks on the key that has been pressed. If the answer is correct, then the computer plays the first two notes of the phrase. The player then repeats that performance. The process continues until either the player misses a note or the entire phrase is completely and accurately performed. The game is designed for one or two players.

Still More Software

In the course of researching this chapter, I discovered the Electronic Courseware Systems Instructional Software Catalog. This catalog is the most far-reaching listing of music education software that I have yet encountered. Much of the software listed in this catalog was designed to complement classroom instruction, but you may nonetheless find it worthwhile for personal use. Call (800)832-4965 to order your copy.

Chapter **12**

Audio Grab Bag

The possibilities that arise when you combine a computer with sound are immense. We've covered the major areas in preceding chapters, but there are still a number of interesting and useful products that don't quite fit into any of our pigeonholes. In this chapter, we'll survey the most intriguing ones.

Clip Music

Clip music is music that others have produced for your use. It is available in all forms—CD audio, digital audio, and MIDI—each with its advantages and disadvantages. Each kind of music comes with its own licensing restrictions.

CD Audio and CD-ROM

There are two forms of music that come on audio CDs—clip music, for use in multimedia projects, and audio samples, for those of you who have samplers or sound cards with sampling capabilities.

Clip Music and Sounds for Multimedia

A number of CD-ROMs and audio CDs can give you the building blocks for complex wave files or multimedia productions. Some contain just music, some contain sound effects and environments, and some have a mix of both. The music on these discs is composed and recorded by professionals with very high quality standards. The purchase price of the disc usually includes the right to use the materials in any multimedia presentations that you put together, but you will generally have to negotiate separately if you wish to include them in commercial products for widespread distribution or for broadcast.

Audio clips in these packages are often presented in multiple arrangements; for instance, you might have three versions of a single theme—in one-minute, 30-second, and 15-second lengths.

Most CD-ROM packages that include a large number of short files include some form of access software to let you find what you need quickly with keyword searches (see Figure 12-1).

One of the largest sound effect collections to be released yet is Aware's Speed-of-Sound, which includes over seven hours of sounds and environments in 27 categories on a single CD-ROM. Cambium's Sound Choice Vol. 1 gives you a database of 29 clips, each of which is available as CD audio, in six formats of wave files (including several that are compressed for improved sound/size ratios), and as a MIDI file.

If you have specific needs that aren't satisfied by any of these sources, contact the companies that produce audio libraries for industrial films and videos (your local librarian can help you find them).

Sample CDs

These are collections of samples of individual notes and rhythm loops for people with samplers or sound cards with sampling capabilities. Not happy with the sound of your MIDI cymbals? Sample from the Sabian Cymbal Sample Library, two CDs full of nothing but cymbal sounds. Want a great cello sound? Choose from an hour's worth on the Cello CD from Big Fish Audio's Orchestral Library. If you're a perfectionist when it comes to sounds, samples of just about every instrument in every pitch range and at every dynamic level are available to you—for a price.

Even more interesting than these, perhaps, are dance groove and drum loop samples. You're undoubtedly familiar with the recent practice, especially prevalent in rap and hip-hop, of sampling a groove from an existing song and adding layers to it, building an entirely new piece in the process. The technique grew out of dance club DJs who specialize in recycling old beats. It may have dawned on you that you have the technology to build music around sampled grooves right in your PC.

As you know, it is generally not legal for you to create a commercial music release based on sampling a rhythm loop from an existing work of art without purchasing rights. However, you can sample grooves, without fear, directly from CDs created just for that purpose. Rap grooves, DJ scratches, techno dance loops, and more are all ready for the taking—again, for a modest fee. Check out the ads in Electronic

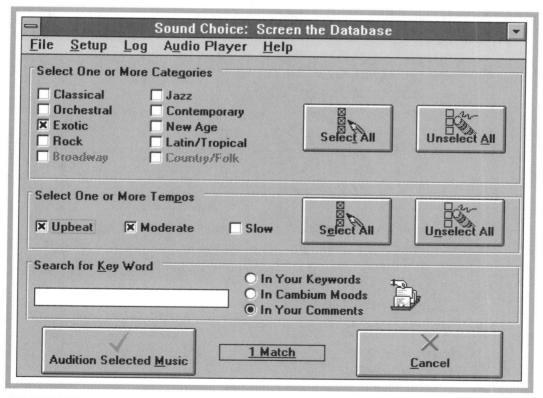

▶ **FIGURE 12-1**

Find the file that you need quickly with the software included with most CD-ROM packages.

Musician or Keyboard to see the latest hot discs, or call Big Fish Audio (listed in Appendix D) for a catalog and demo disc.

There's one caveat about these discs that you must know—CD-ROMs made explicitly for samplers, as many are, will not work in your PC's CD-ROM drive. The formats are different. When purchasing samples and loops, buy only those that come in the form of audio CDs or CD-ROMs made explicitly for PCs.

MIDI Drum Patterns for Musicians

You may be the greatest songwriter in the world and still not have a clue as to how drummers do their thing. This can be a real obstacle to producing great-sounding sequences. This is where products such as 1000 Super Cool Drum Patterns from Cools Shoes Software can help you out.

This product contains 26 Standard MIDI Files, playable by any sequencer. Each file has 40 or so different drum patterns and fills (what the drums play at the end of a phrase or chorus to lead into the next section) that you can copy and paste into your own sequences. You get unlimited rights to use these patterns in any of your own pieces.

These patterns cook, and the selection of styles is amazing. Groove on this: 13 different reggae beats, 11 sambas, dozens of rock styles, five blues, 13 ballads, dozens of funk and jazz styles, African styles, merengue, comparsa, flamenco and many, many more. At about a nickel per pattern, this is one of the bargains of the decade.

In addition to MIDI files, these drum patterns come in drummer 2.0 format, to allow you to easily manipulate them if you have that program (described below).

Other vendors of drum patterns include DrumTrax and Five Pin Press. Contact information is included in Appendix D.

drummer 2.0

This DOS program from Cool Shoes Software allows you to easily create drum grooves with a grid-based interface (see Figure 12-2). You can assemble the grooves into songs with another grid (Figure 12-3). It's an easy way to put together hot rhythms, especially if you use some of the drum patterns in 1000 Super Cool Drum Patterns or another package as a starting point. I especially liked the "auto-fill" function, which lets you ask the computer to play additional notes in any drum parts that you specify. You just tell drummer what percentage of the time to add notes, and it does the work. This works great in conga and bongo parts.

Drummer 2.0 can export its drum pattern files as Standard MIDI Files.

Name	√	Patch	Chn	Pan	Vol
Bass	√	Electric Bass (finger)	1	64	112
Piano	√	Acoustic Grand Piano	2	64	100
Trumpet	√	Trumpet	12	64	90
Loose Kick	√	-none-	10	64	90
Side Stick	√	-none-	10	64	90
Closed Hi Hat	√	-none-	10	64	90
Open Hi Hat	√	-none-	10	64	90
Long Guiro	√	-none-	10	64	90
Shaker	√	-none-	10	64	90

▶ **FIGURE 12-2**

You can create drum grooves using drummer 2.0.

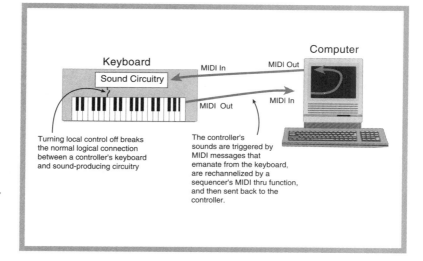

▶ **FIGURE 12-3**

Drummer 2.0 also allows you to assemble the drum grooves into songs.

Turning local control off breaks the normal logical connection between a controller's keyboard and sound-producing circuitry

The controller's sounds are triggered by MIDI messages that emanate from the keyboard, are rechannelized by a sequencer's MIDI thru function, and then sent back to the controller.

Keyboard

Sound Circuitry

MIDI In

MIDI Out

Computer

MIDI Out

MIDI In

Speech Processing

Anyone who has watched the interaction between humans and the ship's computer in *Star Trek* has seen what is probably the ultimate goal of interface designers. Any crew member can simply ask the computer for information, and the computer will understand the question (providing that it is specific enough) and respond in soothing female tones. No one who has seen the film *Star Trek V* can forget Scotty trying to communicate with an Apple Macintosh computer—he starts talking to it; then, when the computer doesn't respond and he's handed a mouse, he starts talking into the mouse. It's hilarious, and it points out how far we are from communicating with computers in a natural way.

The *Enterprise* crew's interaction with their computer presupposes the existence of a number of distinct technologies. First, the computer must recognize each word that any crew member speaks as a word in its dictionary (this is known as "speaker-independent, large vocabulary, continuous speech recognition"). As you'll see, the most advanced programs are approaching this goal, albeit with a number of significant limitations.

Once words are associated with dictionary entries, the *Enterprise's* computer must deduce the meaning of the sentence. We are many years away from this much more complicated task (we don't even know how to represent "meaning" in a computer, much less how to extract it from an English sentence), although we will probably be there long before the 24th century. Then the computer must calculate the answer, the complexity of which depends on the question. Next, the computer must create an English sentence expressing the answer, a task that is somewhat less complicated than understanding the meaning of the question. Finally, the computer must speak its answer. We have programs that can accomplish this last step with varying degrees of naturalness.

On the *Enterprise,* everyone has a personal log. Crew members dictate into these logs, and we're often allowed to eavesdrop on those reflections. These logs contain recordings of the voices of the crew members (or, as we sometimes see, video recordings including both image and voice). The basic technology to do this is in our hands right now—all you need is an infinite budget for hard disks, and you can dictate your diary every night. Get a video capture system and commit to purchasing half-a-gigabyte per day, and you can keep a digital video diary.

Occasionally, when a crew member is investigating a crime or some other unusual occurrence, he will search someone else's logs. The crewperson might ask for all entries that mention Klingons. That, of course, depends on the computer's ability to translate the recorded speech into some kind of searchable representation (such as typed text). This ability is just what you'd need in order to dictate letters into your computer. As you'll see, there are several systems available now that will let you do that, with some limitations and a fairly high price.

One final point before we embark upon voice-processing specifics: have you noticed that when a member of the Enterprise crew responds to a message over her communicator, she never touches the communicator to end the response? It's always <touch>, "On my way," then a purposeful stride out the door. Doesn't this imply that every conversation is transmitted over those communicators? There's no "Off" button! I guess there's not much privacy on a Federation starship.

Talking Computers

It's going to be a long time before a computer can give a credible performance as Hamlet (even Mr. Data on the *Enterprise* can't handle artistic expression), but talking computers that can read text files without making you roll on the floor laughing aren't that far away. Right now, though, computer speech can be pretty darn funny. Even so, it has its uses, primarily as an aid to checking numbers in spreadsheets and to make computers more accessible to people with certain kinds of disabilities. As this text-to-speech capability improves, it will become useful to anyone who has to write letters, memos, articles, or books. When the computer reads your writing out loud, you will quickly spot awkward passages and grammatical errors that you might have otherwise missed.

Monologue for Windows is a text-to-speech program that ships with Creative Labs' Sound Blaster 16 card. Since the disk that I received had no instructions, and there may be thousands of confused readers out there with this software, I will take a paragraph to describe the details of its operation.

When you double-click on the Monologue icon, you get a screen such as that shown in Figure 12-4. We'll only consider the clipboard mode here. Click on the Clipboard button, then click the button in the upper right-hand corner of the window to minimize the icon. Thereafter, any time there's text in the clipboard (copied from Notepad or any word processor), you can right-click the minimized Monologue icon to hear the text read out loud.

Monologue is pretty amusing. It works by analyzing the phonemes (basic sounds) in your text and stringing them together. It pauses at the end of sentences. It has an editable exceptions dictionary to handle words that its phoneme analysis mishandles. This dictionary needs to be a lot bigger—as shipped, you're treated to lots of rib-ticklers. "Don't," for instance, is read as "don tee" (Monologue just reads letter names when it "can tee" figure out what else to do. Interestingly, *Star*

▶ **FIGURE 12-4**

The text-to-speech program Monologure for Windows.

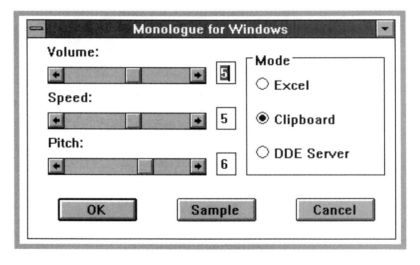

Trek: The Next Generation's Mr. Data can't use contractions either). "CDs" is read as "see dee ess" instead of "see deez." Still, Monologue can read most sentences fairly intelligibly and is good for a laugh. And, it is perfectly able to read back strings of numbers from Excel spreadsheets, a very useful cross-checking aid for someone who has just typed them in from a hand-written ledger and needs to confirm the accuracy of his transcription.

Creative has a another text-to-speech Windows product called TextAssist. TextAssist is based on DECTalk, an advanced, natural-sounding speech synthesis engine that is shipped with (and requires) the Sound Blaster 16 models with CSP chips. Creative also ships DR. SBAITSO and READ, both DOS programs based on the SBTalker software engine, with Sound Blaster and Sound Blaster Pro cards. DR. SBAITSO is a computer-based "psychologist" (it's more a joke or game than a therapist), and READ will accept any text file as input and read it to you.

One text-to-speech product not from Creative Labs is Ralph The Reader, a shareware program available as RALPH2.ZIP in CompuServe's IBM Applications Forum (IBMAPP) Word Processing library, among other places. As of now, there aren't many other players in this arena.

Voice Recognition

Voice recognition is the process of a computer accepting short spoken commands and then performing certain tasks. There are a number of programs available to perform voice recognition on the PC. They can be extremely helpful to disabled people or those who must have the use of their hands while they command a computer, but their utility for the average computer user has yet to be convincingly demonstrated.

Voice recognition programs are generally *speaker-dependent* and must be *trained* for best results, a process in which you speak a command one to three times and associate it with an action. These actions are generally limited to standard macros—anything that you could activate with a keystroke, plus, perhaps, a few additional functions supplied by the programmers. Under Windows you can launch applications or Recorder macros, switch windows, and page forward and backward quite easily. You can also activate the more elaborate macros that can be created for specific products such as Microsoft Word or Excel. Under DOS, you can perform quite elaborate activities in conjunction with powerful macro programs.

Voice recognition programs can typically understand between 100 and 1000 different commands (known in the jargon as *limited vocabulary, discrete utterance* systems). They work fairly well for people in relatively quiet environments but might be error-prone on a noisy factory or convention floor. They include Rover from Digital Soup, Voice Pilot, part of the Microsoft Sound System, and Voice Assist from Creative Labs.

Dictation

Dictation should be just like dictation to a good secretary—you speak, and the computer translates your sentences into typed text. This is a much more demanding task than voice recognition because the size of the vocabulary that you might use is much larger. Instead of recognizing 200 or so phrases, a dictation system must recognize over 30,000 words. The training system has to be much more clever than that used in voice recognition, because it needs to generalize—there's no way that you're going to make the time investment to train the program to recognize each of the 32,000 words individually.

There are several dictation systems available today, from IBM and from Dragon Systems. They are speaker-dependent and also require that you pause slightly between words. Try saying a few sentences with the slightest perceptible pauses between words—just enough to ensure that each word has a definite silence before and after it, however short—and see how it feels. It's rather awkward. This technology has a ways to go, but it is on the road, and it probably won't be too long before you can dictate a letter in natural speech. This may become an important application for both disabled people and others who experience difficulty typing, such as many managers.

Whoop It Up!

The last item in our grab bag takes us from the heady seriousness of state-of-the-art speech processing to the realm of trivial fun. This cool toy won't fulfill any pressing social, business, or musical need, but it will let you customize your sonic environment when you work in Windows. You can attach any wave or MIDI file to all sorts of system events, from alert boxes to window resizing. You may already know that you can attach wave files to some events using the Sound applet in the Control Panel. Whoop It Up! goes much farther, allowing many more events, both system-level and application-specific, to trigger sounds. It can play MIDI files as well as wave files (it can also play video, but the immense size of these files makes them impractical for this fun, but essentially trivial, purpose), and, most importantly, it can choose files at random. Since even the most amusing clip will quickly grow boring with repetition, the ability to switch files this way is appreciated.

Whoop It Up! comes with a substantial selection of musical files, and is a very pleasant and economical little utility. Contact the Advance Support Group, Inc. for more information; they're listed in Appendix D.

Appendix **A**

General MIDI Patch Map

PIANOS

Patch Name

1	Acoustic Grand
2	Bright Acoustic
3	Electric Grand
4	Honky-Tonk
5	Electric Piano 1
6	Electric Piano 2
7	Harpsichord
8	Clavinet

CHROMATIC PERCUSSION

9	Celesta
10	Glockenspiel
11	Music Box
12	Vibraphone
13	Marimba
14	Xylophone
15	Tubular Bells
16	Dulcimer

ORGANS

17	Drawbar Organ
18	Percussive Organ
19	Rock Organ
20	Church Organ
21	Reed Organ
22	Accordion
23	Harmonica
24	Tango Accordion (Bandoneon)

GUITARS

25	Nylon–String (Classical) Guitar
26	Steel–String Acoustic (Folk) Guitar
27	Jazz Electric Guitar
28	Clean Electric Guitar
29	Muted Electric Guitar
30	Overdriven Guitar
31	Distorted Guitar
32	Guitar Harmonics

BASS

33	Acoustic Bass
34	Electric Bass (played with finger)
35	Electric Bass (played with pick)
36	Fretless Bass
37	Slap Bass 1
38	Slap Bass 2
39	Synth Bass 1
40	Synth Bass 2

STRINGS

41	Violin
42	Viola
43	Cello
44	Contrabass
45	Tremolo Strings
46	Pizzicato Strings
47	Orchestral Strings
48	Timpani

ENSEMBLE

49	String Ensemble 1
50	String Ensemble 2
51	Synth Strings 1
52	Synth Strings 2
53	Choir Aahs
54	Voice Oohs
55	Synth Voice
56	Orchestra Hit

BRASS

57	Trumpet
58	Trombone
59	Tuba
60	Muted Trumpet
61	French Horn
62	Brass Section
63	SynthBrass 1
64	SynthBrass 2

REEDS

65	Soprano Sax
66	Alto Sax
67	Tenor Sax
68	Baritone Sax
69	Oboe
70	English Horn
71	Bassoon
72	Clarinet

PIPES

73	Piccolo
74	Flute
75	Recorder
76	Pan Flute
77	Blown Bottle
78	Skakuhachi
79	Whistle
80	Ocarina

SYNTH LEAD

81	Square Wave
82	Sawtooth Wave
83	Calliope
84	Chiff
85	Charang
86	Voice
87	Parallel Fifths
88	Bass and Lead

SYNTH PADS

89	New Age
90	Warm
91	Polysynth
92	Choir
93	Bowed
94	Metallic
95	Halo
96	Sweep

SYNTH EFFECTS

97	Rain
98	Soundtrack
99	Crystal
100	Atmosphere
101	Brightness
102	Goblins
103	Echoes
104	Sci-Fi

ETHNIC

105	Sitar
106	Banjo
107	Shamisen
108	Koto
109	Kalimba (Mbira)
110	Bagpipe
111	Fiddle
112	Shanai

PERCUSSIVE

113   Tinkle Bell
114   Agogo
115   Steel Drums
116   Woodblock
117   Taiko Drum
118   Melodic Tom
119   Synth Drum
120   Reverse Cymbal

SOUND EFFECTS

121   Guitar Fret Noise
122   Breath Noise
123   Seashore
124   Bird Tweet
125   Telephone Ring
126   Helicopter
127   Applause
128   Gunshot

Appendix **B**

General MIDI Drum Map

Note Number	Pitch	Octave	Drum Name	Note Number	Pitch	Octave	Drum Name
35	B	0	Acoustic Bass Drum	60	C	3	High Bongo
36	C	1	Bass Drum 1	61	C#	3	Low Bongo
37	C#	1	Side Stick	62	D	3	Muted High Conga
38	D	1	Acoustic Snare	63	D#	3	Open High Conga
39	D#	1	Hand Clap	64	E	3	Low Conga
40	E	1	Electric Snare	65	F	3	High Timbale
41	F	1	Low Floor Tom	66	F#	3	Low Timbale
42	F#	1	Closed Hi-Hat	67	G	3	High Agogo
43	G	1	High Floor Tom	68	G#	3	Low Agogo
44	G#	1	Pedal Hi-Hat	69	A	3	Cabasa
45	A	1	Low Tom	70	A#	3	Maracas
46	A#	1	Open Hi-Hat	71	B	3	Short Whistle
47	B	1	Low-Mid Tom	72	C	4	Long Whistle
48	C	2	Hi-Mid Tom	73	C#	4	Short Guiro
49	C#	2	Crash Cymbal 1	74	D	4	Long Guiro
50	D	2	High Tom	75	D#	4	Claves
51	D#	2	Ride Cymbal 1	76	E	4	High Wood Block
52	E	2	Chinese Cymbal	77	F	4	Low Wood Block
53	F	2	Ride Cymbal Bell	78	F#	4	Muted Cuica
54	F#	2	Tambourine	79	G	4	Open Cuica
55	G	2	Splash Cymbal	80	G#	4	Muted Triangle
56	G#	2	Cowbell	81	A	4	Open Triangle
57	A	2	Crash Cymbal 2				
58	A#	2	Vibraslap				
59	B	2	Ride Cymbal 2				

Appendix **C**

MIDI Continuous Controllers

General MIDI Controllers

All General MIDI synthesizers and sound cards will respond to the following Controllers:

Controller#	Description
1	Modulation
7	Main Volume
10	Pan
11	Expression
64	Sustain
121	Reset All Controllers
123	All Notes Off

Full List of Semi-Standardized Controllers

The International MIDI Association has created a list of recommended Continuous Controller assignments. No synthesizers or sound cards support all of the control possibilities listed on the following page, but many support a few of them—check the MIDI Implementation Chart in your manual to find out which. Controllers that are supported by all Roland GS-compatible synthesizers have an asterisk in the GS column.

Continuous Controller#	Description	GS
0,32[1]	Bank Select1	*
1	Modulation	*
2	Breath Controller	
4	Foot Controller	
5	Portamento Time	*
6	Data Entry MSB	
7	Main Volume	*
8	Balance	
10	Pan	*
11	Expression	*
38	Data Entry LSB	*
64	Sustain	*
65	Portamento	*
66	Sostenuto	
67	Soft Pedal	*
69	Hold 2	
84	Legato	*
91	External Effects (Reverb Depth	*
92	Tremolo Depth	
93	Chorus Depth	*
94	Celeste (Detune) Depth	
95	Phaser Depth	
96	Data Increment	
97	Data Decrement	
98	Non-Registered Parameter Number LSB	*
99	Non-Registered Parameter Number MSB	*
100	Registered Parameter Number LSB	*
101	Registered Parameter Number MSB	*
120	All Sound Off	*
121	Reset All Controllers	*
123	Notes Off	*

[1] To send a Bank Select message, you must send two Continous Controller messages: First a Continuous Controller 0 with the number of the bank that you want to switch to as the value, then a Continous Controller 32 with any number as the value (the value will be ignored). The bank is not actually switched until the next Power Change message comes in.

Appendix **D**

Resources

Here's contact information for all of the companies that you've read about in this book and a few more, listed in alphabetical order, along with brief descriptions of their products.

Alesis
(800) 5-ALESIS

Alesis manufactures many musical hardware products, including signal processors, mixing boards, and synthesizers. Their most influential product is the ADAT multi-track digital tape recorder, which has brought digital multi-track recording into thousands of home studios.

Alfred Publishing
(818) 891-5999

Alfred publishes musical instruction books, sheet music, music on disk, and various other instructional materials

Animotion
(800) 536-4175

This Windows software publisher makes MCS SoundTrak, a wave editing program that can add Q-Sound processing (see Chapter 3) to any sound file, regardless of the sound card used for playback. Animotion

also publishes MCS Stereo, a program that looks like a rack of stereo components and includes a mixer, CD player, Wave recorder/player, and MIDI file recorder/player. They also publish Sound Savers, a collection of screen savers for Windows or After Dark that varies when sounds are playing through your sound card (disco dancers gyrate to the music from your CD player, for instance).

Aware, Inc.
(800) 292-7346

Aware makes the Speed-of-Sound CD-ROM for Windows, with seven hours of sound effects.

Big Fish Audio
(800) 717-3474

Big Fish publishes CDs and CD-ROMs for sampling.

Big Noise Software
(904) 730-0754

This company's MIDI MaxPak for Windows combines a sequencer with notation, a universal synth patch librarian, tape deck control, JukeMax, and MixMax.

Binary Zoo
(518) 298-2740

Binary Zoo publishes Rock and Bach Studios, a DOS program for ages 7–14.

Blue Ribbon Soundworks
(404) 315-0212

Blue Ribbon publishes SuperJam and EasyKeys, automatic music generation programs for Windows described in Chapter 10.

Cambium
(800) 231-1779

Cambium publishes Sound Choice, clip music CD-ROM for Windows, described in Chapter 12. They'll send you a sampler CD-ROM, Sound Choice Lite, for just a shipping and handling fee.

Coda Music Technology
(800) 843-2066

Coda publishes Finale and Music Prose, notation programs for Windows. Finale remains the most powerful music notation program on the PC. It has quite a substantial learning curve. Music Prose is easier to learn, is quite powerful in its own right, and can share files with Finale.

Cool Shoes Software
(910) 722-0830

Cool Shoes publishes 1000 Super Cool Drum Patterns and Drummer 2.0, described at length in Chapter 12.

Creative Labs
(408) 428-6600

The largest of the sound card manufacturers dominates the market with its Sound Blaster and Wave Blaster family of products. It also sells multimedia upgrade kits, video-capture products, and its newest sound card, the AWE32.

Digidesign
(800) 333-2137

This company dominates the world of professional digital audio recording and editing on the Macintosh platform. Their Session 8 hardware and software product for Windows, described in Chapter 8, gives PC users an entree into the world of professional audio production.

Digital Audio Labs, Inc.
(612) 473-7626

Digital Audio Labs makes several hard disk recording systems discussed in Chapter 8.

Dr. T's Music Software
(800) 989-6434

Dr. T's publishes the Sing-A-Long CD-ROM for children and Composer Quest, an educational game on CD-ROM for a wide age range, described in Chapter 11. They also publish the QuickScore family of sequencing and notation programs for both DOS and Windows.

Dragon Systems
(617) 965-5200

A pioneer in voice recognition and dictation, Dragon Systems makes products for consumers and other manufacturers. Call them for a list of their current offerings.

DrumTrax
(617) 387-7581

This is a good source of drum patterns in Standard MIDI File format.

Eccentric Software
(800) 436-6758

Eccentric publishes A Zillion Kajillion Rhymes, a rhyming dictionary for Windows.

Electronic Courseware Systems
(800) 832-4965

This company publishes the largest catalog of music education software and the Musicus game for Windows, described in Chapter 11.

Five Pin Press
(800) 726-6434

Five Pin publishes MIDI drum patterns. Products include 200 Instant Drum Patterns, 260 Instant Drum Patterns, and Rap Drum Patterns. Patterns come with books displaying all patterns in both grid and musical notation.

Howling Dog Systems
(613) 599-7927

Howling Dog publishes the Power Chords family of programs, described in Chapter 10. Howling Dog also publishes the children's program, Mr. Drumstix Music Studio, described in Chapter 11.

Ibis Software
(415) 546-1917

Ibis publishes a wide variety of well-designed music teaching software for both Windows and DOS. Several of their products are described at length in Chapter 11.

International Business Machines
(800) TALK-2-ME

This spunky little startup company makes the IBM Personal Dictation System, one of the most advanced dictation systems available. It runs only under IBM's OS/2 operating system at the present time. It also has a number of other voice recognition and dictation systems, for both OS/2 and Windows, in various stages of development and release.

International MIDI Association
(818) 598-0088

This is the organization that administers the MIDI specification within the United States. You can purchase official copies of the MIDI specification and assorted extensions from them if you need accurate, detailed, technical information.

Key Electronics, Inc.
(800) 533-MIDI

Key Electronics makes serial- and parallel-port MIDI interfaces for PCs.

Killer Tracks
(800) 877-0078

Killer Tracks publishes Killer Tracks, clip music for multimedia.

Lil' Johnny Enterprises
(800) 645-7697

Lil' Johnny makes the Solo Assimilator, a product that teaches blues guitar, described in Chapter 11.

Lyrrus
(215) 922-0880

This hardware and software company makes products designed for guitarists. Their G-VOX package consists of a pickup that temporarily mounts on your guitar, and an interface to your computer. Their educational software packages (Riffs, Chords, and Tour, described in Chapter 11) analyze the notes that you play and display them on a guitar fretboard on the screen, although these packages can also be used effectively without the hardware. Their new Bridge software, not available at press time, promises to convert your guitar performances to Standard MIDI Files without the inaccuracies and timing delays caused by traditional guitar-to-MIDI converters. Whether Lyrrus can deliver on this ambitious promise remains to be seen.

MediaTech Innovations
(408) 267-5464

MediaTech publishes pattern-based sequencers/drum pattern generators Rhythm Brainz and Rhythm Brainz Plus for Windows.

Medio Multimedia, Inc.
(206) 867-5500

Medio publishes World Beat, a world music festival on a CD-ROM for Windows, created by the author of this book and described in Chapter 11.

MiBAC Music Software
(507) 645-5851

MiBAC publishes Music Lessons, described in Chapter 11.

Midisoft
(206) 881-7176

Midisoft publishes a number of music products for Windows. Their Music Mentor music education program is described in Chapter 11. Their entry-level sequencer, Session, is bundled with Music Mentor and a number of sound cards. Their flagship sequencer, Studio, is quite popular.

MPower
(415) 393-1470

MPower publishes MusicPower for Guitar, a Windows music education product described in Chapter 11.

Music Quest
(800) 876-1376

Music Quest makes MIDI interfaces for PCs.

Opcode Systems, Inc
(415) 856-3333

Opcode publishes The Musical World of Professor Piccolo, a CD-ROM that introduces children to several different styles of music.

Passport Systems
(800) 545-0775

Passport publishes a wide range of popular software for musicians, including notation programs Encore and MusicTime and sequencers MasterTracks Pro and Trax.

PG Music
(800) 268-6272

This company quickly became one of the biggest little companies in the music software business with its automatic accompaniment generator, Band-in-a-Box, described in detail in Chapter 10. In addition to the various versions of Band-in-a-Box for both DOS and Windows, PG publishes Power-Tracks Pro, the most economical commercially-distributed sequencer on the market. Other products include The Pianist, The Jazz Pianist, and The Jazz Guitarist, which are all discussed in Chapter 11.

Roland
(213) 685-5141

Roland's Sound Canvas synthesizer virtually defined General MIDI, and the entire family of synthesizers and sound cards based on that synthesizer has been enormously popular due to the lush sounds on-board. Roland's RAP-10 card is a popular choice because it fulfills all the functions of MPC audio—digital audio playback and recording, General MIDI synthesis, and CD control.

Six String Software
(206) 631-5855

This company publishes GuitarWorks, a DOS program for guitarists. GuitarWorks includes an electronic chord dictionary and can play back songs while displaying the notes on a guitar fretboard, in tablature, and as chord diagrams. It comes with the book *How To Play Guitar*, by Roger Evans.

Software Toolworks
(800) 234-3088

Software Toolworks makes the Miracle Piano Teaching System, described in Chapter 11.

Soundtrek
(404) 623-0879

Soundtrek makes The Jammer, an intriguing music generation program for both DOS and Windows, described in Chapter 10.

Steinberg/Jones
(818) 993-4091

Steinberg/Jones publishes the Cubase family of sequencer/notation programs.

Tascam
(213) 726-0303

Tascam manufactures a wide range of recording products, from portable mini-studios (mixer and multi-track cassette recorder in one tidy package) to its popular DA-30 DAT Recorder and its DA-88 Digital Multi-track Tape Recorder.

Temporal Acuity Products
(800) 426-2673

This company has been producing music software for DOS for quite a few years. They publish the MusicPrinter Plus DOS sequencer with notation. They also publish a wide variety of music education software, including The Music Learning Series, Inner Hearing, Rhythmaticity, and Piano Works, all described in Chapter 11.

Turtle Beach
(717) 767-0200

Turtle Beach is one of the major manufacturers of sound cards and music software for PCs. Their cards include the Multisound Monterey, Multisound Classic, Maui, and Tahiti, and their software includes the wave-editing program Wave and the four-track recording system Quad, described in Chapter 8.

Twelve Tone
(800) 234-1171

Twelve Tone publishes the popular Cakewalk family of sequencers for both DOS and Windows. The Windows versions include notation. Cakewalk is unique among sequencers in that it provides a programming language, CAL, which hard-core users can utilize to transform sequences in ways limited only by their imaginations.

Appendix **E**

Staying In Touch

For the lowdown on computers and music on a timely basis, magazines and special interest areas on computer networks are key. Here are my recommendations:

Online Services

These offer the most timely information (virtually up-to-the-minute, in fact) on a wide variety of topics. You can get opinions and advice from other individuals, which is a great aid to making purchase decisions, and help and information from the many companies who maintain an online presence. The downside is that you often have to wade through a lot of muck to get to the good stuff, and that you usually pay by the minute while you're doing so. Still, if you can keep yourself from become addicted to networking, these services can be extremely worthwhile and can also pay for themselves many times over through tips that save wasted time and money, as well as the business connections that you might make.

CompuServe

Voice: (800)848-8990

This is a very valuable service because of the size of its membership and because of the number of companies who use it to offer technical support and customer information. It has a vast number of files online, including shareware, product demos, and archives of discussions about significant topics (the best headphones, sound cards, etc.). There are a number of music-related forums on CompuServe, including the MIDI Forum and the Music and Arts Forum.

America Online

Voice: (800)827-6364

This rapidly-expanding service has many discussion areas dedicated to music and offers access to a number of Internet services, described below. An excellent user interface makes it extremely easy to explore. Because you need AOL's own software to access the service, contact the voice number listed above for your starter kit.

Microsoft Download Service

Modem: (206)936-6735

This is the place to go for updates of system files for both DOS and Windows. In particular, if you're looking for the Microsoft Audio Compression Manager or the latest CD-ROM driver, this is a good place. It's free, but you have to pay for the phone call to Redmond.

The Internet

No one knows for sure where the Information Highway is going, but it's a good bet that the wild and crazy Internet is going to emerge as one of its most significant components. The Internet is the next frontier—the Wild West of probing minds. Its anarchic, community-created nature has turned it into a constantly-changing, self-organizing group consciousness. As unprecedented numbers of new users and commercial ventures explore the grounds, the nature of the virtual community is bound to evolve in ways that will surprise just about everyone. It's a wild ride.

The varieties of ways of connecting to the Internet and the services available are too varied to mention. If you're a college student or an employee of a company with a commitment to the Internet, you can probably obtain free access through your organization. Otherwise, start off your explorations by at least obtaining access to the newsgroups (discussion groups). From there you'll be able to get pointers to other areas on the Internet that might interest you. Also, there are many excellent recent books that describe resources on the Internet in detail.

Some of the newsgroups whose names begin with "rec.music" will probably interest all readers of this book.

Forms of access to the Internet are rapidly changing. Hundreds of new services, and new ways of packaging access for you, are springing up each month. America Online, discussed in its own right earlier, offers access to Internet e-mail, newsgroups, and several other services. Delphi offers access to all Internet services but doesn't have a particularly user-friendly interface. There are also services such as free.org at (715)743-1600 which will provide you with free access to the Internet (with no fancy user-friendly interface—we're talking Unix commands here). Free.org pays its bills by selling long distance services (although you can call them over any carrier), and they'd love to have you as a customer.

Magazines

These information sources may not be quite as instantaneous and fashionable as the electronic ones, but they provide you with timely, well-organized, well-written, and useful information (note: the author of this book writes for several of these publications on a freelance basis).

Electronic Musician
Subscriptions: (800)888-5139

This magazine provides excellent coverage of all topics that involve music and technology, especially synthesizers, software, and signal processing. It aims to provide something for everyone, from introductory tutorials to expert reviews.

Keyboard Magazine
Subscriptions: (800)289-9919

This is an excellent reference for keyboardists of all stripes, with an emphasis on artists, synthesizers, samplers, and software.

Multimedia World

Subscriptions: (800)766-3294, ext. 205

This covers multimedia on the PC, is available on newsstands, and is designed for the general public. It contains reviews of titles, tools, sound cards and other hardware, along with discussions of larger topics, trends, and their implications.

New Media

Subscriptions: (609)786-4430

This covers multimedia on all platforms. It is sent without charge to qualified new media professionals in the United States and is available to others by paid subscription. New Media is an excellent source for multimedia developers or musicians who want to keep abreast of this rapidly expanding market for compositions and other music products.

Index